COINED

Also by Kabir Sehgal

A Bucket of Blessings

*Walk in My Shoes: Conversations Between a Civil Rights Legend
and His Godson on the Journey Ahead*

*Jazzocracy: Jazz, Democracy, and the Creation of a
New American Mythology*

COINED

THE RICH LIFE OF MONEY AND
HOW ITS HISTORY HAS SHAPED US

—— KABIR SEHGAL ——

GRAND CENTRAL
PUBLISHING

NEW YORK   BOSTON

Grand Central Publishing
Hachette Book Group
1290 Avenue of the Americas
New York, NY 10104

www.HachetteBookGroup.com

Printed in the United States of America

RRD-C

First Edition: March 2015
10 9 8 7 6 5 4 3 2

Grand Central Publishing is a division of Hachette Book Group, Inc.
The Grand Central Publishing name and logo is a trademark of Hachette Book Group, Inc.

The Hachette Speakers Bureau provides a wide range of authors for speaking events. To find out more, go to www.hachettespeakersbureau.com or call (866) 376-6591.

The publisher is not responsible for websites (or their content) that are not owned by the publisher.

Library of Congress Cataloging-in-Publication Data

Sehgal, Kabir.
  Coined : the rich life of money and how its history has shaped us / Kabir Sehgal. — First Edition.
      pages cm
  Includes bibliographical references and index.
  ISBN 978-1-4555-7852-8 (hardback) — ISBN 978-1-4789-5935-9 (audio book) — ISBN 978-1-4789-8342-2 (audio download) — ISBN 978-1-4555-7850-4 (ebook)
1. Money.   2. Quality of life.   3. Rich people.   I. Title.
  HG203.S44 2015
  332.4'9—dc23
                                    2014045984

ISBN 978-1-4555-5860-5 (international ed.)

For Douglas Brinkley,
mentor and friend

Contents

Part III SOUL: *A Symbol of Values*

Foreword

In 1974, I was teaching economics at Chittagong University in Bangladesh. In order to reach the campus, I had to travel through Jobra, a typical Bangladeshi village next to the newly built university campus. That same year a terrible famine caused millions across Bangladesh to suffer, and when I realized I could do nothing to ease all that suffering, I felt the arrogance of knowledge and learning begin to melt away. I wanted to overcome this feeling of uselessness by helping at least one person at a time.

I started walking around the village every day with that tiny mission in mind. There were so many things to be done that I hardly knew where to begin. Then I noticed loan-sharking was being practiced widely in the village, which was an ugly thing to watch—a mechanism that exploited the poorest people. Using my one-person-at-a-time approach, I started lending to people out of my own pocket, and that is how the idea of microcredit was born.

My work as a banker to the poor has helped me reevaluate money. The traditional definition of money found in economics narrowly categorizes it as an instrument to be used either to maximize our self-interest or to give away as charity. Money, however, can also be applied to advance important social goals, such as reducing poverty and preserving the environment—but these objectives require innovative applications and a willingness to look at money from new perspectives and through the lenses of multiple disciplines. Kabir Sehgal's new book, *Coined: The Rich Life of Money and How Its History Has Shaped Us*, does precisely that.

I first met Kabir in New York City in 2010. He showed deep concern about the misery that the financial crisis of 2008 brought to millions of people around the world, and he agreed with me that we needed to redesign financial institutions to make them more responsible and inclusive. He went even further, wanting to determine why and how money shapes our lives, perhaps even reassessing the role it should play in our lives. He mentioned his interest in writing a book that would enrich our understanding of money, broaden our perspective, and augment our financial literacy.

The book that resulted from his efforts is a unique and fascinating study of money, not just as an instrument for buying and selling but also as an extension of humankind through the ages. This book reflects our multi-dimensional nature, as it is an exploration of money and exchange through the perspective of various disciplines from biology and anthropology to history and theology. Kabir examines the uses of money, its invention, its change over time, its future forms, why it is such a powerful force in our lives, and, ultimately, how it should be used.

Kabir examines the past and present of money and projects its likely future. I am most interested in the future incarnation of money: what it can be, and how it holds the power for changing society. That is the role of money I recognized through microcredit, a construct that can empower people and bring about meaningful and sustainable change in a society. That is how I see its power through social business with non-dividend companies that are dedicated to solving human problems. As more people read this book and broaden their understanding of money beyond the goal of accumulation, I hope that they will start social businesses in the future.

But whatever the future of money might be, Kabir Sehgal has done us a great service in writing this book. He has presented in this book everything that money has meant to people over the centuries and with a panoramic perspective. He has prepared the ground for us to take it forward, to give new meaning to money, to assign it new roles in our lives, and to imagine the future of money as a foundation upon which we can build the future of the world we all cherish. Thank you, Kabir.

Muhammad Yunus
Nobel Peace Laureate
Founder of Grameen Bank

COINED

It is more easy to write on money than to obtain it;
and those who gain it, jest much at those who only know how
to write about it.
—*Voltaire*[1]

The image propagated by tradition is that of a city of pure gold,
with silver locks and diamond gates, a jewel-city, all inset and
inlaid, as a maximum of laborious study might produce when
applied to materials of the maximum worth. True to this belief,
Beersheba's inhabitants honor everything that suggests for them
the celestial city: they accumulate noble metals and rare stones,
they renounce all ephemeral excesses, they develop forms of
composite composure.
—*Italo Calvino*[2]

To Whom It May Concern,
We regret to inform that the mounted centenary coins displayed
at the museum are missing from their place. Whoever is in
possession of the same is earnestly requested to return them to
us in view of the historical importance of those particular coins
which were presented personally to the Superior General of the
Missions of Charity by the President of India, on the occasion of
the Centenary Celebration of Our Mother Teresa.
We can make a gift of coins of the same value on return of those
coins. We assure that the entire matter would be kept private
and confidential.
—*Letter posted at Mother Teresa's Motherhouse*
in Kolkata, India

Introduction

Red light.

Jakarta.

Running late.

An emaciated barefoot beggar paces in front of my taxi while carrying a baby in her arms. We make eye contact. I look away. In the other direction, I see several more beggars standing in line, index fingers raised.

Odd.

Street sounds blend harmoniously with a fainter, distant call to prayer. The *adhan*, now in its minor third interval, reminds me of Islam's role in this city—a vibrant amalgamation of nearly 10 million residents.

Here I am, far from home, smack-dab in the middle of them.

Green light.

Off and away.

Or not.

"Let's go, bro," I urge the driver. But he sits, heavy foot on brake, while others blare their horns. The beggar approaches. Expecting the inevitable knock, the curled hand, I look away again.

The front door opens.

Um.

My protest is ended by her taking a seat, fiddling with the air-conditioning.

Four of us. Driver, pedestrian, baby, and I sit in silence as the car motors away. Is this a kidnapping? If so, it is the quietest and most orderly kidnapping ever. Maybe I should flip through the Lonely Planet guide to Indonesia. Where is the self-defense section?

We speed onto the expressway and into the carpool lane, and it suddenly becomes clear.

It's not a kidnapping. It's a transaction. For a cut, this pedestrian-now-passenger has enabled the driver (and me) to use the fast lane. She is one of Jakarta's many small-time hustlers. These folks don't care where they go. Neither does my driver. And in a certain sense, neither do I.

We are all after the same thing. We are all out to make a buck. The pedestrian is happy to travel ten kilometers for a few rupiah, my taxi driver one hundred kilometers more for a fare, and me ten thousand kilometers for an investment opportunity.

At first it may appear that money is merely an instrument of exchange, the turnstile of the transaction, moving from hand to hand. But money is far more than just an item to be swapped. Seen through a more panoramic lens, money plays a social, mental, natural, and even artistic role in this exchange.

Because of money, I encountered three people whom I probably would not have met otherwise. Though I didn't add them as Facebook friends (Indonesia is one of Facebook's largest markets), money helped to create a relationship where one didn't exist previously. Money spurred and shaped our interactions.

Money also stimulates the brain: The thought of expected gain activates the nucleus accumbens, part of the reward center of the brain. The thought of making money probably stimulated the nucleus accumbens in the brains of the driver and pedestrian. The thought of losing money, thinking that I would be robbed, activated my amygdala, the fear center of the brain.

Money plays a natural or evolutionary role. At the most basic level, humans are driven by a need and desire to survive. And all humans must exchange with each other in order to survive. The four passengers, in a sense, relied on each other: I wanted a ride, the driver wanted a fare, the pedestrian wanted a cut, and the baby wanted a place to sleep. Money helps us obtain the resources to survive, from a bite to eat to a place to rest. While money is a human invention, all organisms rely on exchange in order to survive. From sea urchins and algae to birds and flowers, exchange is fundamental to life on this planet.

In this corner of the world, in Indonesia, birds and flowers are even on the money. In 1960, Bank Indonesia issued rupiah banknotes with indigenous organisms: sunbirds, green jungle fowl, tuberose, bougainvillea. Money, in this case, was a symbol not just *of* value but of things that *are* valuable to Indonesian society, like indigenous flora and fauna, a national crest and motto, or a founding president. On some rupiah notes is the

Garuda Pancasila, the national emblem of Indonesia, which depicts an eagle clutching a ribbon. The Garuda is actually a symbol of the Hindu god Vishnu—a peculiar image for the nation with the largest Islamic population in the world to put on its money. But the symbol reveals a chapter of Indonesia's cultural history, and how Hinduism spread to this island nation in the second century AD. In fact, the symbol can be traced back to the eagle and snake myth found in ancient Mesopotamia during the third millennium BC. It's a symbol that has spread across many geographies and been incorporated by several cultures over thousands of years. For example, the back of the US one-dollar bill features the Great Seal, with an eagle at its center. In its beak is a ribbon that looks like a snake. The symbols on money are cultural fossils—links to our past. They can serve as a guidepost for our future, reminders of the virtues to which citizens should aspire.

I never wanted to work at an investment bank. In fact, I cried on my first day on the job. After completing my graduate degree in London, I moved to Mangalore, India, to start an online education company with my buddy. We ran out of money, so I applied to be a computer coder at investment banks in London to cover our bills. I received two offers: Lehman Brothers and J. P. Morgan. I wish I could say that I picked J. P. Morgan due to my remarkable foresight and careful consideration of its historical importance, fortress balance sheet, and stellar management, but I decided based on office location. J. P. Morgan's office was in Central London whereas Lehman was in Canary Wharf, a financial district in East London. And I didn't want to ride the Tube.

On my first day, it sank in—I was working at a bank. There's nothing wrong with working at a bank, but it just wasn't for me. I would have to wear an ironed collar and write "Best Regards" to close my emails. I would have to learn how to use financial jargon and manage my managers. It was all so very corporate, different from what I had envisioned for my life. I grew up wanting to be a character in Michael Lewis's *The New New Thing*, a story about Silicon Valley tycoons like Jim Clark and Marc Andreessen. Instead, I had just walked into what I thought would be *Liar's Poker*.

After a few months in London and a quick stint in San Francisco, I was placed at the emerging markets equities desk in New York in 2008. I was a stockbroker who sold the stocks of corporations in developing markets to large institutional investors like pension funds, mutual funds, and hedge funds managing billions of dollars in assets. I worked diligently, but in the back of my mind, I thought I wouldn't be around for long.

But then the world started to shake. First, the J. P. Morgan office in New York sits above Grand Central Terminal, so you can feel the rumble when a train approaches. And second, Lehman Brothers failed (as did my Indian enterprise), and the great financial crisis was under way. I had a unique position. I had a desk in a row on a trading floor in a building that belonged to a bank in the middle of the crisis. I didn't just have a courtside seat. I was in the game. It occurred to me then, as it does now, that I was a part of history. I decided to stay (and wasn't fired).

Being new to global markets, I had trouble keeping up with the alphabet soup of news: AIG, AAA, CDS, TARP, VOL, ZIRP. I created an "SGO" or "Shit Going On" folder on my laptop in which I saved stories to read over the weekend. I was alarmed with the damage wrought by the financial crisis, and I had difficulty grasping how it could have happened in the first place. I rode the No. 6 train and saw grown men crying while they carried cardboard boxes of office supplies. I remember watching on television the misery in the eyes of Americans who had lost their homes. Seven years later and now a vice president, I am still working out the meaning of it all.

I made it a personal project to learn about the financial crisis and its root causes. I began an odyssey that took years and culminates in this book. I started by reading books on the financial crisis and quickly learned that historically, busts are as much a part of the financial system as booms: from tulip mania, which gripped the Netherlands in the 1630s, to the dot-com crash at the turn of the twenty-first century. I read historical works such as Charles Kindleberger and Robert Aliber's *Manias, Panics, and Crashes* and Roger Lowenstein's *When Genius Failed.* These older texts deepened my interest in economic history and reintroduced me to the works of economic philosophers like Adam Smith, David Ricardo, John Stuart Mill, Karl Marx, John Maynard Keynes, Friedrich Hayek, Murray Rothbard, and Milton Friedman. In total, I read hundreds of sources looking for answers. The more I read, the more I wanted to know.

My investigation into financial crises provoked me to ask a more sweeping question: What is it about money that we can't master? There's something about it that makes us act in bizarre and irrational ways. I looked for answers in the texts of behavioral economists like Daniel Kahneman, Amos Tversky, and Richard Thaler, who study the psychology of people when making economic decisions. Their research led me to that of neuroeconomists like Brian Knutson and Paul Glimcher, who examine and interpret brain scans of people while they make financial decisions. Since all decisions, including financial ones, are made in the brain, I delved into the research of evolutionary economists like Haim Ofek, who examines how the brain developed over thousands of years, and whether money was an output of an evolutionary process. My quest for depth resulted in breadth. I grew fascinated with the many approaches through which one can understand money.

It became apparent that to focus only on financial crises or to consider money with a traditional economic lens belies the full range of what money means to us. Besides, the world didn't need another book on the 2008 financial crisis.

Money is like a musical note. In one note, there are more notes vibrating at other frequencies; we just can't hear them. Similarly, there is more to money than there may first appear. Take, for instance, $2,500. It means something diffcrent if it's booked as revenue, income, taxes, plunder, bribes, earmarks, or an honorarium—even though it's the same amount. Whether someone hoards $2,500 or donates it to the Red Cross may reveal their values, character, and even religious beliefs. Say someone pays $250 to his mother-in-law as payment for her preparing Thanksgiving dinner. If this is acceptable behavior, it provides anthropological insights into the society itself: Norms of the marketplace have replaced those found in the familial sphere. In this case, money has altered a societal norm and modified human behavior.

The necessity of money, and its multiple frequencies, led me to an even broader question: What is it about money that makes the world go 'round? My obsession for money, not making it but understanding it, was governed by this question. It's this question that is at the center of this book.

The traditional definition of money is that it's a medium of exchange, unit of account, and store of value. It likely originates from economist William

Stanley Jevons's 1875 text, *Money and the Mechanism of Exchange*. The definition adequately describes the economic function of money. During my taxi ride, the rupiah acted as a medium of exchange, the valuable item that changed hands. It also acted as an Indonesian unit of account because it provided a standard measurement for the service being rendered, in this case, the taxi ride. We didn't haggle about how much 10,000 rupiah was worth. It also acted as a store of value in that I could keep it in my wallet and retrieve it hours, weeks, even years later and it would have roughly the same value (not considering inflation and other developments that impact the value of money over time).

But as my taxi experience suggests, money doesn't just play an economic role, and the traditional definition seems limited. It doesn't account for various other ways one can interpret money.

A wider perspective begets a broader definition: I define money as a symbol of value. A symbol is used to represent something else. It's an abstraction from the thing that it represents. Value is the importance or worth of something. Money is therefore a sign of something valuable and important.

This simple yet expansive definition isn't original. But it gets us past seeing money purely as a monetary instrument. It helps us to listen in to money's various frequencies and set the frame for the collage of topics found in this book. Despite the kaleidoscopic lenses in which money is viewed within this book, it can be understood throughout as a symbol of value. Each chapter unpacks money through the prism of a different critical perspective in order to see the same topic in a new light. And that's the purpose of this book: to coin a multiplicity of ways to think about money.

One of these ways is to see money as alive. It lives. It sleeps. It breathes. It adapts. That's because we as humans are ever changing. Ever since the creation of money, we have adapted it to better fit our needs, from precious metals to plastic. But just as we think we determine the form of money, it also shapes us. Our skin conductance increases at the thought of money. Our brains register money as a stimulus, so much so that the brain scan of someone about to receive a hit of cocaine is virtually indistinguishable from someone about to gain money. Money has done to us what Pavlov did to his dog: Anticipated gain stimulates and conditions the brain.

Some scholars contend that money may have led to the creation or spread of religions. As coinage was invented in Greece, India, and China, leaders like Pythagoras, Buddha, and Confucius gained legions of followers. Dealing with money is a central theme of many religious lessons. In the Gospel of Matthew, eight of the ten parables reference money or wealth in some way. That money may shape our religious beliefs and rewires our neural circuitry demonstrates its omnipresent and dynamic force on our lives. It intrudes in almost every part of our lives from birth, presenting gifts to a newborn; to death, receiving an inheritance; to the hereafter, buying indulgences to save the soul.

I personify money with the subtitle *The Rich Life of Money and How Its History Has Shaped Us* to highlight its influence. I also invoke a biographical device to serve as the organizational skeleton for this text. This book, this life of money, is divided into three sections: Mind, Body, and Soul.

In Mind, I ask "Why?" That is, why do we use money? I answer this question by using biology, psychology, and anthropology. In chapter 1, I travel to the Galapagos Islands in search of the origin of exchange. It's a peculiar place to start, but before examining money, one must understand the nature of exchange. On these islands, I meet scientists who teach me about the evolutionary biological process and how exchange is fundamental to life on this planet. I boil things down to the cellular level to understand why organisms exchange with one another and enter into symbiotic relationships—usually to obtain food and resources to survive. In the natural world, energy functions as currency. But in the human world, money is also a primary currency. In order to deal in money, humans must be able to think symbolically. Thus I trace the evolution and expansion of the brain, and how the first signs of symbolic thought are found in cave drawings that were made tens of thousands of years ago.

In chapter 2, I go inside the brain, examining the psychology and neuroscience of financial decision making. The subconscious operates quietly beneath the surface, making financial decisions even when we think we're not. For example, the weather impacts how much one tips a waiter. The type of music playing in a store influences what type of wine one buys. There may even be a gene that determines whether someone is predisposed to making riskier financial decisions. The promise of neuroeconomics, the nexus of neuroscience and economics, may tell us more than conventional economic models ever did about human behavior. Neuroeconomics may reveal why we use money in the first place—or at least how to be more aware of the hidden forces guiding our financial decisions.

In chapter 3, I examine the social brain, the collective wisdom of crowds. Some anthropologists contend that debt, not barter, was the forerunner to money. I discover how various cultures deal with social debt or gifts: the Maori people of New Zealand, residents of the Trobriand Islands in the Solomon Sea, the Kwakiutl people of the Pacific Northwest; even netizens who use Napster and Kickstarter. I examine the edge of where the gift economy ends and the market economy begins. When market values reign supreme, and everything has a price, it can lead to the dark side of debt. When social debt is transformed into market debt, it may result in disgusting practices like debt bondage and slavery.

In Body, I ask "What?" That is, what is money? I answer this question by focusing on the physical forms of money throughout the ages, and also on the possible futures of it. Chapter 4 is the story of hard money, made from precious metals. I visit the gold vault beneath the Federal Reserve Bank of New York and see the elaborate measures the government takes to safeguard yellow metal. I trace the origin of metal as money from ancient Mesopotamia to ancient Egypt. In the seventh century BC, coinage was invented in Lydia. It spread throughout Greece and the Mediterranean world in the subsequent centuries. During the Roman Empire, coins were debased and manipulated for political reasons. In altering the physical form of money, man was also trying to shape society and control others.

Chapter 5 is the story of soft money, which is not linked to metal. I discover the early uses of paper money in tenth-century China. It was used widely by Kublai Khan to unify his empire during the thirteenth century. But paper money is only one part of the modern monetary system. Eighteenth-century France is an example of how paper money can reboot a flagging economy. John Law's monetary system may have lasted only four years, but it achieved a financial resurrection, thanks in part to soft money. The modern financial system relies on soft money, so I briefly survey the history of the dollar until it was unhooked from gold in 1971, and explain how the Federal Reserve and banks work together to create money today.

Chapter 6 is the story of the future—the good, the bad, and the incredible. If the world suffers an economic cataclysm, we may return to using goods and services. In the 2008 financial crisis, the price of gold soared. Many returned to bartering, the exchange of hard commodities, instead of just using money. If the world avoids disaster, it's likely that money will be increasingly plastic and invisible. In the emerging world, there is a lack of credit cards but a plethora of mobile phones. The future of money will be realized when mobile phones become the preferred method of payment for billions around the world. The future of money may also resemble science fiction: the rise of a "neural wallet" in which everyone is plugged into a grid that enables people to trade ideas and energy.

In Soul, I ask "How?" That is, how should we use money? I answer this question by turning to the humanities, such as religion and art. Money isn't just a symbol of value but a symbol of our values, depending on how it's used and expressed. In chapter 7, I highlight how major religions provide ample instruction on how to handle money. I recount lessons from the Bible, Torah, Koran, and Vedas. In all these scriptures, there seems to be a spiritual logic of *less is more* or *enough is enough* when it comes to material wealth. For example, Jesus advises a rich man to sell his earthly treasures and follow him. In Hinduism, it's through experiencing *artha*, or material pleasures, that one is awakened to the need to renounce it and achieve *moksha*, or liberation.

In chapter 8, I travel with an archaeologist to rural Bangladesh in search of a lost civilization that Ptolemy once described. It's through a hoard of coins discovered at the ruins, the symbols on the money, that one can identify this civilization. The symbols, the art, help to elevate money to its valuable, monetary status. They also express a nation's identity and cultural history. For my job I have traveled more than 700,000 miles to more than twenty-five developing nations, from Turkey to Thailand, South Africa to Sri Lanka. I use my spare moments to meet with coin collectors. I ask them which coins best represent their countries, and what the symbols on these coins mean. This book begins with a historical explanation of symbolic Paleolithic cave art, and it ends with a geographical safari in which I interpret the creativity found on monetary art.

This book does not advance a grand theory, nor does it provide completely unique perspectives. It synthesizes the work of others that is detailed in the selected bibliography, and to whom I am grateful. Indeed, there is an infinite amount of topics that I could have included, or the subjects that I did choose could have been investigated with more depth. Each chapter could be the subject of an entire book. But every chapter is meant to spark your curiosity, not satisfy it.

The financial crisis ignited my curiosity and exploded my perception of money. It caused me to think about an ancient topic in new ways, to hear the different frequencies of money. Master musician Duke Ellington's adage, "No boxes," became my mantra. My quest led me to examine money from cell to community, from life to death, from inner spirit to outer space. I blurred the lines among sciences, social sciences, and the humanities. I traversed every hemisphere, over twenty-five countries. I explored its past and dreamed about its future. This book presents a multidimensional and interdisciplinary portrait of currency through the ages. It seeks to deepen your understanding of the history of money, and to show how it continues to shape our future in often imperceptible ways. I hope this book will explode your perception of money, and help you coin new ways to think about it.

PART I

MIND

The Roots of an Idea

CHAPTER ONE

It's a Jungle Out There

The biology of exchange

I keep the subject of my inquiry constantly before me, and wait
till the first dawning opens gradually, by little and little, into a full
and clear light.
—*Isaac Newton*[1]

But man has almost constant occasion for the help of his
brethren.
—*Adam Smith*[2]

But several seedling mistletoes, growing close together on the
same branch, may more truly be said to struggle with each other.
As the mistletoe is disseminated by birds, its existence depends
on them; and it may metaphorically be said to struggle with other
fruit-bearing plants.
—*Charles Darwin*[3]

An example of symbiotic exchange in the natural world:
fish cleaning a green sea turtle.

The bay buzzed with underwater activity as sea lions and colorful fish rushed past me. A current of frigid water enveloped me as I swam in the direction of the ocean. Looking for a warmer spot, I whirled around and headed for a narrow crevice that was receiving more sunlight. But instead I scratched my foot on a jagged boulder, and stayed put—waiting. I held on to black lava rock that had been covered with a bed of slimy algae. And then I saw it.

My quest to understand the origin of money began underwater. I wasn't looking for the booty of a sunken pirate ship, but another type of treasure. My friend took a deep breath and dove eleven feet to the bottom of a ridge, where she scooped up a small dollar-green-colored object with her bare hands. She surfaced and swam to me so that I could see it more closely.

"This is what we were looking for," she said.

She would certainly know, as marine ecosystems are her field of expertise.

My friend's name is Rachel Gittman. And for her, it ain't about the money.

"Nobody goes into science for the money," she says, laughing. "I didn't have much to begin with."

Rachel grew up on a farm in Prince George County, Virginia, where she spent much of her time outside, in nature, exposed to the elements. "As a child, I was fascinated by nature and wanted to understand more about the natural world." Now in her late twenties, she is a PhD candidate in ecology at the University of North Carolina at Chapel Hill. And she would help me understand more about the world, and more about money.

But in order to learn from her, I had to trek to her.

I began my search for the roots of money in a peculiar place. An obvious place to start my quest to understand money would have been the Great Rift Valley in East Africa, to search for artifacts that were used as currency, and where many early human fossils have been discovered; or in western Turkey, once the site of the Kingdom of Lydia, where coinage was likely invented in the seventh century BC. But to start my quest in these places would be like tuning in to a baseball game in the eighth inning. NASA calculates that eight hundred generations span the thousands of years of human existence. Of these, more than six hundred resided in caves and only the last few generations saw words in print.[4] Put another way, humans have existed for 0.004 percent of earth's history.[5] I voyaged to a place where modern humans have made a smaller imprint, where I could observe the organic origin of exchange.

I found myself in the Pacific Ocean, near the equator, far from the Ecuadorian coast, in an undulating motorboat appropriately named *Destiny*. I was journeying to Isabela Island, part of the Galapagos Islands, to meet Rachel.

I picked these islands for a reason. They were the same islands that inspired Charles Darwin to arrive at his theory of evolution by natural selection. He wrote in his book *On the Origin of Species* that his journey aboard the HMS *Beagle* and his observations of the Galapagos would "throw some light on the origin of species—that mystery of mysteries."[6] An expedition to the Galapagos might also throw some light on the roots of money, and specifically, the nature of exchange.

It was a picture-perfect day under an enormous blue sky, with an ocean breeze to soften the heat. Rachel met me at the dock, wearing a Carolina-blue UNC baseball hat, similar-colored T-shirt, black shorts, and sunglasses. She was in the Galapagos as part of a research project to study marine life in mangrove ecosystems. We ambled down a sandy road, and after thirty-five minutes, my lesson began.

"Exchange happens everywhere on these islands," said Rachel. "From the bottom of the food chain to the top."

So we started at the bottom.

We walked through the mangroves, over a sleeping sea lion (and its poop), under a blue-footed booby that had taken flight, around three dozen marine iguanas, until we arrived at Concha de Perla, a small bay in the southeast part of Isabela Island. We put on our snorkels and flippers—and dove in.

When Rachel surfaced, she held in her hand a dollar-green sea urchin. She had told me about them, but I couldn't find one on my own—I benefited from her expertise. This would be my first lesson of how exchange happens in the Galapagos. The sea urchin needs energy to survive, so it eats algae. The sea urchin is a herbivore and grazes on the algae, transferring the energy to itself. It's not the only organism that feeds on algae, as the damselfish competes with the sea urchin. A damselfish sometimes picks up a sea urchin by its spine and takes it elsewhere, away from the algae.[7] But this is an example of how one organism benefits at the expense of another.

To find an example of symbiosis, when the exchange of two different organisms benefits both, I only had to submerge and look around. Resting on a lava rock was a sea turtle with a shell two feet in diameter. It had exposed its fins so that five wrasse fish could eat parasites on it, cleaning the turtle. Left to fester, the parasites could cause to form on the turtle's shell a calcium carbonate barnacle that doesn't usually harm it, but some species of barnacles have been known to cause damage. In some cleaning stations, a cleaning fish even swims into the mouth of the larger fish being cleaned, so that it can remove parasites in hard-to-reach areas.

Rachel explained to me that symbiosis is a crucial component of marine ecosystems, as many organisms rely on each other to survive and reproduce. She told me about the exchange between coral polyps and zooxanthellae. Though it's difficult to observe with the naked eye, she walked me through it. Corals form hard skeletons by secreting calcium carbonate, which then form reefs that serve as the habitat for thousands of marine species. Zooxanthellae (pronounced zo-uh-zan-THELL-ee) are microalgae that live in the tissue of corals. Through the process of cellular respiration, the coral produces carbon dioxide. The zooxanthellae use carbon dioxide in photosynthesis. The by-products of photosynthesis are oxygen and organic compounds that provide energy that the coral needs.[8] The zooxanthellae supply the coral with food. The coral provides the zooxanthellae with shelter.

My quest to understand money begins with asking why we use it in the first place. To use my baseball analogy again, it's difficult to determine the objective of baseball just by looking at a bat. The aim of baseball is to score more runs than the other team. The bat is a tool that helps accomplish this. Similarly, a dollar bill is an instrument that facilitates exchange.

At the most basic level, humans exchange with one another to acquire the items that we need to survive, like food and shelter. While money is a human invention, all organisms exchange in order to survive. We as humans rely on other organisms to stay healthy, like microorganisms found on our skin and inside our mouth. More than 100 trillion live in the intestine, where bacteria help digest nutrients, metabolize energy, and synthesize vitamins. The bacteria in our gut may also keep out parasitic bacteria.[9] Our intestine provides bacteria a place to live, and it helps keep us well.

In the parlance of Dr. Seuss, exchange happens on a boat, with a goat, in a hut, and in the gut. It is everywhere and so much a part of life on earth, we often don't notice it. From the beginnings of life, when sperm hits the egg, to the end of it, when maggots feast on a corpse, exchange is at work.

To be sure, there is a distinction between exchange that happens between humans and that which happens among other organisms. The difference is that the human brain makes us aware of exchange. It enables us to think tactically about it. As the human brain became capable of symbolic thought, it was possible for us to see the potential value in things. Commodities like salt, barley, and cacao were early forms of currency. As humans began to produce more than they could consume, a surplus handful of barley became an item that might be traded to acquire something else. The surplus became a symbol of value. Its value was realized when it was exchanged for something else. It became currency.

It is easy to understand the transfer of energy taking place in an exchange of one organic commodity for another, when they are then consumed naturally as food. There's no denying that the need for energy serves as a primary catalyst for exchange among all species, both humans and nonhumans. The difference, again, is that humans can trade energy tactically, seeing the symbolic value of it and turning it into realized value. Early humans who traded food items like meat and barley were exchanging energy but in a new way. That they exchanged the energy-rich commodities in a more deliberate manner points to the evolving nature of humans.

Evolutionary economist Haim Ofek asks in his masterful book *Second Nature*: "Was exchange an early agent of human evolution, or is it a mere *de novo* artifact of modern civilization?"[10] He raises the possibility that exchange is an evolutionary force: Organisms that exchange are more likely to survive and reproduce, and pass down an "exchange trait" to future generations. Exchanging—working together—is evolutionarily advantageous. And there is compelling evidence that social people actually live longer.[11] Later in his book, Ofek reasons that human exchange may be a continuation and advancement of that found among the earliest organisms. The development of exchange from microorganisms, to the animal kingdom, to Paleolithic tribes, to Wall Street traders reveals a fascinating progression of an evolutionary force.

Ofek notices patterns in *how* organisms of the same species exchange. Ants and humans, for example, both rely on division of labor in order to more efficiently accomplish a task. Some members of the same species forage for food and others rear the young. Individual organisms that are responsible for certain parts of the larger task become specialists in that part. A specialist creates specific tools in order to accomplish this task.

In the case of humans, we became aware that exchange increases our chances of survival. This awareness would lead to the creation of tools that fostered cooperation, maybe even to outcompete other species. At first these tools would be used to accomplish a simple task, but the brain's capacity for symbolic thought enabled humans to see these instruments as more than just physical objects. Perishable commodities gave way to nonperishable items like agricultural tools, weapons, and jewelry, which all functioned as early currencies. Humans could see the symbolic value of these tools—they could be exchanged for other valuable items. As the human brain became more sophisticated, and as civilization became more complex, there would be a need for a uniform and universal tool that would facilitate exchange more broadly. This tool was money.

It's an intriguing theory—that exchange is part of our evolutionary algorithm. And, ultimately, money is an output of exchange. Ofek's theory provoked me to consider an alternative, biological explanation for why we use money in the first place. To understand the basis for money, I would need to learn about the origin of exchange.

In the Beginning

Long before money was invented or humans roamed the earth, organisms exchanged with one another in order to survive. Some 3.8 billion years ago, the first signs of life emerged: single-celled prokaryotes, such as bacteria that lack nuclei. Two billion years ago, multicellular eukaryotes appeared. These cells make up fungi, plants, animals, and people. It was through symbiosis that eukaryotes formed. Eukaryotes developed when one prokaryote ingested another prokaryote. Instead of being destroyed, the smaller cell stuck around forever as a specialized structure known as an organelle, like a houseguest who never moved out.

The organelle in question is the mitochondrion. Biologists suspect it used to be a prokaryote. Mitochondria resemble prokaryotes and reproduce like them, dividing independently of the greater cell, which means it's semi-autonomous, but it relies on the cell for many of its proteins.[12] Eventually mitochondria lost their ability to live outside the greater cell. The family adopted the houseguest. Thankfully, it does some chores.

One of those chores is providing food for the family. The mitochondria provide energy to the greater cell. It has two membranes, which are like walls in a house. One membrane is folded to boost its surface area, so that it can produce more energy in the form of adenosine triphosphate (ATP). All organisms need energy to reproduce and operate. A molecule found in all living cells, ATP delivers energy from foods to the cell. Like the coral and zooxanthellae, the cell provides shelter, and the mitochondria supply energy.

This theory about the creation of eukaryotes is known as symbiogenesis, the union of two cells to create one, and it explains the basis of earthly life. Russian botanist Boris Mikhaylovich Kozo-Polyansky first proposed symbiogenesis in the early twentieth century.[13] It's a plausible and widely accepted explanation of how eukaryotes developed. Kozo-Polyansky's theory implies that symbiosis, working together, is foundational to the life of all multicellular organisms.

The Garden of Symbiosis

A discussion of symbiosis seems incomplete without including that found between two multicellular organisms: insects and plants. Sure, some plants like ragweed and grass rely on wind rather than insects to spread their pollen, but that's inefficient. These plants have to produce excess pollen so that the wind will carry enough to exactly the right flower.

Plants need insects to reproduce. Insects need plants to eat. Flowers advertise with pleasant aromas and colorful pigments, inviting insects, as well as birds and bats, to visit. Flowers furnish them nectar, which is a sugary water solution derived from sunlight. A sampling of nectar shows quantities of sugar that range from 18 percent to 68 percent. Nectar, with its saccharides, proteins, amino acids, and enzymes, provides energy for insects to persist. Bees turn nectar into honey, which is in essence conserved energy, like a reserve generator, which switches on during winter when flowers have wilted.

Bees need not only nectar but the nutrients stored in the amino acids of pollen. Produced by the anthers of a flower, pollen is the male fertilizing agent. Many of the twenty-five thousand species of bees use nectar and pollen as the sole type of nutrition for their young. Bees have body hair that helps collect pollen. The pollen is stored in the corbicula, a type of pollen container connected to a bee's back leg. Bees transport pollen like couriers making an express delivery. Trade terms of the flower: I'll give you food. You deliver my package.

This relationship has been studied dating back to at least the eighteenth century. The large body of research has led many scientists to conclude that it's impossible to imagine a world in which plants and insects existed without each other. The symbiosis is an example of coevolution, a mutually beneficial partnership. The history of this exchange goes back more than 100 million years, to when specimens of female insects were found to be carrying pollen, a sign that they were likely searching for food for their young.[14]

Bees and flowers—like the cell and mitochondria, coral and zooxanthellae, sea turtles and wrasses, and humans and intestinal bacteria—help each other to survive.

The Currency of Nature

In all these examples of symbiosis, energy is being exchanged. It can be said that energy is the currency of nature.[15] To highlight the role of energy in symbiosis, consider again the electric exchange between bees and flowers. When a bumblebee lands on a flower, it buzzes in a higher pitch to shake the pollen out of it. One estimate is that 8 percent of flowers are pollinated using this method.[16] The bee's flapping wings even jolt the flower with electricity. A flower has a negative charge compared to the air surrounding it. Bees have a positive charge. When a bee lands on the flower, negatively charged pollen attaches to the bee.

Researchers decided to test whether electricity actually makes a difference in the symbiotic relationship between flowers and bees. They created a flower bed with fake flowers. Half the flowers had a solution akin to nectar; the others had a repellent one. The bumblebees foraged randomly in the flower bed. When the researchers introduced a negative charge to certain flowers, bees visited them more frequently. When the charge was removed, the random foraging resumed. After the bee departs, the flower keeps the positive charge for more than a minute, as if to hang a "Do Not Disturb" sign for the next guest.[17]

Bees and flowers are also part of a greater exchange that encompasses all living organisms. The grandest example of symbiotic energy transfer is that of photosynthesis and cellular respiration. Consider the chemical reaction of photosynthesis:

$$6H_2O + CO_2 + \text{light particles} \rightarrow C_6H_{12}O_6 + O_2$$

In the first part of the reaction, there are water (H_2O), carbon dioxide (CO_2), and light particles. Water enters the plant through its roots. Carbon dioxide is absorbed by a green plant's leaves, like those that the bee visits. They combine with invisible particles of sunlight called photons, which are captured by pigment molecules such as chlorophylls in green plants. When combined, they produce glucose, $C_6H_{12}O_6$, to be used immediately or saved for later to create more complicated foods like fruit. Oxygen (O_2) is a by-product of photosynthesis. Though this is a basic explanation, photosynthesis is essential in creating oxygen and energy, the currency of nature. All food chains start with organisms that create organic molecules from inorganic material—like the algae I swam through in Concha de Perla.

Cellular respiration is photosynthesis in reverse. It's the process of breaking down foods to release energy. Animals ingest organic molecules like fruits and vegetables and, with oxygen, convert them into carbon dioxide and ATP. Consider the chemical reaction of cellular respiration:

$$C_6H_{12}O_6 + 6O_2 \rightarrow 6H_2O + 6CO_2 + ATP$$

Glucose breaks down through a process called glycolysis into molecules known as pyruvates, which are processed in the mitochondria, which emit carbon dioxide. The energy found in glucose is transported through an electronic transport chain that creates oxygen as a by-product. The chain eventually yields ATP. Photosynthesis and cellular respiration constitute a virtuous cycle of symbiotic exchange that makes life as we know it possible.[18] It converts sugar molecules into energy usable by organisms like bees, converting a foreign currency into a more usable one.

Energy and money are both currencies that circulate and flow. The word *currency* comes from the Latin word *currere*, which means "to flow" or "to run."[19] Both energy and money are valuable, and organisms compete to obtain them. Though the earth absorbs a significant amount of solar energy, only a small percentage makes it to organisms in need. So there is intense competition for it: Some plants grow taller to attract more sunlight, shading and starving other plants. Remarkably, the starved plant informs its stem to grow more quickly, a response that botanists call "shade avoidance syndrome."[20]

If an organism must use energy immediately after obtaining it, the creature is dangerously dependent on the source. If the source is interrupted, the organism may die. That's why many organisms store energy. Whales amass fat for their protracted journeys. Birds and squirrels store food in caches, like a savings account to draw upon in times of need. Storing energy allows organisms a degree of sureness in the face of uncertainty. Because it's valuable, desirable, and storable, energy bears a similar role to money in the human world.

Money may be an evolutionary substitute for energy. As our ancestors evolved from hunting and gathering food to cultivating and preserving it, humans produced more than they could consume. The surplus took on symbolic importance. An extra barrel of salt mined was more than a mineral to be consumed. It could help preserve other food, other sources of energy. One of the first civilizations of the Neolithic Age in 9000 BC was Jericho, and it became a trading center for Dead Sea salt. Humans were eating more meat like pigs and cattle, and salt preserved it.[21] There was a strong demand for salt, so it became a currency.

Salt had gone from being just a rock, and a way of conserving food, to an item that could obtain more of it. Salt blurs the line between commodity and currency because it has historically been used as both. Instead of humans consuming the mineral immediately, like an animal might, they *thought* about what else they could do with it. They could see that salt could represent something else, like pepper. By focusing on the commodity aspect of salt, one can see how one form of energy is exchanged and turned into another:

$$C \rightarrow C$$

The *C* stands for "commodity." In this barter trade, both the salt and the pepper are represented by C. You trade salt for pepper. You are still trading commodities that fulfill their evolutionary purpose of sustaining humans and helping them survive. But, like energy, the commodity has been converted from one form into another by trading it. In a more advanced society that uses money, the exchange is still a conversion of energy forms. In his book *Capital,* volume 1, Karl Marx considers the conversion of commodities into money as the most basic form of monetary exchange:

$$C \rightarrow M \rightarrow C$$

Again, the *C* stands for "commodity" which is sold and turned into M, or money, like coins. This money is used to buy another commodity, like pepper.[22] As you will see, the human awareness that C was convertible and exchangeable was a first step in the creation of M. But I use this example to highlight how a source of energy like barley can be converted into different forms through exchange. Money, too, can be converted into various forms. Even today, money is used to obtain perishable commodities, which in essence are forms of energy that we need in order to live. Though modern money has been abstracted from its evolutionary role, it is still the tool we use to acquire the calories that we need.

The Human Connection

Darwin's phrase "the survival of the fittest" is often used to describe the competition with others. For basic necessities like food to a rank in the social ladder, humans struggle against others at times. Darwin adopted the phrase at the suggestion of British philosopher Herbert Spencer, who believed evolution was a universal theory. Spencer believed in what later became known as "Social Darwinism," that evolution shaped not only humans but society: A simple society evolved into a more complex one. A more pernicious interpretation is that the stronger or more "fit" persons will reap more rewards.

However, Darwin meant the phrase as a broad explanation to account for the biological development of all species—not as a description or justification of human society.[23] Instead, Darwin recognized that symbiosis and cooperation were critical to survival. He found that organic cells were microcosms, systems that work together. He even advanced a theory of pangenesis, in which tiny particles called gemmules were marked with data and fused with reproductive cells. The fusion of cells was how parents transmitted familial instructions to their offspring, such as beak size and eye color.[24] His theory was later replaced with insights into genetics, but it underscores Darwin's realization that cooperation is fundamental to life. In *The Descent of Man*, Darwin takes it further, positing that sympathy within the same species is an output of evolutionary forces: "[Sympathy] will have increased, through natural selection; for those communities which included the greatest number of the most sympathetic members, would flourish best and rear the greatest number of offspring."[25]

In his landmark book, *The Evolution of Cooperation*, political scientist Robert Axelrod concludes that cooperation helps people survive and is therefore evolutionarily beneficial. His conclusion is supported by the results generated from a simulated tournament he ran.

He used the well-known Prisoner's Dilemma game in his tournament. Prisoner's Dilemma starts with you and your friend being arrested. The police question you separately. You face a year in prison, but if you snitch on your friend, your sentence will be reduced. Your friend is offered the same deal. If you both snitch, you will both receive longer sentences. But if you both remain silent, and cooperate with one another, you will both benefit. It's a dilemma because you don't know what your friend will choose.

In 1980, Axelrod planned a computer tournament to see which strategy is best, whether you should cooperate with your friend or not. He assigned points to each of the four outcomes:

(1) If both you and your friend cooperate, you are both rewarded with three points; (2) if you snitch, and your friend cooperates, then you receive five points, and your friend receives zero; (3) conversely, if you cooperate, and your friend snitches, then you receive zero points, and your friend receives five points; and (4) if you both snitch, you both receive one point. The incentive to snitch is significant: You will receive points regardless of whether your friend snitches or cooperates.[26]

Scholars from several academic disciplines, such as evolutionary biology and economics, who were knowledgeable about Prisoner's Dilemma submitted strategies that were pitted against each other in more than two hundred iterations of the game. The winning strategies remained in the tournament, and the losing ones were discarded. Axelrod writes, "This process simulates survival of the fittest . . . At first, a rule that is successful . . . will proliferate, but later as the unsuccessful rules disappear, success requires good performance with other successful rules."[27] He found that the experts who submitted strategies took too competitive an approach and assumed that the other prisoner would snitch.[28]

The winning strategy was known as "Tit for Tat." Even when contestants were aware that Tit for Tat had won the initial round, they couldn't beat it in subsequent ones. The strategy calls for cooperation on the first move and reciprocation on subsequent moves. Tit for Tat shows that it pays to cooperate. But if someone attacks you, you should strike back to punish them. But if then the person reverts to cooperation, you should forgive them and cooperate, too. Axelrod recognizes that self-interest is the basis for cooperation. It helps your individual situation if you both cooperate. He writes, "You benefit from the other player's cooperation. The trick is to encourage that cooperation. A good way to do it is to make it clear that you will reciprocate."[29]

Though Axelrod's tournament was a theoretical game, it had profound implications. His book has had more than twenty thousand citations across a broad range of academic disciplines, including those who have considered whether cooperation was part of the evolutionary algorithm. At first glance, Axelrod's results support Ofek's theory that cooperation is evolutionarily advantageous.

Axelrod and evolutionary biologist William D. Hamilton translated their findings to biology. They provide the example of fig trees and wasps, which are symbiotic organisms. Wasps pollinate the tiny flowers inside figs. In return, they have shelter to lay eggs, so their larvae have an immediate source of nourishment. A wasp could "snitch" by underpollinating the flowers found inside figs. The tree could "snitch" by stopping the growth of a fig that has been underpollinated, killing the larvae of the wasps.[30] Both these organisms seem to be reflexively following Tit for Tat. Evolutionary biologist Richard Dawkins agrees with Axelrod's results and writes that "many wild animals and plants are engaged in ceaseless games of Prisoner's Dilemma, played out in evolutionary time."[31]

It's not just wild animals, but apparently humans, too. In Axelrod's tournament, even when it paid not to cooperate, for some reason, cooperation among humans prevailed. That may be because humans are aware that cooperation increases the chances of survival. Unlike most animals, humans can think before they act, and they reason that it's better to cooperate. The results reinforced the view of economist Ludwig von Mises, who writes in *Human Action* that "human beings are potential collaborators in the struggle for survival because they are capable of recognizing the mutual benefits of cooperation."[32] We seem to be biologically wired to cooperate, and an awareness of this helps improve our chances of enduring as a species, even though, as many biologists contend, individuals cooperate because of their own self-interest, not because of what may ultimately benefit the species.

Indeed, cooperation and socializing increase our chances of survival. Dr. Dean Ornish found that a leading cause for heart disease was isolation from others.[33] In her book *The Bond*, Lynne McTaggart writes that "healthy adults with good support networks have lower blood cholesterol levels and higher levels of immune function than those without emotional support."[34]

In one study, stroke patients who were isolated from others were more likely to have another stroke than patients who were more social.[35] Another report combed more than one hundred studies that compared human relationships with health outcomes. It concluded that any type of social relationship can increase survival rates by 50 percent. Being alone, not having a social and supportive network, is analogous to smoking more than a dozen cigarettes per day and can increase the likelihood of obesity.[36]

That cooperation helps us survive squares with Kozo-Polyansky's theory of symbiogenesis at the cellular level. Dawkins believes it proves true at the gene level; he contends that the "selfish gene" is responsible for cooperation: Organisms of the same species share similar genes, and even though they are self-interested actors, their cooperation helps to perpetuate their gene pool.[37] "Survival of the fittest" describes the gene, not the organism. All organisms, from intestinal bacteria to humans, usually exchange in order to pursue their own self-interests, but one effect is that it can perpetuate their genes in future generations. Because cooperation boosts our chances to survive, a "selfish gene" may have spread through our population as a way to perpetuate the gene pool. This "selfish gene" that encourages cooperation may be part of our evolutionary algorithm.

Researchers have tried to determine whether primates have a gene that makes them more prone to cooperate. They examined more than two hundred species of primates and concluded that social behavior is a function of genetics. They didn't locate a specific gene, but they ruled out other variables. For example, baboons exhibit the same social living patterns no matter their geography or environment. In one study, researchers noted the foraging behavior of 217 species of primates. They found that about 52 million years ago, foraging likely became more social. They hypothesize that primates lived together in order to increase their chances of survival. If they lived alone, it may have invited more predators. This more social foraging pattern, they write, "facilitates the evolution of cooperative behaviors and may provide the scaffold for other distinctive anthropoid traits including coalition formation, cooperative resource defence, and large brains."[38]

The DNA of humans is 99 percent the same as chimpanzees', so researchers also hypothesize that human exchange may be driven by genetics.[39] In one study, they found a gene that accounts for cooperation and altruism. Researchers asked more than one hundred participants to memorize and repeat a group of numbers. If they successfully repeated the numbers, they would earn cash. After earning the reward, they were shown a charity advertisement that had a picture of a little girl from Peru. The participants were given the option to donate anonymously part or all of their earnings to charity, though the researchers could still track who donated. Before the study, researchers had collected DNA swabs of all participants. Researchers focused on the COMT gene, which has two variants, COMT-Val and

COMT-Met, which are evenly distributed among humans.[40] They found that participants who had the COMT-Val variant donated twice the amount of money, and that more than 20 percent of people who had this variant donated their entire reward.[41]

Another possibility for why humans cooperate is the "love hormone" of oxytocin. It's created in the brain and disbursed into the bloodstream, though there are oxytocin receptors found in neurons in the nucleus accumbens, which is part of the reward center of the brain. Oxytocin levels in the bloodstream are typically minimal and require a stimulus to be increased. Mothers experience heightened levels of oxytocin while breast-feeding. When people hug a friend or check Facebook to catch up with friends, they also experience increased levels of oxytocin.[42]

In one study, there was a positive correlation between participants who donated money and the amount of oxytocin in their bloodstream.[43] In one study that focused on causation, participants who were provided doses of oxytocin were 80 percent more generous in donating money to a stranger than those who received a placebo.[44] Researchers have even tested whether oxytocin alters the behavior of those in the Prisoner's Dilemma game. Oxytocin increased cooperation in those players who had met their partners before the game. However, it exacerbated noncooperative behavior when players had not met previously. These results suggest that oxytocin can reinforce a preexisting social bond, but it can't create one from scratch.[45]

If there is a cooperation gene, perhaps it would explain why we form families, tribes, clubs, and countries. As the human brain became more advanced, perhaps the gene was expressed through more sophisticated behaviors like reciprocity, and concepts like equality and morality.[46] It's difficult to work out from where these behaviors originate, but it's clear that humans eventually realized that cooperation increased their chances of survival. And they created tools to foster working together.

Divide and Conquer

Darwin was struck with how life could have developed on the Galapagos archipelago, a microcosm of biological diversity. Because island habitats are isolated from the mainland, they appear to have fewer factors that could impact the development and differentiation of various species. Darwin later grasped that many of the species were unique to the islands yet were similar to creatures on the nearby continent.

Darwin inspected the wildlife closely, comparing the anatomy of birds and recording their size to the millimeter. He famously theorized that the fourteen species of finches found on these islands were interrelated but discernibly different. He noticed the finches had different-sized beaks. He realized that beak size was determined, in part, by each species' niche. For example, big-beaked finches were able to crack open tough seeds. These finches survived a drought on Daphne Major Island and their population flourished.[47] Beak sizes appeared to be an evolved trait that allowed each species to better survive in its environment.[48]

"Beaks are tools," explained Rachel. We had left Concha de Perla, hitched a ride in the back of a red pickup truck (we were still dripping wet and the driver didn't want to ruin her backseat), and ate at a small café called El Tundel de Mayra to continue our discussion. Her lab mate Lindsey Carr joined us for a lunch of ceviche, french fries, and Coca-Colas. Originally from Southern California, she has made these South American islands a home away from home. Lindsey has spent more than 365 days in the Galapagos over five years. She is on track to be the first American to receive her PhD in marine biology from research done in the Galapagos. She patiently explained to me how exchange works across these islands. When I reflected on our conversation weeks later, I realized she was teaching me Economics 101.

"Tools enable specialization," elaborated Lindsey. "When you become a specialist, you narrow your niche and reduce your competition, if everyone else is specializing their niche, too."

She was talking about Darwin's finches, but she could have been talking about Adam Smith's butcher. Both Darwin and Smith lived in Scotland and were influenced by eighteenth-century Scottish Enlightenment intellectuals. Darwin even cites Adam Smith in *The Descent of Man*.

Adam Smith opens *The Wealth of Nations* with meditations on the division of labor. To him it springs from the penchant to exchange. Smith believed that division of labor introduces specialization into a society. Not everyone needs to be a butcher. We simply visit one when we want veal shanks. Similarly, the butcher visits a dentist when he has a toothache. The butcher and dentist need tools, and necessity, it is said, is the mother of invention. The butcher has a meat cleaver to hack through muscle tissue. The dentist has a dental mirror to peer into his patients' mouths. Specialization leads to the need and development of tools—from beaks to cleavers to mirrors.[49] One tool, in particular, may have paved the way for the creation of money.

The First Palm Pilot

A son of British missionaries and an intellectual disciple of Charles Darwin, archaeologist Louis Leakey traveled to Kenya in 1926 to excavate near Lake Elmenteita, in the Great Rift Valley. Three years later his team unearthed a collection of hand axes that were estimated to be 500,000 years old.[50] Similar bifacial hand axes that date back hundreds of thousands of years have been discovered in excavations across Africa, Asia, and Europe.[51] In 1931, Leakey discovered a hand axe at the Olduvai Gorge in Tanzania that dates back 1.2 million years; it is now housed at the British Museum in London. It was made from phonolite, a chunk of green lava, and sculpted by hitting or "knapping" round pebbles against it. The process results in a teardrop-shaped axe with a pointed tip and jagged edges. The pointed edge could be used like a drill to dig holes in the ground. The sharp sides could be used to bludgeon an animal, tear its hide like a rudimentary meat cleaver, scratch bark from a tree, or possibly etch artwork on a cave wall.

Much can be inferred from ancient hand axes. First, they are older than the human species, as *Homo sapiens* dates back only 200,000 years.[52] Second, this tool suggests its toolmaker had a creative capacity. Third, the toolmaker could have used the hand axe as a type of currency. Fourth, these toolmakers may have had other tools that facilitated cooperation. Fifth, the hand axe may have helped to alter the human diet, to one that provided more fuel to the brain, which would lead to the invention of money.

The research into the social behavior of primates indicates that our ancestors lived in groups. They eventually realized that cooperation increased their chances of survival. To foster cooperation, they specialized in different areas, creating a division of labor: Some were hunters that caught game;

others reared children. The creation of hand axes helped hunters kill and prepare larger game, which provided nourishment to the larger group. Division of labor and cooperation, wrote Mises, "are man's foremost tool in his struggle for survival."[53]

Making a hand axe requires cognition and dexterity. Around 1.7 million years ago, our ancestors began to walk upright, perhaps as a way to conserve energy while foraging for food. Temperatures had cooled, and there were fewer forests. Walking upright would have helped in searching for prey, peering out over open grassy areas. A consequence of bipedalism is that our ancestors were freed to begin using their hands in new ways, such as creating new tools. They were able to manifest thoughts into physical forms using their hands. In his detailed book *Landscape of the Mind*, archaeologist John Hoffecker writes that "humans developed the highly unusual ability to externalize information in the brain—probably as an indirect consequence of bipedalism and foreign limb specialization related to toolmaking—and this ultimately became the basis for the mind."[54] Like a sculptor who carves a statue from a block of marble, our ancestors must have visualized a hand axe before it was made. As the brain of the toolmaker became more capable and complex, the tools also became more sophisticated. Axes were refined over the years; the designers may have passed down knowledge on how to create them through apprenticeship. More recent hand axes in the archaeological record were thinner and made from different raw materials, with finer craftsmanship. Most axes have clear symmetry that is the result of preparation and experience, debatably the product of a toolmaker with an appreciation for aesthetics.

Some scholars contend that hand axes had symbolic value. The brain's capacity to think symbolically turned these tools into items that could be exchanged. It's unlikely that everyone created their own hand axe: The specialist toolmaker may have exchanged hand axes for other goods like raw materials, food, and shelter.[55] The wide geography in which hand axes have been discovered shows that they were widely used, there was strong demand for them, and they were worthy of exchange. Scholars even contend that hand axes may have become a type of ceremonial art or currency.[56] Many large axes that are too difficult to grip have been discovered, and could have been symbols of one's wealth, status, or ability to protect one's kin. A larger hand axe may have even helped to attract a mating partner.[57]

If our earliest ancestors could create hand axes, maybe they had other tools—like language. In one study, the brains of archaeologists were scanned while they knapped hand axes. The results show that the same part of the brain responsible for making tools is responsible for comprehending and processing language. If you can craft tools, you can form words. Like the hand, the vocal tract was a tool that helped manifest thoughts externally.[58] It's difficult to know when our ancestors gained the capacity to speak, because the vocal tract is composed of organs that disappeared over time and aren't part of the archaeological register.

The hand axe also helped to alter the diet of our Paleolithic ancestors. Archaeologists have unearthed evidence of butchered elephants, other large game, and freshwater fish during this period.[59] Caches of tools, including hand axes, were located where animal remains were likely taken for processing.[60] Several hand axes have been found near the Thames River in what's now England. Lakes and river valleys provided fresh water that attracted not only early humans but animals as well. Our ancestors probably hid in nearby woods, stalking prey for their meat and furs. While their diet was largely vegetarian, hand axes were a means by which meat was obtained and introduced into consumption.

The transition to meat intake was a significant phenomenon in the development of early humans and the eventual creation of money. Meat has a higher caloric density than plants. The discovery of fire enabled our ancestors to cook meat and make it a more common part of their diet. The ability to store and cook food may have been a trigger for the shrinking of our ancestors' stomachs, since the human stomach is 60 percent of the relative size found in other primates.[61] However, the increased meat consumption provided energy to a growing organ, the brain. Hungry for glucose, our brain consumes 20 percent of the body's energy, roughly twelve watts, almost enough to power a lightbulb.[62] But our brains weren't always as large. Fossil remains of our earliest ancestors show head cavities that are unquestionably smaller than those of modern humans.

There are various reasons besides human diet for why the brain expanded. Among them are climate and competition. During the Paleo-lithic era, our ancestors migrated around the world, as evidenced by many unearthed remains and hand axes. They encountered a range of environ-ments, from the cooler temperatures of the North to the arid climates of Africa. The Smithsonian compares the variations of the earth's climate based on evidence in ocean sediments with the brain size of early humans, using 160 skulls. The brains of early humans increased most quickly from 800,000 to 200,000 years ago, around the time *Homo sapiens* finally emerged.[63] This period was also a time when the earth underwent several ice ages.[64] Others theorize that our brains enlarged because of social competition to acquire more resources.

The expansion of the brain gave rise to consciousness and symbolic thought. It's this capacity that led to the creation of money.

Symbolically Thinking

In 1879 in northern Spain, eight-year-old Maria Sanza de Sautuola and her father went for a walk west of Santander, in Altamira. She dashed ahead by herself, entered a nearby cave, and found an incredible artistic rendering on the ceiling. It was the first known discovery of Paleolithic-era cave drawings. The drawing was made approximately 13,000 years ago, over the span of many centuries. The rendering is of fifteen bison and other large animals. They were depicted using mineral oxides and are polychrome in color. The images are lifelike in detail, and some even have a three-dimensional effect.[65] They are so realistic that many accused Maria's father, Marcelino Sanza de Sautuola, who was an amateur archaeologist, of forgery. It was thought that our Paleolithic ancestors weren't capable of making such intricate artwork. Eventually the images were verified, and UNESCO has declared the area a World Heritage Site.

Archaeologists have since found more than one hundred caves with artwork that dates between 40,000 and 12,000 years ago. Like the Altamira drawings, some feature color that was made by mixing earth mineral oxides with blood or other liquids. Some were created using charcoal and by scratching stones against the wall. Also found in caves have been artifacts like beads made from ivory and bone, as well as musical instruments and weapons. More than 90 percent of Paleolithic spears have some decoration. A figurine of a woman with large breasts was found in a cave in southwest Germany and typifies a fertility motif in Paleolithic renderings.[66]

Common depictions in Paleolithic art are large animals, portly women, and triangular vulvas; they likely represent food and sex. The conspicuous absence of men in the depictions and prevalence of women and their genitalia highlights the importance of reproduction to early humans. Surely not all women were portly, yet 95 percent were depicted thus, leading archaeologists to surmise that large women could be symbols of fertility, health, and an ability to rear children. In a study of more than fifty images of Paleolithic women, the waist-to-hip ratio was found to average 0.655, almost identical to the ratio that men in contemporary studies found most appealing.[67] Paleolithic depictions of women were a symbolic ideal like today's swimsuit models.

The archaeological register is filled with our ancestors' attempts at externally manifesting thought—such as through decorative hand axes—as early as 1.7 million years ago. Paleolithic art revealed the state of the early human capacity for external manifestation. Humans were highly creative, and that would alter everything.[68] Humans could see a bison, remember it, and then re-create it artistically at a later point. This ability to render thoughts in the real world, to create art, is unique to humans.

Civilization has been defined as the "storage of symbols outside the brain."[69] Whether it's a hand axe or a coin, these items were first constructed with mental scaffolding. These mental representations were passed on as symbols and ideas to others, who could hone them and pass them down to future generations. Human society was becoming a decentralized neural network, and tools enabled humans to work cohesively as one unit—like an ant colony. The evolutionary force of exchange that began in the cell had gone social to create a "super-brain," or collective mind of society. Hoffecker observes:

> The *mind* is the super-brain: the integration of brains facilitated by language and other forms of symbolism created the mind. Although the super-brain is composed of a group of individual brains that are

the product of evolutionary biology, it exhibits properties that are unknown or had not been evident in organic evolution.[70]

One of these properties was the human ability to externalize thoughts writ large, throughout society. By the time the Neolithic era begins, the advanced faculties of humans would lead to new ways to cooperate and new tools to facilitate it. It had taken millions of years, but two factors necessary for the creation of money were in place: cooperation and symbolic thought.

Humans were aware that cooperation increased their chances of survival. They could now create symbolic and social tools to abet their biological goals. It was this capacity that turned the currency of energy into commodity money (C-C), which we eventually transformed into coins and paper (C-M-C). These symbols of value represented what they could obtain. The creativity that the brain unleashed would even lead to putting artistic symbols on monetary ones—the signs and insignias found on ancient and modern currency alike. Just as Paleolithic artists drew on caves, today we illustrate on money.

My expedition to the Galapagos helped me glimpse the biological origin of a relatively modern instrument. It was these islands that helped Charles Darwin recognize that natural selection was a common link among all species. It's on these same islands that Rachel opened my eyes to the ubiquity of exchange in nature, and how all organisms rely on each other to survive.

On a tour of the Galapagos Science Center, a joint facility between the University of North Carolina at Chapel Hill and Ecuador's Universidad San Francisco de Quito, on San Cristobal Island, I met more biologists who shared additional examples of exchange. The laboratory technical director and I sat on wooden stools in the marine biology lab while I peppered him with questions. He boiled it down simply for me: "If exchange helps organisms survive, then it must be part of the evolutionary algorithm."

Humans became aware that cooperation was evolutionarily advantageous, so they created tools like language and hand axes to foster it. Humans have continuously created new tools to make it easier to exchange, to cooperate, and to increase our chances of survival. The changing forms of money over thousands of years are improvements to make exchange more convenient and efficient.

At first these tools helped us trade energy. Nourishment is the catalyst for symbiotic exchange for most organisms. As humans produced more than they could consume, not living hand-to-mouth, they traded food items like salt and barley. This commodity money was nonsymbolic, since it directly filled the ultimate need of survival. As our brains gained the capacity for symbolic thought, humans didn't just exchange food, but also other tools, like hand axes, spears, or agricultural devices. These items were an abstraction from the original evolutionary need—to eat and survive. Yet they were symbols of what they supplanted.

Over time, the symbolic mind and the "super-brain" of humanity would see value in more than just these tools. They would see the value in creating a universal tool that would be accepted by all mankind. What started as commodity money became bullion, and eventually coins, paper, and digital currencies. This monetary tool would become a further abstraction from its evolutionary purpose. It would be limited only by our imagination, and the organ that makes that possible.

CHAPTER TWO

A Piece of My Mind

The psychology of money

Because to be truly rational, you can't hold a conviction without
significant empirical evidence.
—*Alan Greenspan*[1]

He weighs losses about twice as much as gains, which is normal.
—*Daniel Kahneman*[2]

Brain imaging gives us the hope of opening up the black box.
—*Brian Knutson*[3]

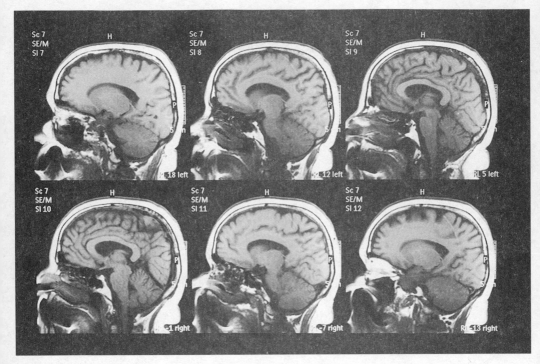

Neuroeconomists use brain scans to understand how the brain makes financial decisions.

In ancient Egypt, the brain was considered insignificant. To prepare for mummification, it was sucked out via the nose and discarded. Instead the heart was preserved, because it was believed to be the seat of the soul and carrier of the consciousness.[4]

By now we know, of course, that the brain facilitates thought and catalyzes action. It's where symbols like money are created and interpreted. Money is a manifestation of the mind. It makes sense, then, to explore how the brain processes money, interprets its value, and understands the *idea* of it. A telling method to determine how the brain registers the *idea of money* is to discern why and how we make financial decisions, which ultimately shape our lives.

Only recently have researchers used brain scans to understand how the mind processes money. Yet, despite not having this technology, economists have long made assumptions about human behavior, which indeed is directed by the brain. In Economics 101, most students learn about *Homo economicus*, or the economic man who makes self-interested decisions, which makes sense from an evolutionary standpoint, since acting in this manner should maximize one's chances for survival. This supposition that humans are rational, logical actors is also the basis of many economic forecasts.

All too often, these forecasts are wrong. For example, the economists at the Federal Reserve, International Monetary Fund, and several Wall Street investment banks didn't foresee the great financial crisis of 2008 or its macroeconomic consequences.

Even as late as September 2008, months after the collapse of Bear Stearns, the median forecast for US economic growth in the fourth quarter was 0.2 percent, as reported by Blue Chip Economic Indicators, versus the annualized decline of 6.2 percent actually recorded, the largest drop since the 1982 recession.[5] Their forecasts failed in part because they were based on the questionable assumption that the market is self-correcting and composed of rational actors.

It raises this question: If economists better understand the mind, could they make more accurate forecasts? To answer this question, consider three economic thinkers: Alan Greenspan, Daniel Kahneman, and Brian Knutson. Greenspan spent many years at the helm of the Fed and long believed that markets were self-correcting and composed of rational actors. But in the wake of the 2008 financial crisis, this line of thought was discredited, and Greenspan has since modified his views. Kahneman is a behavioral economist who studies the psychology of decisions and has documented how humans make many irrational financial decisions. Knutson is a neuro-economist who uses brain imaging to visualize how humans make financial decisions.

Neuroeconomics presents great potential for the future of the economics discipline as a whole. By improving our grasp of how the brain processes the idea of money, perhaps economists will make more accurate forecasts. But the development of this field is a slow process, and, in the short run, it will complement rather than supplant the assumptions and forecasts of more traditional economists. Nevertheless, it's worthwhile to examine these three perspectives to see how our thinking about money continues to evolve.

Let's Get Rational

Alan Greenspan wasn't expecting this type of phone call. The date was March 16, 2008, and an official from the Fed was on the line. Greenspan was informed that the Fed would lend $29 billion for J. P. Morgan to purchase Bear Stearns. It was a jarring moment because he hadn't seen the crisis coming. To be sure, some investors recognized the problems with subprime assets and foresaw the market decline—and even made lots of money by betting against the conventional wisdom. Yet Greenspan describes the crisis as "almost universally unanticipated" in his 2013 book, *The Map and the Territory*.[6] He raises the questions, "What went wrong? Why was virtually every economist and policy maker of note so off about so large an issue?"[7] He answers his questions, in part, by blaming economic forecasts.

But let's consider another question: Why do we forecast in the first place? Even though Greenspan acknowledges that forecasting is fraught with uncertainty, he asserts that "our nature demands it."[8] This economist assumes that there is a biological reason for predictions.

He's right. In one study that demonstrates our nature to forecast, researchers scanned the brains of people who were provided squirts of juice and water in predictable and unpredictable patterns. There was heightened activity in the nucleus accumbens, a region deep within the brain involved in processing rewards, when subjects encountered a predictable pattern.[9] In brief, an accurate forecast resulted in a jolt of pleasure. The evolutionary logic seems to be that when we identify predictable patterns, uncertainty is reduced, which increases our chances of survival.

Even though money has become an abstraction of its original evolutionary purpose, we humans register that it's critical to our survival. "Money represents the means of maintaining life and sustaining us as organisms in our world," states neuroscientist Antonio Damasio.[10] We want to know our financial future because it can aid in our survival.

Forecasting has been integral to the modern financial services industry since the early twentieth century. It was a period of tumult, as the United States economy fluctuated between robust growth and financial panics. Businesspeople grew concerned with the instability because they had to plan for the future, minimize the chances of an idle workforce, and maximize capacity in times of strong demand. In his illuminating book *Fortune Tellers*, Walter Friedman explains:

> Economic forecasting arose when it did because while the effort to introduce rationality—in the form of the scientific method—was emerging, the insatiable human longing for predictability persisted in the industrializing economy. Indeed, the early twentieth century saw a curious enlistment of science in a range of efforts to temper the uncertainty of the future.[11]

Early forecasters were influenced by meteorology and even used weather jargon when making economic predictions. They also had access to growing amounts of economic data, as government agencies tracked and published metrics on, for example, commodity prices.[12] After the Panic of 1907, in which the stock market fell nearly 50 percent and many banks failed, retail and institutional investors were desperate for ways to mitigate uncertainty. They found solace in forecasters who leveraged and analyzed rich sets of data. As Friedman puts it:

> Forecasts...were more than predictions of the future. They were assumptions about what the economy was and how the economy worked. By pointing out trends in data and creating charts and models, forecasters made capitalism seem natural, logical, and most of all, predictable.[13]

Over time, these forecasts were improved and refined, and many businesspeople came to rely on them for making important decisions—even treating these predictions as facts. However, unlike many hard sciences, economic forecasting is less reliable because it's based on something that's continuously changing: human behavior.

Nevertheless, the supposition that people are rational and able to weigh trade-offs between choices is the foundational model of human behavior on which modern economics is built. After all, economics is typically the study of how we make decisions to allocate limited resources to satisfy limitless desires. Conventional economics incorporates a widely studied model of human behavior: (1) Consider how each option can increase your happiness; (2) mull your constraints, such as time and money; and (3) choose what gives you the most happiness.

According to many economists, rational people form a rational market. And rational markets lead to rational or "right" prices. The price of a stock reflects the best collective intelligence of the market. Whether a stock goes up or down, the market dictates the "right" price. This belief formed the efficient market hypothesis, advanced by economist Gene Fama in his 1970 paper titled "Efficient Markets: Theory and Evidence," which contends that stock prices reflect all available public information.[14] Because the price is a manifestation of the wisdom of crowds, one can't outperform the market— because it's already "right." A more straightforward name for the hypothesis is rational markets theory. This view shaped much of twentieth-century economic thought, from university campuses to Wall Street. It influenced the deregulation of the financial services industry and the growth of financial instruments like index funds and derivatives.[15] In his *The Myth of the Rational Market*, Justin Fox writes:

> The belief in the so-called rational market...was about more than just stocks. It held that as more stocks, bonds, options, futures, and other financial instruments were created and traded, they would inevitably bring more rationality to economic activity. Financial markets possessed a wisdom that individuals, companies, and governments did not... [From this] flowed the conviction that...prices were in some fundamental sense *right*.[16]

In other words, the market knows best. While many economists advanced parts of this theory, one stands out in packaging it for Wall Street. Harry Markowitz, a graduate student at the University of Chicago in the 1950s, trained his mathematical abilities on the financial markets. He read the works of Benjamin Graham, the father of value investing, and gleaned that investors diversify their holdings to diminish their risks but rarely consider the risk of the entire portfolio. He developed a formula for calculating the risk on a stock portfolio, taking into account the expected return of each stock, the uncertainty of that outcome (risk), and the degree to which the returns on the stocks would move in the same direction (correlation).[17] He originated the modern portfolio theory that investors still use to optimize portfolios for risk and return: Portfolio managers could weigh their options and constraints, and choose the securities that would provide the greatest expected returns with the least risk. He and Fama were later awarded Nobel Prizes in Economics.

Modern portfolio theory sounds reasonable. But surprisingly, even Markowitz found it hard to follow when he considered how to invest for his own retirement:

> I should have computed the historical co-variances of the asset classes and drawn an efficient frontier. Instead, I visualized my grief if the stock market went way up and I wasn't in it—or if it went way down and I was completely in it. My intention was to minimize my

future regret. So I split my contributions 50/50 between bonds and equities.[18]

The inventor of modern portfolio theory didn't use it. Even though he was aware of the supposedly rational thing to do, he chose a seemingly irrational one.[19] That a Nobel laureate economist acted in such a way demonstrates the problem with assuming that humans are completely rational actors. In one Japanese study, researchers evaluated 446 residents of affluent Tokyo communities, people you might expect to act in a completely rational and self-interested manner, and concluded that only 31, or 7 percent, acted in line with the *Homo economicus* model of human behavior.[20] "Economists' models are just awful. They completely forget how important the human element is," says Paul Wilmott, an expert and educator in quantitative finance.[21]

The economic forecasters who didn't anticipate the 2008 crisis made the same mistake. In 2009, eight accomplished economists wrote a paper titled "The Financial Crisis and the Systemic Failure of Academic Economists," in which they lambaste the use of mathematical models that didn't account for differences in the ways that people make decisions. They assert that many forecasters assumed that all market actors, including individuals and institutions, would behave in a rational manner. Wharton School professor Sidney Winter, who agrees with the authors, reasons that "rational behavior is not that dependable, or else people would not do self-destructive things like taking out mortgages they could not afford, a key factor in the financial crisis. Nor would completely rational executives at financial firms invest in securities backed by those risky mortgages."[22] The eight economists make the case that forecasters should account for variations in human psychology and behavior:

> The major problem [with forecasting] is that despite its many refinements, this is not at all an approach based on, and confirmed by, empirical research. In fact, it stands in stark contrast to a broad set of regularities in human behavior discovered both in psychology and what is called behavioral and experimental economics...Economic modeling has to be compatible with insights from other branches of science on human behavior. It is highly problematic to insist on a

specific view of humans in economic settings that is irreconcilable with evidence.[23]

At the height of the global financial crisis, in the autumn of 2008, Alan Greenspan responded to an inquiring congressman as to whether the prevailing wisdom of rational markets had failed: "That's precisely the reason I was shocked, because I had been going for forty years or more with very considerable evidence that it was working exceptionally well."[24] In his postmortem of the 2008 financial crisis, Greenspan writes that the prevailing forecasts didn't account for the "animal spirits" that John Maynard Keynes once described as "spontaneous urge to action rather than inaction, and not as the [rational] outcome of a weighted average of quantitative benefits multiplied by quantitative probabilities."[25] In sum, human behavior is guided at times not by logic and so-called rationality but by other forces, such as emotions like fear and euphoria. Greenspan summarizes his epiphany:

> We like to describe ourselves as fundamentally driven by reason to an extent not matched by other living creatures. This is doubtless true. But we are far from the prototype depicted by neoclassical economists: that of people motivated predominantly by considerations of rational long-term self-interest. Our thinking process, as behavioral economists point out, is more intuitive and syllogistic... The economics of animal spirits, broadly speaking, covers a wide range of human actions, and overlaps with much of the relatively new discipline of behavioral economics. The point is to substitute a more realistic version of behavior than the model of the wholly rationality-driven "economic man" so prominent for so long in economic courses taught in our universities.[26]

It remains to be seen whether forecasts that incorporated more "human" factors would have predicted the financial crisis—though it doesn't take a sophisticated model to realize that housing prices won't continue to rise forever. Nevertheless, many forecasters recognize the failure and folly of their previous predictions. They seek new ways to understand human psychology and behavior when making financial decisions.

Oh, Behave!

In 1955, a young psychologist and lieutenant in the Israeli army, Daniel Kahneman, was tasked with determining which candidates would make successful officers. He arranged a team of eight candidates without their ranks displayed and directed them to raise a large log over a tall wall without it touching the wall or ground. Kahneman took a logical approach to evaluating the candidates: He observed who took charge and who followed others, which formed the basis of his predictions regarding who would become successful officers. When compared to the actual performance results of officers many months later, his predictions fell well short, almost no better than a guess. Despite knowing that his method of evaluation wasn't predictive of performance, he continued doing it. His actions remind me of that often-used quotation, "The definition of insanity is doing the same thing again and again and expecting a different result." Kahneman refers to his irrational behavior in another way, calling it an "illusion of validity."[27]

The illusion of validity is a cognitive bias, which is a deviation from the expected behavior of a rational actor or blind spots to logic. Even though Kahneman was aware that his method of evaluating candidates was suboptimal, he was biased toward using the old method. Cognitive biases are a starting point for behavioral economics, which is more of a psychological than a purely economic approach to understanding how people make financial decisions. Kahneman and his colleague Amos Tversky spent years uncovering, chronicling, and explaining hundreds of cognitive biases. Both are widely credited as pioneers of behavioral economics. Tversky passed away in 1996, and in 2002, Kahneman was presented the Nobel Prize in Economics without ever taking an economics class.

In his bestselling book, *Thinking, Fast and Slow*, Kahneman presents a new model to understand how the mind works. He distinguishes between "System 1" and "System 2" in the way the mind works. System 1 makes automatic, fast decisions that happen subconsciously—like turning the pages of this book. System 2 makes slower, more complex decisions that happen consciously—like how to balance your retirement portfolio. We like to think that System 2 guides our financial decisions, when in fact in many cases it's System 1.

Because they were proposing a new way of understanding human cognition, Kahneman and Tversky's ideas have had a profound impact on a range of fields, including economics. Their paper on "Judgment Under Uncertainty: Heuristics and Biases," published in 1974, lists twenty cognitive biases and is one of the most frequently cited across a range of academic disciplines. Kahneman explains how their research questioned the very root of traditional models used to understand human behavior:

> Social scientists in the 1970s broadly accepted two ideas about human nature. First, people are generally rational...Second, emotions such as fear, affection...explain most of the occasions on which people depart from rationality. Our article questioned both assumptions... We documented systematic errors in the thinking of normal people, and we traced these errors to the design of the machinery of cognition rather than to the corruption of thought by emotion.[28]

The "machinery of cognition," System 1 and System 2, presents a different way of understanding how we make decisions. Our choices aren't just rational or irrational but are made consciously and subconsciously. Many of our financial decisions are guided by forces of which we aren't fully aware. For example, in one study, waiters found that customers tip more when exposed to sunshine.[29] The weather affects our mood, which makes us more likely to give a bigger tip. Another study reveals that weather may play a role in the performance of the market. Comparing historical weather patterns with the performances of primary stock exchanges in twenty-six different countries shows that markets outperform considerably on sunny days, an annualized return of 24.8 percent over cloudy days. No serious investor asks how the weather makes them feel before making an investment decision, but the subconscious has already answered that question and acted on it.[30]

The subconscious also guides the financial choices of shoppers. Researchers found shoppers were more likely to buy French wine while hearing French music and German wine when hearing German music.[31] Another study finds that music can influence how wine drinkers perceive the taste of wine, describing the taste of the wine similar to the feel of the music.[32] These findings are old hat to advertisers. In the television series

Mad Men, Don Draper makes a bountiful living by trying to influence the subconscious of consumers with positive associations of products.

To facilitate System 1 thinking, we have created mental shortcuts to save energy to process thousands of decisions per day. These shortcuts are called "heuristics," which are frequently defined as "rules of thumb." Though several heuristics work well, like ducking when someone yells "Watch out," some are less helpful and irrational, and produce cognitive biases. By observing these heuristics that result in cognitive biases, Kahneman and Tversky provided a new way of understanding how humans make financial decisions.

To illustrate the significant impact that heuristics (and resulting cognitive biases) have on financial decisions, let's consider but four: (1) availability heuristic; (2) illusion of skill; (3) loss aversion; and (4) money illusion. The availability heuristic explains why my father always plays the lottery. I'm sure that he's aware that there is a one in 175 million chance that he will win. But when he enters the Shell gas station to buy his ticket, he isn't thinking about the long odds. Instead, he remembers that once he matched a few numbers and received a $475 payout. He thinks about the winners he hears about on the five o'clock news. The more readily examples are remembered, the more likely a particular outcome seems.[33] Most of us are unable to calculate large statistical problem sets in our heads, so the availability heuristic guides our decisions.

Heuristics can also result in a cognitive bias known as an "illusion of skill." Kahneman analyzed data on twenty-five investment advisers from eight years at a wealth management firm. Metrics on the data were used in determining each adviser's yearly compensation. Incredibly, Kahneman calculated zero correlation between their advice and investment outcome. He presented his findings to the firm's executives and writes, "This should have been shocking news to them, but it was not."[34] The managers continued their irrational behavior, rewarding an "illusion of skill"—paying their employees compensation that didn't reflect their actual performance.[35] Unfortunately, there's plenty of evidence to suggest that an "illusion of skill" pervades the asset management industry: 95 percent of mutual fund managers underperform a standard index fund that has no active manager over a fifteen-year period.[36] Despite poor performance, many fund managers continue to make handsome fees. The "illusion of skill" in the fund management space reveals an irrational behavior of market participants: rewarding underperforming managers. Indeed, a fund manager's poor performance may eventually lead to withdrawals from his or her fund. But that poor performance continues to be lucrative for long periods shows how financial decisions aren't governed by completely rational and logical forces. Kahneman explains that this bias is "deeply ingrained in the culture of the industry. Facts that challenge such basic assumptions—and thereby threaten people's livelihood and self-esteem—are simply not absorbed. The mind does not digest them."[37] What seems like irrational behavior, disregarding the facts that reveal the poor track records of wealth advisers and fund managers, can be seen in another light. The management teams at these funds are trying to protect their own jobs and maintain their livelihoods, which is a perfectly rational and motivating factor, so they look the other way.

Another heuristic, "the money illusion," has been widely studied by economists for almost a century.[38] It holds that people think of money in nominal rather than real terms, not considering inflation, the general increase in prices in an economy. For example, Kate makes a salary of $45,000 in one year when inflation is 1 percent. The next year she makes the same amount but inflation reaches 4 percent. Kate continues to purchase the same quantity of goods and services, as if prices have not gone up, but her income in real terms has decreased. The money illusion, when widespread among many people, may lead to market manias. In 2008, two economists proposed that people may have decided whether to rent or buy property by contrasting monthly rent versus mortgage payments without properly considering how inflation affects the real cost of payments in the future.[39] For example, a drop in inflation lures Kate and many others to buy property as they conjecture that low nominal interest rates have made owning a home more affordable. In reality, Kate should consider her real interest rate, which will give her a true idea of whether her mortgage is actually a better deal than renting. Without considering real interest rates, Kate and others can mistakenly believe that buying a home is the better choice, which drives up prices and can potentially lead to a housing bubble.

It's not just the housing market that may be subject to the money illusion; in the stock market money managers may not consider the real rate of a company's earnings. During inflationary periods, money is worth more now than in the future, so investors calculate what future payments are worth now in a process called "discounting." Some economists contend that investors may discount with nominal rather than real rates.[40] It's hard for me to fathom professional money managers not accounting for the real rates. Yet the money illusion could lead to a situation where stock prices don't reflect the underlying fundamental value of the company. In other words, a cognitive bias may be the root of mispriced assets or even a labor dispute: Only 19 percent of Canadian union contracts between 1976 and 2000 included cost-of-living adjustments. Maybe employers wielded a significantly stronger upper hand in negotiations, or perhaps union negotiators demonstrated a cognitive bias, forgetting about the erosion of purchasing power over time in an inflationary environment.[41]

Until recently, it's been impossible to peer into the black box of the brain and glean how it weighs and makes financial decisions. Such is the province of neuroeconomists, which I'll explain in the next section, but some brain imaging studies can help us better grasp what's going on in the brain of someone exhibiting the money illusion. Brain images reveal the neural underpinning of this cognitive bias. In a study, the brains of participants were scanned while they were instructed to solve problems in which they could win money. In one scenario, they could earn money and buy goods that were relatively cheap from a catalog. In the other scenario, they could earn 50 percent more money and buy goods from the same catalog, except the prices were 50 percent higher. Despite the increase in nominal amounts, the participants' purchasing power stayed constant, and they were briefed at the beginning of the experiment that the value of money wouldn't vary. There was considerably more activity in the prefrontal cortex of the brain during the scenario involving larger nominal amounts than during the scenario with smaller nominal amounts.[42] Even though the real value of money remained constant, the brain reacted to variations in nominal amounts. This study shows that higher nominal prices register more activity in the part of the brain that is involved in processing rewards and valuing goods; the prefrontal cortex is also considered the seat of reason, and its activation may induce us to be more cognizant of higher prices. It may also explain how the brain processes "sticker shock"—heightened neural activity and awareness when confronted with an unexpectedly high price of a good. Most of us have experienced sticker shock, so it may not come as a surprise that activity in the brain is heightened, but now there is brain imaging to show *how* the brain is processing these financial decisions, which is a first step toward making better predictions regarding human choice.

Finally, the heuristic for which Kahneman and Tversky are best known is loss aversion. It's also known by its more academic name, "prospect theory," which basically says that when making decisions, people value perceived gains and losses differently.[43] The evolutionary logic of loss aversion seems to be to minimize harms and costs as a way to increase chances of survival. Consider a coin toss in which you could either lose $20 or win $22. Though the payoff is in your favor, and the rational model of human behavior would suggest you take the bet, most would reject this gamble. Kahneman and Tversky found that when offered a coin toss that could result in losing $20, participants asked for an average of $40 for winning.[44] There is a stark unevenness in how folks value losses and gains, as they try to avoid loss even if there's good probability of gaining.

Loss aversion may also explain widespread market behavior. Mebane Faber of Cambria Investment Management has found that there is more volatility in stock prices during bear markets than during bull markets.[45] One reason for this, according to financial writers Gary Belsky and Thomas Gilovich, might be that traders make increasingly risky bets because they want to avoid realizing their losses: "If you're a stock trader who's lost a lot, the temptation to gamble big in the hopes of recouping money is very powerful."[46] For example, during the 1990s, the demise of Barings Bank was brought about by a rogue trader doubling his bets, trying to avoid realizing amassed losses.[47] In periods of uncertainty, rational actors shouldn't gamble more aggressively.

Loss aversion isn't found just in the financial world. Cutting welfare benefits is difficult because the political cost of reducing is high. Those who are likely to suffer a loss are more likely to mobilize in defense of benefits. Politicians herald the expansion of benefits but duck blame when the entitlements are cut.[48] Even professional golfers are subject to loss aversion. A comprehensive study of more than two million putts during PGA tournaments, controlled for location and other factors, shows that golfers are 3.6 percent more successful when putting for par, facing the prospect of underperforming on the hole, than for birdie, which could put them ahead in the round.[49]

Loss aversion is regulated by neurological mechanisms. Several parts of the brain are involved in weighing and making decisions, from the ventral striatum in the limbic system, which is involved with anticipated and realized gains, to the amygdala, which processes expected and realized loss.[50] Researchers scanned the brains of two women with lesions to their amygdala, effectively turning it off.[51] Healthy control participants were more likely to accept a gamble in which they won $50 and lost $10 than one in which they won $20 and lost $15, whereas the two women with lesions were more likely to engage in riskier bets, even those in which the potential losses were greater than potential gains.[52] The amygdala, which is known to promote fear learning, appears to play the same role in financial decisions, steering us away from loss.

These cognitive biases reveal humans for what they are—at times, unaware and irrational actors. Instead of acting according to a rational model, we show great variation in our psychology and behavior. Kahneman and Tversky recognized these differences by observing and detailing human behaviors over the years. Their findings provide a more realistic version of human behavior, something that Greenspan said was needed. But it will be difficult for economists to account for hundreds of cognitive biases in their financial models. What's needed is a sophisticated yet straightforward way to understand how people make financial decisions.

For that, consider the work of behavioral economist Richard Thaler and his concept of mental accounting. Instead of seeing every dollar as just another dollar, people view their dollars differently, classifying them into discrete buckets like safety income and risk capital, the way a corporate treasurer classifies capital for different purposes, such as salaries, taxes, or research and development.[53] People, like corporations, treat each category of money differently. My father's decision to play the lottery can be explained not only by the availability heuristic but also by mental accounting. He explains his decision: "I'm not using my retirement money to buy tickets." It's as if he's created a mental "discretionary account" with which to gamble. Even though the amount of cash in question may be the same, mental accounting makes us treat money differently. Thaler's theory neatly illustrates that we conceive of money in different ways, and economists should recognize that not every dollar is alike.

Richard Thaler, Daniel Kahneman, Amos Tversky, and other behavioral economists have made important contributions to our understanding of human behavior as it relates to money. But their findings only go so far—and don't fully explain what's going on in the mind to direct these behaviors. To continue our quest to understand money in new ways, we must go inside the black box of the brain.

Brain Man

Brian Knutson (pronounced Kih-NOOT-suhn) is a man on a mission: to understand how the brain makes financial decisions. A professor of psychology and neuroscience at Stanford University, he is one of the most visible and important neuroeconomists. Neuroeconomics is an interdisciplinary study of how the brain makes financial decisions. If one were to take attendance at a neuroeconomics faculty meeting, present might be neuroscientists, behavioral economists, "traditional" economists, psychologists, biologists, chemists, and computer scientists. The various approaches are helpful because trying to understand how we make certain decisions can be incredibly complex.

The interdisciplinary nature of neuroeconomics is a good reminder that humans make financial decisions for a variety of reasons. Since we gained the capacity for advanced thought, we like to think that our decisions are processed in the neocortex, the seat of our consciousness. But it's the subconscious, System 1, that works on autopilot and navigates many financial decisions without our fully realizing it.

Not only are many of our financial decisions made subconsciously. Our motivations may also be driven by forces of which we aren't fully aware. In one British study involving money, eighteen participants were instructed to press a handgrip. But first they were shown the images of a coin of low value, a penny, or a coin of a higher value, a pound, signifying the amount they could win. They would receive money proportionate to how hard they squeezed the grip. In some cases, the displayed image lasted until the participant was conscious of which coin it was. In other cases, it was flashed too quickly for the participant to be fully aware, confirmed by the fact that they self-reported that they couldn't identify which coin was displayed. Despite not being consciously aware of which coin was at stake, participants still squeezed harder for the higher-valued coin.[54] The subconscious was still able to register how much was at stake.

The money also induced a physiological change among the participants. Researchers found that the skin conductance of participants increased when the higher-value coin was displayed. In another study, one group of university students was asked to count eighty $100 bills, the other group eighty pieces of paper. Some students from both groups were instructed to place their hands in water heated to 122 degrees Fahrenheit. Those that handled money reported that the water wasn't as painful as those who counted paper.[55] These findings indicate that the thought and the touch of money alter our physiology in seemingly imperceptible ways.

But what's going on in the brain during these experiments? In the hand-grip study, researchers used brain scans to discover that the ventral pallidum (which is part of the ventral striatum that includes the nucleus accumbens) registered more activity when a pound was displayed, and seems to be the part of the brain that supports conscious and subconscious motivation. They conclude that the "human brain is able to translate expected rewards into physical effort, without the need for the subject's awareness."[56] Money is motivating us to act, shaping our decisions and behavior without our fully realizing it.

"MRIs are a game changer," says Knutson. Functional magnetic resonance imaging (fMRI) measures the oxygen usage of the surrounding cortical tissue; brain cells need oxygen to work.[57] Using this technology, neuro-economists can look deep into the brain, in the "subcortical" level, below the cortex, to see what's happening when we make financial decisions. The *New York Times* describes the range of activities that neuroeconomists have examined with brain imaging: "These researchers are busy scanning the brains of people as they make economic decisions, barter, compete, cooperate, defect, punish, engage in auctions, gamble and calculate their next economic moves."[58]

I've already discussed how neuroeconomists have conducted a variety of experiments to determine the neurological underpinning of the money illusion, loss aversion, and subconscious financial motivation. They've even studied what happens in the brain when money is destroyed. Researchers scanned the brains of twenty participants while watching videos of paper money and regular paper being folded and torn. When participants saw money being destroyed, there was heightened activity in the temporoparietal network of the brain, which activates when using tools like screwdrivers, hammers, or knapping hand axes. Money of higher denomination generated more neural activity, too.[59] The researchers say, "This lends plausibility to a genuinely psychological interpretation of the explanation of money as a tool... The fact that the brain does treat money as a tool for tracking exchange on a precise scale suggests that a tool explanation of money is more than just a useful metaphor."[60]

Despite these intriguing findings, we are still in the beginning stages of neuroeconomics, and there is much more to learn about how the brain processes money. There are about 100 billion brain cells, known as neurons, in the human brain. A neuron fires when it receives impulses that excite it.[61] Neurons translate this firing into chemical signals that can excite other neurons by traveling across small spaces between them known as synapses, which are like swapping stations where messages are relayed. With an average of five thousand synapses per neuron, there are approximately 500 trillion synapses overall.[62] The links between neurons are critical to storing and facilitating knowledge, such as how to use money. Incredibly, more information is processed in one brain than on the Internet.[63] Just as the links between websites can change, so, too, can the neurons involving money be rewired to recognize salt, gold, dollars, or almost anything as a currency. This is known as neuroplasticity, the brain's ability to make new connections. When neurons fire together, they are said to wire together.[64]

During childhood, we learn about money as a symbol of value, maybe through formal instruction but more likely through observing a parent. Some neurons fired when you saw your mother buy milk with dollars. Over time, the brain associated money with what it could obtain. Developmental psychologists Stanley Greenspan and Stuart Shanker have studied infants to see how they create symbols. One of the conditions they found necessary to "create a meaningful symbol" was that it must be "invested with emotions."[65] Without emotions, symbols are just images. Mom isn't just a tall lady with long brown hair; she provides comfort through food and shelter. A dollar bill isn't just paper with green ink. It's what you give to your kids to reward them for doing their chores, or it's how you insult someone when you give too little a tip. Money isn't just the output of logic and reason; it brims with emotional meaning. They found that children learn to imbue images with additional meaning, turning them into symbols that are "seasoned with more . . . emotional experiences."[66]

The topic of emotions and decisions is what led Knutson to become a neuroeconomist. As a graduate student, he was already studying facial expressions and emotions when one of his advisers suggested that he dig deeper into how the brain processes feelings. Thus began his career in affective neuroscience, or the neurological aspects of emotion. During his postdoctoral fellowship at the National Institutes of Health, he worked with brain imaging techniques and realized that they could provide a glimpse into how the brain functions. He always had an interest in the cognition of emotions, and now he had the capacity to see what is really happening in the black box of the brain. I learned about Knutson's story from him. He joined me for dinner in New York and navigated me through the complex field of neuroeconomics. He boiled down his research into two questions that guide his work:

1. Which brain mechanisms anticipate good and bad events?
2. Does their activity influence choice?

The first question is an anatomical one. He wants to know which regions of the brain activate when it anticipates a positive or a negative event. By using brain scans, he can see which regions are correlated with each event. Neuroeconomists have found that the nucleus accumbens activates when anticipating a gain, while the anterior insula also activates at the prospect of loss.

In an experiment, Knutson and his team scanned the brains of eight participants while they were presented with the prospect of winning or losing money. The opportunity of receiving cash presumably would increase dopamine levels, a neurotransmitter linked with excitement, in the nucleus accumbens of participants.[67] Accordingly, the mere *anticipation* of making money led to a surge of activity in this region. Financial writer Jason Zweig visited Knutson in his Stanford laboratory and underwent a similar experiment, which he describes in *Your Money and Your Brain*: "In fact, Knutson's scanner found, the neurons in my nucleus accumbens fired much less intensely when I received a reward than they did when I was hoping to get it."[68] The idea of gaining money is more of a neural stimulant than money itself.

It's almost as if the thought of obtaining money induces a "high," like a drug. Neuroscientist Hans Breiter and his research team looked into this comparison. They scanned the brains of twelve people while they played a game in which the dozen could win or lose money. The scans show heightened activity, again, in the nucleus accumbens but also in other regions. Remarkably, the brain images were similar to those of drug addicts who were given a hit of cocaine.[69] Zweig writes that "the neural activity of someone whose investments are making money is indistinguishable from that of someone who is high on cocaine or morphine."[70] One doesn't have to take harmful chemicals in the form of drugs to generate heightened activity in the nucleus accumbens. Knutson has found that the prospect of winning money is incredibly stimulating: "We very quickly found out that nothing had an effect on people like money—not naked bodies, not corpses. It got people riled up. Like food provides motivation for dogs, money provides it for people."[71] Money has become our Pavlov's bell, activating the nucleus accumbens and conditioning our behavior as we salivate at the opportunity to feast on more.

Researchers have found that the anterior insula, in the middle of the brain, fires at the prospect of loss. Researchers scanned the brains of nineteen participants while they were given various ultimatums related to an amount of cash. During each trial, there were two participants: the proposer, who makes an offer on how to split the money, and the responder, who decides whether to take the proposal. The researchers state that the "standard economic solution" would be for the proposer to offer a low quantity, and the responder to consent, since some money is better than no money.[72] But they found that low offers, approximately 20 percent of the total amount, are rejected 50 percent of the time. Even though the responders knew that by rejecting these offers neither participant would receive any money, they still refused, which demonstrates there is a powerful force guiding their decisions. The responders were reportedly insulted and angry with the low, perceived-to-be-unfair offers. By rejecting these offers, the responder penalizes the proposer and nobody receives money. From an evolutionary standpoint, rejecting the offer may be a way to maintain status in a community as someone who should not be mistreated.

The brain scans reveal that the dorsolateral prefrontal cortex activates when a responder receives an offer. This part of the brain is usually linked with deliberate, conscious thought. However, the anterior insula fired when the responder received an unfair offer. This region of the brain is often linked to negative emotions and activates when experiencing pain, disgust, humiliation, thirst, and hunger. Zweig notes that the insula is full of spindle cells, which have a molecule that's found in lesser amounts in the brain than in the human digestive system, which bring about contractions to process food: "When you get a 'gut feeling' that an investment has gone sour, you might not be imagining. The spindle cells in your insula may be firing in sync with your churning stomach."[73] The responders who had higher activity in their anterior insula rejected unfair proposals with greater frequency.[74] It's as if the insula overrides the prefrontal cortex, emotions trumping reason. This study illustrates what behavioral economists have long observed: that our financial choices are influenced by other factors beyond pure reason. Thanks to brain imaging, now we can see the neurological underpinning of how one of those factors, emotions, influences financial decisions.

Knutson makes the case that emotions are key to understanding financial decision making when he writes, "Some still assume that emotion is peripheral, but the time has come to recognize that emotion is central... Emerging physiological, behavioral, and neuroimaging evidence suggests that emotions are proactive as well as reactive."[75] He has found that positive emotions promote risk taking, and negative emotions induce risk aversion.[76] In one of his studies, fifteen heterosexual males were shown a picture and then asked to make a high-risk or low-risk financial gamble. The pictures consisted of positive stimuli, like erotic images that induced excitement, negative stimuli of snakes and spiders, and neutral ones of household appliances. Sure enough, the positive stimuli increased activation in the nucleus accumbens and financial risk taking.[77] The study shows that incidental cues can influence financial decisions and that emotions should be taken into account when one is trying to predict human behavior.

It's one thing to observe which regions of the brain are activated; it's quite another to forecast human decisions. In 2004, an editorial for *Nature Neuroscience* read, "Cognitive science is not yet close to explaining or predicting human decision-making in the real world."[78] That may have been the case at the time, but Knutson has found that one can predict financial choices by examining the brain, and he's successfully answered the second question that he shared with me over dinner. During one of his experiments, twenty-six people had their brains scanned while making shopping decisions. First, they were presented products on a screen. Next, the price was displayed. Last, there was an option to buy. When the product was displayed, the nucleus accumbens fired, excited by the potential reward. When the price was presented, part of the prefrontal cortex activated, indicating that the information was being processed by the reason center of the brain. But when the price was too excessive, the activity in the prefrontal cortex lessened and increased in the insula; there was sticker shock or disgust at the requested amount. The researchers found that neural activity in each of these regions accurately predicted the eventual consumer choice: "These findings suggest that the activation of distinct brain regions related to anticipation of gain and loss precedes and can be used to predict purchasing decisions."[79]

Neural activity predicts investment decisions, too. Knutson and his neuroeconomist colleague Camelia Kuhnen realized what Alan Greenspan came to learn, that "investors systematically deviate from rationality when making financial decisions."[80] But they wanted to know what neurological mechanisms accounted for this behavior. In a study, they asked participants to make an investment decision, choosing among two stocks and a bond. The participants were informed that they would receive gains or losses (subtracted from their volunteer fee) commensurate with their decisions.

The brain scans show that the nucleus accumbens was activated before participants made riskier decisions, such as choosing a stock with a poor historical performance. The researchers conjecture that as casinos surround their customers with rewards like free drinks, it may generate activity in the nucleus accumbens and lead to riskier behavior. In the study, the insula activated before low-risk decisions like choosing the more conservative bond. The activity in the nucleus accumbens and insula accurately predicted the choices of participants. The researchers square their findings with prevailing economic models that assume rationality: "The results therefore indicate that, above and beyond contributing to rational choice, anticipatory neural activation may also promote irrational choice. Thus, financial decision making may require a delicate balance—recruitment of distinct circuits may be necessary for taking or avoiding risks, but excessive activation of one mechanism or the other may lead to mistakes."[81] Their brain scans show *how* the brain makes irrational decisions, and why it's wrong to assume that humans act in a completely rational manner.

Knutson and Kuhnen took their research even further. Joined by neuroscientist Gregory Samanez-Larkin, they discovered that irrational investment decisions may be a function of genetics. The questions guiding their research: "Do genes influence cognitive abilities, do they shape the way people learn in financial markets, or do they determine risk attitudes?"[82] They focused on the neurotransmitter serotonin, which is widely believed to play a role in happiness and may be central to understanding financial decisions. One serotonin gene, 5-HTTLPR, comes in two types, long and short. Everyone has two copies of the gene in different combinations, long or short. Researchers collected saliva samples from sixty volunteers and asked them to allocate $10,000 among cash, stocks, and bonds. Those with two short 5-HTTLPR copies parked about 24 percent more money in cash, had fewer credit lines, and maintained higher FICO scores than those with two long copies. Those with short copies were found to experience more negative emotions on a consistent basis than those with two long copies. These negative emotions may have led to their risk aversion. They also demonstrated a greater degree of neuroticism, a personality trait characterized by anxiety and apprehension.[83] Yet the researchers trod carefully with their conclusions, saying that genetics isn't the only factor guiding behavior, since not all participants acted as their genes would have suggested.[84] Nevertheless, their research shows that biological factors should be considered when trying to understand how humans make financial decisions.

In Brains We Trust

Thanks to the research of many neuroeconomists, the black box of the brain isn't so mysterious anymore. We have a better understanding of how the mind processes financial decisions. But the question remains: Will these neurological insights help economists make more accurate forecasts? Neuro-economists can predict financial choices based on what is happening in the brain. It might follow, then, that the market, which is composed of many minds, could be forecasted in a more accurate manner.

Though neuroeconomics is still in its early stages, some reputable traditional economists have taken notice. Yale economist Robert Shiller says that a "neuroeconomic revolution" will reshape economics. University of Minnesota economist Aldo Rustichini echoes these sentiments: "This new approach, which I consider a revolution, should provide a theory of how people decide in economic and strategic situations. So far, the decision process has been for economists a black box."[85]

But few economists have actually incorporated neuroeconomic insights when building their forecasting models. I've never seen a Wall Street economist or research analyst account for neurological insights in their predictions. Leading neuroeconomist Colin Camerer explains: "I would say that neuroeconomics is about 90 percent neuroscience and 10 percent economics. We've taken a lot of mathematical models from economics to help describe what we see happening in the brain. But economists have been a lot slower to use any of our ideas."[86]

In 1947, economist Paul Samuelson published *Foundations of Economic Analysis*, which served as an intellectual foundation of the efficient or rational market theory. In 2010, neuroeconomist Paul Glimcher published *Foundations of Neuroeconomic Analysis*, which, he hopes, will prompt economists to include neurological insights in forecasting models. He writes that, indeed, "economics is, in the words of the 19th-century economist Thorstein Veblen, finally becoming an 'evolutionary science,' and that science has already shown itself to be a powerful tool for understanding human behavior."[87]

Maybe it's just a matter of time until economists incorporate findings from neuroeconomics. After all, in 2013, Alan Greenspan wrote in his book about his epiphany, which echoes what neuroscientist Jonathan Cohen said ten years before, in 2003, "Most economists don't base their theories on people's actual behavior. They study idealized versions of human behavior, which they assume is optimal in achieving gains."[88] However, some economists dismiss the field, arguing that brain scans reveal which neurons are firing and not why, and neuroeconomic studies haven't been able to predict human behavior writ large.[89]

But that is changing. The *Chronicle of Higher Education* highlights a study in which the brain scans of teenagers were used to predict an increase in music sales.[90] Researchers found a correlation between activity in the nucleus accumbens of participants and album sales across the country.[91] The findings, in the words of the researchers, "suggest that the neural responses to goods are not only predictive of purchase decisions for those individuals actually scanned, but such responses generalize to the population at large and may be used to predict cultural popularity."[92] If neuroeconomists can forecast retail music sales, one day they may be able to predict stock prices, or at least provide more color as to why a market is performing in a particular manner. Glimcher says, "If we had access to that data, when people pick stocks, can these models predict macro-level changes in stock prices from individual-level models of agents picking stocks...? There's reason to believe it might work."[93] It will take more time for insights from neuroeconomics to be absorbed into economic models. But neuroeconomics has already enriched our understanding of money.

As our brains enlarged, we became aware of the benefits of cooperation, creating tools like money to facilitate it. But money isn't just the output of reason and logic. We also gained the capacity for complex thoughts, turning tools like money into symbols of value that are imbued with emotional meanings. Without knowing what's happening in the brain, economists long made assumptions about human behavior, and, implicitly, about how the mind processes money. But with the advent of brain imaging technology, we can look at the mind in the mirror and better understand its ways. We've come to learn that the way in which we use money is influenced by a range of factors, including emotions and genetics.

But there are other things that shape how we think about and use money—like social norms, cultural rituals, and societal beliefs. Despite our physiological similarities, humans think of money in different ways. Our quest to understand money, then, must account for this variety, so we will move from studying the brain to surveying the social one, the "super-brain" of society. Without a doubt, the one thing I've learned from my research regarding the *idea* of money is that everyone has their own.

CHAPTER THREE

So in Debt

The anthropology of debt

I don't do favors. I accumulate debts.
—*Sicilian proverb*[1]

The gift is to the giver, and comes back most to him—it cannot fail.
—*Walt Whitman*[2]

Annual income twenty pounds, annual expenditure nineteen nineteen six, result happiness. Annual income twenty pounds, annual expenditure twenty pounds ought and six, result misery.
—*Charles Dickens*[3]

A Native American potlatch ceremony in British Columbia.

When I lived in London, there was this guy I knew. Tall, handsome with a faint hint of a unibrow. He joined my buddies and me for drinks after work. One by one, we took turns signaling the bartender and logging an order of four pints of Guinness. After downing a few and feeling slightly wobblier, we were ready for one last round. Everyone gazed in the direction of the only person not to have paid for a round, this guy.

A friend asked him, "Can we get another round?"

"Sure, but I'm not paying for it."

Awkward silence.

After determining that this guy wasn't kidding, the same friend concluded, "That's weak, mate. I'll get the last round." And on went the conversation. But this guy had turned into *that* guy—the one who doesn't cover a round of drinks for friends.

That guy, I must admit, was me.

I ran this crude social experiment in the friendly confines of a local pub to see what happens when there's a gross violation of an implicit agreement to pay. Of course I ended up paying for a round of drinks, joking away my previous remark. But for a few moments, I moved from being a stand-up guy in the eyes of my pals, taking part in a social ritual, to being a freeloader, abusing the generosity of others.

There is no law written anywhere that says you must buy the next round of beers. But most of us know what's expected. My friends and I were engaging in an exchange as primitive as it is modern: accepting a gift and reciprocating the favor; incurring a short-term debt and repaying it later. The use of money, in this case, was governed by the social mores of our little tribe.

Money is interpreted differently across the world, in various parts of the "super-brain." The ways in which people use money reveal how they conceive of it. Anthropologists have trekked to distant corners to study the uses of money, discovering unusual practices and documenting how money plays an important role from birth to death. In India, money is given to new-born babies and their parents. In Japan, money is gifted to newly married couples.[4] In Nigeria, many corpses are buried with money.[5] Money marks many important moments of our lives and in countless ways.

Despite the numerous ways in which money is used today, it functions universally as an instrument to settle debts. Printed on the dollar bill is written as much: "This note is legal tender for all debts, private and public." Dollars are issued by the Federal Reserve, and they show up as a liability on the Fed's balance sheet. The collateral that backs the bills is found on the asset side of the balance sheet. These assets are mostly securities issued by the US Treasury and federal agencies.[6] In other words, dollars are obligations of the US government, and they are backed by the debt of government institutions and the faith of the government. In the current US monetary system, money and debt cannot be disentangled.

Those little words printed in black ink are also a reminder of money's alternative past. For centuries, economists have contended that bartering was the precursor to money. But there was actually another financial instrument in wide circulation: debt. Thousands of years before the invention of coinage, there were interest-bearing loans in ancient Mesopotamia. Debt was the forerunner of money. Today we may see money and debt as two different things, but they share a common origin. That the dollar is a liability, an obligation of the Federal Reserve, reveals how fundamental lending and borrowing have been throughout man's history.

That's because debt isn't just a *financial* obligation, it's a *social* one. In this chapter I use an anthropological approach to examine both types of obligations. I examine different spheres of debt exchange: (1) the familial sphere, the basis of the gift economy; and (2) the commercial sphere, or the foundation of the market economy.[7] I focus more on the gift economy because it's more nuanced and open to interpretation. But it ends up shaping our perceptions of money, and even influences how we view our friends and family.

It's evident that auto loans and mortgages are financial debt instruments with listed prices found in the market economy. It's less clear how to quantify a social debt or credit brought on by receiving or giving a gift.

The practice of gift exchange, enacting a social debt, can be found in most cultures, from the intricate gifting culture of East Asian countries to gifting a friend a beer in East London.

Regardless of which sphere one finds it in, debt brings with it a sense of obligation. For as long as we've been around, we have taken on debts, both social and financial, and have been obliged to honor them. And obligations have moral overtones. Not to reciprocate a gift like a beer can be interpreted as breaking an implicit, unspoken social understanding. Not to repay a loan breaks a contractual agreement. Not to honor thy debts is *wrong*. To reciprocate and repay is to *make good*. Then again, it's also *wrong* to take advantage of people through usury and predatory loans. I save the religious strictures on debt for another chapter, and instead focus on what happens when a social debt is computed as a market one. This can result in the dark side of debt, using money as a bludgeon to control others.

An Alternative Origin

In most introductory economics classes, the history of money goes something like this: Once upon a time, in a land far away, people bartered goods, but sometimes each party didn't have exactly what the other wanted, so they invented money. You can trace this line of thinking to Aristotle and classical economists like Adam Smith, who contended that a division of labor led to more specialized tools, which necessitated money to facilitate increasingly complex trades. Adam Smith writes in *The Wealth of Nations*:

> The butcher has more meat in his shop than he himself can consume, and the brewer and the baker would each of them be willing to purchase a part of it. But they have nothing to offer in exchange, except the different productions of their respective trades...In order to avoid the inconveniency of such situations, every prudent man in every period of society, after the first establishment of the division of labour, must naturally have...a certain quantity of some one commodity or other, such as he imagined few people would be likely to refuse in exchange for the produce of their industry.[8]

Smith goes on to say that through exchange, commodities such as nails in the Scottish Highlands became early currencies. And over time, these commodities were replaced with small pieces of precious metals. My evolutionary biological investigation into the origin of money even supports this notion that bartering commodities, perhaps food items and hand axes, paved the way to using money. A romanticized, simplistic notion of tit-for-tat bartering seems to be a forerunner to monetary exchange: Here's three silver coins, and good-bye.

However, writing in the *Banking Law Journal* in 1913, a British economist questioned this theory. Alfred Mitchell-Innes asserted that there is no historical proof for Smith's axiom, and that it is, in fact, false. He notes that Smith's example of nails was even debunked by William Playfair, an editor of *The Wealth of Nations*. The nail makers were poor. The makers had to rely on suppliers to furnish them with the raw materials to make the nails. The suppliers also provided credits to the makers for bread and cheese while they were making the nails. The nail makers were in debt. When the nails were completed, the nail makers paid back the suppliers with the nails.[9] Mitchell-Innes writes, "Adam Smith believes that he discovered a tangible currency, [but] he has, in fact, merely found—credit."[10]

His paper received a modicum of attention, though it did receive plaudits from economist John Maynard Keynes. But it was long since forgotten for almost a century. It resurfaced in the twenty-first century, when notable economists like L. Randall Wray and anthropologists such as David Graeber saw its merit. Wray asserts that money and debt may be one and the same— that money is simply a measure of debt.[11] In Graeber's book *Debt: The First 5,000 Years*, he draws attention to the work of several anthropologists who have studied barter. One of them is Caroline Humphrey of the University of Cambridge, who writes, "No example of barter economy, pure and simple, has ever been described, let alone the emergence from it of money; all available ethnography suggests that there never has been such a thing."[12] Graeber connects the dots, saying that this lack of proof calls into question the conventional theory of how money originated. And it suggests such a foundational theory as to how money developed is a myth.[13]

However, before dismissing bartering-led-to-money entirely as myth, Graeber provides a bit of nuance. Indeed, many folks have bartered as a means of exchange, swapping one good for another. But it's usually with strangers—someone you may not ever see again, so the goods must be something of value.[14] I once bartered a beer in exchange for someone buying me a ticket to a baseball game. The cashier didn't accept credit cards, so the guy behind me paid for me with cash, and I promptly went to the first restaurant at the stadium and bought him a cold one with my credit card. To barter with someone you know may suggest a deficit of trust. Why not do a deal on credit? That requires confidence and faith, as the Latin root of *credit* means "to believe" or "to trust."

Not trusting your counterparty, not doing a deal on credit, can introduce a competitive aspect to bartering, in which barterers try to seize the upper hand. Graeber mentions the Pukhtun men of Pakistan, who barter with nonrelatives. They swap items in similar categories, like a shirt for a shirt. They also swap items of different categories, like donkeys for a bicycle. Winning a trade, getting the more valuable good, is reason to crow.[15] They aren't following the first step of Tit for Tat. They've assumed there won't be a second iteration of the game and are content to maximize the gain on the first move. In a credit system, the first move requires trust and cooperation.

Graeber, like Mitchell-Innes, asserts that before there was money, there was debt. Interest-bearing loans first appear in ancient Mesopotamia, thousands of years before the invention of coinage in the Kingdom of Lydia. In Mesopotamia, those who worked in temples, palaces, and prominent households calculated loans based on the prices of commodities like silver and barley. It also turns out that putting beers on a bar tab is an age-old practice, common in ancient Mesopotamia as well.[16] He ultimately concludes that debt predated or at least developed simultaneously with money. Given the historical importance of debt, it's necessary to understand its various dimensions.

Debts of a Different Type

In West Africa, it's forbidden to exchange cloth for yams. In the Solomon Islands, it's prohibited to trade taro for turmeric.[17] These peculiar rules are examples of spheres of exchange, in which items are assigned to a category and can be traded with items of the same category but not those in another group. Several cultures draw distinctions between spheres of nourishment and those of material goods. For instance, Tiv people of Nigeria have three spheres of exchange: (1) food items like grains and vegetables; (2) more lasting, prestigious items like brass rods and horses; and (3) "dependent persons" like children. The Siane people of New Guinea also have three spheres: (1) food items like bananas and taro; (2) luxury items like tobacco and nuts; and (3) ornaments like seashells and headdresses.[18] To mix spheres not only demonstrates ignorance but can also be insulting, as if you're trying to take advantage of the person with whom you're trading.

To transact smoothly in any society, it's important to know what's exchangeable for what: You don't exchange a Bentley for a hug (but you might give someone a hug if they give you a Bentley). There are different spheres of debt exchange in contemporary societies. Consider these two exchanges:

1. Miriam invites you over for a home-cooked meal of honey barbecue meat loaf.
2. You agree to a fixed-rate mortgage to finance payment on a new house.

The first exchange is in the familial sphere, with friends and family outside the marketplace. Because of Miriam's generosity you feel an obligation to reciprocate with a benevolent gesture of your own, like bringing a bottle of Petite Sirah wine, writing her a handwritten thank-you note on embossed stationery, or inviting her to a summer picnic in Central Park sometime in the future. The gift, the transfer of wealth or valuable goods, is only one part of the exchange. Also being exchanged may be respect, thanks, admiration, or a range of other things. This gratitude-induced obligation serves as the basis of what's known as the gift economy, found in ancient and contemporary societies all over the world.

The second exchange, involving the home mortgage, occurs in the commercial sphere, usually with strangers. There is an obligation to make the mortgage payments in full and on time. This legally induced obligation is part of what we today call the market economy. When we compute a debt obligation with money it can take the form of financial instruments like student loans, auto loans, and credit card bills.

Both exchanges result in an obligation of varying strengths to repay. But the method of payment is different. In the familial sphere, you would repay Miriam with an in-kind gift, and the interaction might then be considered complete, though it is likely to sustain a virtuous circle of future giving and receiving. But to mix market practices within the familial sphere can make for awkward situations. Say after aperitifs, appetizers, delicacies, and dessert you ask Miriam how much you owe her. You take out a billfold, count aloud eighty-five dollars, and press the cash into the palm of her hand. If Miriam is like most of my friends, you will offend her for treating her hospitality as if it were a good that can be purchased at the local Trader Joe's. You introduced a market practice, paying for services rendered with cash, into a social situation.

Of course, these two spheres are not mutually exclusive. They keep bumping up against each other. Companies try to blur the lines between these spheres for their benefit. Treating a client like a dear friend or family member is a characteristic practice of effective salespeople everywhere. And frequent-flier and other reward programs are designed to instill a sense of loyalty and obligation that gives you pause before you return to the marketplace. These companies are trying to enter your familial sphere so that you will view them more favorably and less like a stranger. The more you trust them, the more they can sell you. But even still, Best Buy isn't the same thing as your brother.

The Gift

Marcel Mauss was a multidisciplinary man, chock-full of ideas. Part sociologist, part anthropologist, part philosopher, he wrote in 1924 *Essai sur le don*, or "The Gift," which still serves as a foundational work for anthropologists who study gift exchange.[19] A gift can have political, economic, social, even religious dimensions, and studying it requires a broad, panoramic lens. A gift can take on several meanings because it reflects the intent of the giver, which can range from benevolence and munificence to solicitation and contempt. For example, say Miriam invites you to dinner to butter you up before she requests that you help her son gain admission to a select university that you attended. Her gift, the lovely dinner, now drips with additional meaning. And if you had known her intentions before the dinner, you might have rejected the invitation.

Gift economies have their unique flavors of rituals and customs, but Mauss observed that they usually involve three types of obligations or principles: to give, to receive, and to reciprocate.[20] These obligations make up the cycle of the gift economy. The constant movement of gifts, which I will trace across several cultures, suggests that the currency of gifts, and debts of the familial sphere, bear a similarity to the movement of money in the commercial sphere. However, the difference is that movement or "transactions" in the gift economy usually sustain relationships. After you receive a cappuccino from a friend, the relationship is sustained and even strengthens, and you're obligated to reciprocate the gesture at a later date. When a gift is given, despite money never changing hands, there is still another currency in circulation: familial or social debt. In the market economy, after you buy a caramel Frappuccino from a Starbucks barista, the relationship ends and you go your separate ways.

Mauss recognized how gifts sustained the relationship among the Maori people of New Zealand and nature. The Maoris speak of gifts as having a *hau*, or spirit. Hunters who catch game from the forest give some meat to priests, who perform rituals on it. By doing so, the priests arrange a *mauri*—for example, game prepared during a ritual ceremony or sacred stones—which is a physical manifestation of the forest's *hau*.[21] They offer the *mauri* back to the forest as a demonstration of gratitude for nature's gift. Not to demonstrate proper gratitude can upset nature and diminish its future bounty.[22] In general, a gift's *hau* is said to have a yearning to return to its place of origin, encouraging recipients to reciprocate the gift. The forest, hunter, and priest are all givers and recipients, playing their roles in the cyclical movement of the gift. Several scholars have attempted to debunk Mauss's spiritual interpretation in favor of a more secular understanding: Not to reciprocate a gift would harm the reputation of the recipient.[23] Even still, the movement of a gift shows the currency of the gift economy in full circulation.

We see the circulation of gifts on a larger scale in the Trobriand Islands, near New Guinea, where anthropologist Bronisław Malinowski found locals practicing a gift exchange called the Kula. Two types of ceremonial gifts, or *vaygu'a*, necklaces and armbands, are exchanged among families on the many islands that make up the Massim archipelago, and they function like a type of currency.[24] Both gifts move in a loop around the islands: Red shell necklaces move in a clockwise manner, and armshells move in a counterclockwise fashion. The gifts are exchanged for each other: Receiving a necklace should be reciprocated by giving an armshell now or up to one year in the future. It can take up to ten years for gifts to make it all the way around the islands, as folks travel long distances via canoe to other islands.[25] The cycle of gift exchange, incurring social debts and repaying them, gives shape to the society—knowing where folks stand in relation to each other, like a large credit system. To hoard a gift for too long risks your reputation or credit. Not to give means ending one's social ties and withdrawing from the community. Giving is expected and is part of being an upstanding member of the group.[26]

The constant movement of gifts in the gift economy is in contrast to the buying and hoarding we often associate with Western societies. In the Trobriand Islands, and in many so-called archaic societies, Malinowski observes that *"to possess is to give."*[27] Translated into modern parlance: Pay it forward and keep the gift moving. In his illuminating book *The Gift*, author Lewis Hyde contrasts divergent cultural views regarding the movement of gifts with a thought experiment. Say an early English settler visits a Native American community, where he is given a pipe. The settler gladly accepts the pipe and displays it proudly at his home. When members of the Indian tribe visit his home, he learns that they expect him to give them the pipe. He bemoans the Indians' disrespect for private property. To him, to receive a gift is to remove it from circulation, maybe even turning it into a commodity that can be sold later. He sees them as what has been called an "Indian giver," someone who wants their gift back—a phrase with a stereotypical and negative connotation that may stem from Lewis and Clark's expedition, when they encountered difficulties trading with Native Americans.[28] In Hyde's thought experiment, the Indians bemoan the settler's disrespect for the movement of the gift and the wider community. To them, to hold a gift is to continue giving and regifting, sustaining relationships.[29] Here we have the familial and commercial spheres coexisting, albeit uneasily.

To give, in some societies, is part of a formalized way to gain status. Anthropologists in the nineteenth century, including Mauss but starting with Franz Boas, who studied the Kwakiutl people, a native tribe of British Columbia, spilled considerable ink explaining the potlatch (not to be confused with a "potluck," which is of English origin). A potlatch is a ceremonial gift exchange that historically took place among native communities in the Pacific Northwest. Potlatches were organized for noteworthy occasions like births, weddings, and funerals. But the purpose of most potlatches was to make or demonstrate a social claim, for instance, the ascension of a new chief after the death of the previous one, like a coronation ceremony in which a new king is crowned.[30] The new chief was usually the firstborn son, and it was his role to preside over the potlatch. Social mobility was limited, and potlatches reinforced hereditable claims to power through rituals.[31]

Most native communities of the region had their own twist on the potlatch, but there was some similarity in format. The chief and his wider kin group, or *numima*, as it's known in the Kwakiutl society, invited guests to witness the important occasion. The potlatch became a public spectacle in which the chief or "donor" and *numima* prepared a feast and led rounds of oration, singing, and dancing. At the end, the donor distributed gifts to guests, as a symbol of generosity and a signal for the guests to leave. Gifts reflected the prestige of the donor instead of the desires of the guests. Therefore, higher-valued items like meats and skins were often given as gifts. Kwakiutl coppers were another notable gift, made from metal sheets adorned with the names of previous owners. Over many generations these coppers changed hands through a series of many potlatches. Enshrined on the coppers is a history of gift exchange during this era.[32]

Indeed, potlatches helped to integrate families and build solidarity among the wider community. But they also served as a way to distinguish among members, to identify an individual's status and rank. Gifts were distributed in order of each guest's rank, so the recipient knew exactly where he or she stood in the eyes of the donor, as no two guests had an identical rank. Recipients also contrasted the gifts they received among themselves, as a way to gauge their own relative status.[33] For example, in one potlatch feast, a seal's breast was served to the chief, whereas the flipper was given to the second in command. Members with lower rank received lower-quality cuts of meat.[34]

Giving gifts, and openly "destroying" one's wealth, is a virtue in these Kwakiutl societies. It contrasts with the notion in Western societies of gaining status through accumulating wealth.[35] In fact, from the late nineteenth to mid-twentieth century, potlatches were deemed illegal in Canada's Indian Act because they supposedly stood in the way of cultural assimilation. Destroying wealth was seen as a blatant disregard for private property.[36] Upon further analysis, there's a competitive spirit to the potlatch. Although gift giving in the potlatch has the patina of generosity, many tribes became competitive about it, trying to outdo their previous potlatch and those organized by their neighbors, lavishing their rivals with outsized largesse. However, as the native communities shrank in population, due in part to diseases contracted from foreigners, claims to status and rank were blurred. Sometimes there weren't enough members to fill all the positions of status. Disputes between members who claimed the same rank or status were settled by whoever organized the better potlatch. What had initially served as a way to limit social mobility, the potlatch had become a ladder for it.[37]

Over time, as these native communities traded with Western settlers, some newly procured items, like clocks and, later, sewing machines, were injected into potlatches, along with norms found in the commercial sphere. These goods gradually took on traditional meanings, and eventually a donor's prestige was derived mostly from the monetary value of his gifts. Status now came from a market price instead of a hereditable claim. Coppers were measured on scales, and gifts were seen through the lens of money and the market economy. The potlatch had been transformed. Market norms had made inroads into the familial sphere.

Gift economies aren't found only in societies from centuries ago. Such modern public displays of gift exchange that sustain a web of relationships can be found on the World Wide Web and online platforms. Founded in 1999, peer-to-peer music-sharing service Napster dramatically altered music consumption: Instead of buying music in the marketplace, users shared or gifted their collections of MP3 music files with one another. After down-loading a song from someone else, it was added to one's collection, and others could download it. Though one didn't part with the song when it was shared, it amounted to a gift for the recipient. There was constant movement, like in the Kula, as songs were gifted and regifted. Instead of a circle, Napster's gift economy had a rhizomatic or rootlike structure, with users spread around the world.[38] One researcher interviewed Napster users to better understand their motivations. Users spoke of the Napster "commu-nity" to highlight that sharing and gifting built a sense of solidarity.[39] Others decried the practice of downloading music but not sharing one's own collec-tion of music. One user said, "If they're not into sharing, they should not be allowed to reap the benefits."[40] Napster users developed norms and obliga-tions similar to the societies studied by Mauss and Malinowski. Certainly, many believed Napster users were engaging in music piracy, stealing from the marketplace and sharing freely with the community. Facing lawsuits and court orders, Napster shut down. In this example, it's the producers in the market economy that suffer from familial attitudes on sharing writ large. A valuable piece of intellectual property was shared around the world with little monetary regard for its creator.

We see the reverse, the commercial sphere benefiting from the familial sphere, with the online crowd-funding platform Kickstarter, which enables people to give money to artistic projects. Artists create short videos that explain their vision. Many have achieved incredible fund-raising success: One musician seeking $100,000 raised $1 million; a video game designer looking for $400,000 raised north of $3 million. More than $800 million has been raised on the platform.[41] Kickstarter takes a fee for every suc-cessful fund-raising campaign, acting as a market agent that benefits from the money flowing through the gift economy. Those startled by the rise of Kickstarter need only remember the pervasiveness, draw, and obligations of the gift economy.[42] When your artist friend asks you for money, you may feel obligated to help. There's no large economic benefit to the giver, but the gift sustains the relationship with the artist, who provides the artistic gift along with a steady stream of updates to benefactors, and small gifts like free albums or the dedication of a song.

In all these examples, the movement of gifts relies on gratitude, or what sociologist Georg Simmel termed "the moral memory of mankind."[43] After receiving a gift, there's a resulting gratitude-induced obligation that the recipient remembers. Though gratitude carries a warm and generous connotation, make no mistake of its strong force, a "gratitude imperative" to reciprocate a gift.[44] A gratitude-induced obligation creates a tie of morality between the giver and the recipient—symbolically represented by the bow and ribbons found on presents.[45] Admittedly, gratitude-induced obligations work only up to a point. When a group gets too large, it's nearly impossible to remember how every exchange affected each relationship, and where everyone stands in the mutual web of indebtedness. Gratitude necessitates remembrance and is necessary to restoring the debt balance between the giver and the recipient.

There's even a rough way to track and calculate one's social debt balance. Remember from earlier that you and Miriam are counterparties in a familial or social debt exchange: Her kind gesture credits her balance and debits yours, like a social bank account or credit system. In conversation, we even use language as if we're keeping track of balances in such a system. We use metaphors involving debt to describe our relationships with others: I *owe* you one; I am in your *debt*; I'll make him *pay*.[46] We may even *think* in terms of such a credit system. Leading linguists contend that metaphors aren't just artful ways of expressing ourselves; they also shape how we think.[47] Many folks keep an active mental account as to whom they owe and who owes them. Some even write it down: J. P. Morgan CEO Jamie Dimon reportedly keeps a list of "people who owe me stuff" in his suit pocket.[48] He realizes that gifts or social credits minimize the friction of dealing with individuals solely through the market economy: The cost of doing a deal is less expensive if someone already owes you. That a Wall Street titan recognizes and keeps track of favors or "chits" shows how important the gift economy can be in greasing the wheels of the market economy.

When President George W. Bush was reelected in 2004, he said matter-of-factly, "I earned capital in this campaign, political capital, and now I intend to spend it."[49] He wasn't just using an expressive metaphor but providing a window to his thoughts and second-term policy agenda. "Political" or "social" capital invokes the same debt metaphor. Though termed "capital," it isn't owned like a piece of property.[50] You can't cash it in with everyone or convert it easily into another currency like money. Its value is embedded in the relationship with whoever is on the other side of the obligation. If that person walks away from the obligation, the credits that you accrued may be worthless. It takes at least two to tango in these social debt arrangements. And because you can't exactly "own" this type of social debt, at least in these examples, this metaphorical capital returns us to the notion that *to possess is to give*: The value of social capital is realized by having someone else fulfill their obligation, to repay the gift and to keep the cycle going.

Constantly keeping track of one's social debt balance can be a source of anxiety. First, it can be difficult to reciprocate and find the right "payment" or gift. One study found more than a dozen sources of anxiety resulting from gift giving; they range from unfamiliarity, not knowing the recipient well or their preferences, to selectivity, when the recipient is highly selective in their tastes.[51] For example, finding an appropriate gift for a new boyfriend or girlfriend can be difficult indeed. Too inexpensive a gift sends a signal that you didn't sacrifice or spend enough on them. Too expensive a gift and you risk scaring them away because the money you've spent could signal too much commitment or seriousness at an early stage. Second, one may not want to incur a social debt obligation, as it may shift the power to the benefactor. And one may reject the gift outright. In a study on the role of gift exchange in courtship, some women resisted a man's attempt to buy them dinner, preferring instead to "go dutch" and split the bill. To some, the gifts aren't just a way to ingratiate but an effort to control the relationship.

Anxiety from gift exchange can push folks to escape *to* the market economy, which can offer anonymity and fewer lingering obligations. In Montreal, for example, some have turned to professional moving services instead of relying on friends to help them move. Historically, Montreal's large working-class population was forced to move residences frequently. Most rental leases were for one year and started in the summer, and many found themselves moving at the same time. These days, moving in Montreal has become something of a hobby and part of the culture. Labatt Breweries of Canada has run advertisements with moving residences as the theme. A famous song by Robert Charlebois sounds a cultural note with his tune "Deménagér ou rester là," which means "Move out or stay put."[52] Since moving houses is labor-intensive, the mover will turn to the gift economy and ask his or her friends and family to help during the move. One mover praised the cooperative nature of the gift economy: "These people who helped us, I've helped them move in the past...Wow! People are here for you. You're not in a mess. You're not alone."[53] But exchanges in the gift economy don't always flow smoothly. If friends and family don't show up, one may lose faith in them and feel slighted by their reluctance to help. Others don't want the resulting obligations associated with friends and family members who have helped during the move. Mira, a forty-nine-year-old architect, says: "It would be complicated to entrust [my cousin] with the painting job because he won't charge me the market price...I don't want to feel obliged. I don't want to feel that I will have to give back."[54] Escaping the gift economy for the market economy shows the lengths some folks will go to to avoid social indebtedness.

Remember Your On

In all my travels and research, the most fascinating and curious gift economy that I encountered was in Japan. Not only do we find the constant movement of gifts and the seesaw between gratitude and anxiety, but there's a high degree of thoughtfulness and detail that goes into procuring and giving gifts. Unpacking Japanese gift exchange reveals complex ideas about social debt and gratitude.

In the mid-twentieth century, anthropologist Ruth Benedict detailed Japanese conceptions of debt, known as *on* and *giri*. *On* is defined most broadly as an obligation. It's the social burden that one carries from others, such as managers or parents. A worker who receives a benefit from his manager, say a promotion or bonus, is said to carry an *on* to his manager. To remember your *on* is to feel gratitude toward whoever provided you with the benefit, and eventually to reciprocate.

The burden of *on* makes many reluctant to get entangled with others, as in refusing to accept casual acts of kindness from a stranger who offers a beer or a cigarette. Even today, some conceal their trips abroad from friends to avoid having to bring gifts.[55] Benedict says that the Japanese have various ways of expressing thanks, such as *arigato*, which means "Oh, this difficult thing."[56] Another word for thanks, *sumimasen*, has an apologetic connotation and is loosely translated as "I'm very sorry" or "This doesn't end." The feeling of obligation is so deep, it seemingly cannot be repaid.[57]

To repay an *on* can be long and complicated. A man is said not to know how to repay the *on* to his own parents until he himself has children. To care for your children is to repay parental *on* that you accrued when you were a needy child. During World War II, many Japanese recognized their imperial *on* toward the emperor of Japan. Every gift distributed to the soldiers, from sake to cigarettes, was an advance of the imperial *on*. To die in a kamikaze mission was to repay an imperial *on*.[58]

Benedict describes two types of repayment: *Gimu* is a repayment of an *on* that can never be totally repaid, debts you take on at birth, like *on* toward parents; *giri* is a repayment of *on* with some measure of equivalence.[59] She distinguishes between *giri* to the world, repaying one's contemporaries and extended family, and *giri* to one's name, maintaining your honor, reputation, and good name. *Giri* is even embedded in the names of certain familial relations: Instead of "father-in-law," it's "father-in-giri."[60] Not to give a *giri* risks one's reputation or "credit" of not knowing how to act and honor *on*. *Giri* payments are even dressed up as Valentine's Day presents or *giri choco*, which means "obligation chocolate," when women give sweets to men with whom they're not romantically involved. One survey showed that 84 percent of women give gifts to people who have aided them, repaying an *on*, yet only 28 percent give to someone with whom they're romantically involved.[61] On March 14, a month after Valentine's Day, the tables are turned and the men reciprocate with white chocolate gifts for women.

Repayment is expected even when you experience personal tragedy. My American friend's mother died while he was living in Japan. When he returned to work, there was a pile of envelopes, known as *okouden bukuro*, with cash gifts that his colleagues had given as condolences. He learned that the proper protocol is to spend half of this money on return gifts such as handkerchiefs for his colleagues, known as *hangaishi*, or "half return."

Anthropologist Katherine Rupp picks up from Benedict, exploring the art form of gift exchange in Japan. Not all Japanese people take part in ritualized gift exchange, but she identifies noteworthy patterns. The Japanese gift economy spells real business: The summer (*chûgen*) and winter (*seibo*) gift seasons account for 60 percent of earnings for many department stores. Stores start their *seibo* advertising campaigns early and hire staff to keep up with demand, just like the Christmas season in the United States. Folks are flush with cash because they receive bonuses worth two or more months of salary.[62]

These giving seasons began in China, possibly as a Buddhist tradition, and were an opportunity to show gratitude to one's deceased ancestors. During the Meiji Restoration in Japan, in the nineteenth century, the government urged citizens to replace Buddhist shrines with more nationalist Shintō ones, in order to create a sense of commonality. Over time, gift giving became less of a way to honor deities. It became a way to bestow favor on one's parents and ancestors, or simply to repay an *on*. Younger people today have even updated, contemporized, and merged *seibo* with Christmas, since both happen around the same time of the year.[63]

In Japan, gratitude isn't just symbolically represented by the bow and ribbons tied around a gift, but by *how* the gift is wrapped—an indication of the high attention to detail found in this gift economy. Gifts for weddings and funerals are tied with a unique knot known as *musubikiri*, meaning "to tie completely," and which cannot be unraveled easily.[64] Gifts for birthdays, graduations, and newborns ought to be tied with *chōmusubi*, or a "butterfly knot," which can be unraveled readily, suggesting that these events happen more frequently.[65] To tie a funeral gift with a butterfly knot is foreboding, meaning that another death may occur. Similarly, a wedding gift tied with a butterfly knot doesn't bode well for the success of the marriage.

Gifts with wrapping paper from top department stores indicate that the giver has spent considerable time and money on the selection. Top department stores are adamant about wrapping gifts themselves in order to control quality and maintain their reputation. On the wrapping paper is usually the store brand and address, so that the recipient knows from which branch location it was purchased. And new hires are trained over many days on how to wrap presents properly.[66] The person who receives the gift is expected to unwrap it deliberately and thoughtfully. Other cultural practices include giving money in odd numbers; even numbers are considered unlucky because they are divisible. And envelopes containing money for weddings should have in the top right corner a small depiction of an abalone, which is a symbol of auspiciousness. All of this to say, it can be a highly elaborate process to give a gift and enact a social debt in Japan. Even though there's not a formal accounting system, the Japanese gift economy acts as if there is one in place—gifts are evaluated closely. The only thing missing is a price.

Into the Wilds of the Market

Computing obligations with money can transform them into debt instruments found in the market economy, from a mortgage to buy your house to a bank loan to renovate it. Financial debt has been with us since the beginnings of civilization. Interest-bearing loans predated the invention of coins by thousands of years.

Around 5000 BC, in what's now known as the Middle East, various types of debt instruments emerged. Friendly loans with no interest were common, but these resembled gifts: Despite not having a price, there was still an obligation to repay. Interest-bearing loans started with agriculture and farming: seeds, nuts, olives, grains, and cows borrowed by destitute farmers who repaid the loan with interest—in the form of the surplus from their harvest.[67] Loaning agricultural goods, however, was fraught with difficulty. The gains on an agricultural loan were uncertain due to unpredictable weather.[68]

As civilization took root, the need for lending grew. Short-term interest-free loans remained since they helped people, particularly family members, cope with a crisis. But again, these loans were more like gifts. To recognize the importance of interest-bearing loans to ancient societies, consider the Third Dynasty of Ur.

Around 2100 BC, after the decline of the Akkadian Kingdom, a dynasty emerged in the city of Ur, in what is now southern Iraq, which lasted for 104 years. It's a period known as the "Sumerian Renaissance."[69] City leaders incorporated advanced architecture, like brick buildings with sloped arches, and built walkways so that people could amble to work. Surviving documents from this period also show a society rich with literature, language, religion, and commerce.

Many documents mention a merchant known as Turam-ili. Fifty-nine tablets constitute the Turam-ili archive, now housed at Yale University. Nearly 20 percent of these records are loan documents. Turam-ili was known as "ugula dam-gàr," which translates to "overseer of the merchants."[70] Turam-ili acted as an agent for others, buying and selling goods, and extending credit to those in need. He and other merchants made loans to finance payments and the transfer of items, a necessary function to keep any economy humming. Moneylending among merchants and others was attractive because income generated from interest-bearing loans could be used to procure even more land, animals, and slaves.[71] Money made money.

During this time period, loans that required interest payments were structured in various ways. Some stipulated that borrowers make interest payments in the form of labor: Silver-based loans usually required a debtor to provide a skilled laborer; barley-based loans required the labor of an agricultural worker. Historian Steven Garfinkle says that loans that required nonlabor interest payments can be classified as "productive" and "consumptive." Productive loans were made in silver by merchants or institutions and for the enhancement of a debtor's living situation, such as improving their home. Consumptive loans were made in barley and intended to help a debtor make ends meet before the harvest.[72] These loans also helped to reinforce the status of people in a hierarchical society, as creditors could increase the dependency of laborers.

Garfinkle calls credit a "functional necessity," since almost everyone relied on it, destitute farmers and wealthy individuals alike.[73] Affluent folks may have been trying to finance their high cost of living, or reloaning to others at higher rates. Creditors included wealthy families, merchants like Turam-ili, and large institutions.

The temples, the palace, and the households of governors and officials were the principal institutions of Sumerian society, and they were the major creditors, in some cases functioning like banks.[74] They took in taxes and dues in the form of grains, animals, and silver. They also accrued income from land that had been given by kings or won during a war. They even distinguished between items that could be exchanged and those that couldn't, publishing exchange rates and establishing the basis for trade. Acting as institutional lenders, they made interest-bearing "consumptive" loans to individuals so they could make ends meet until the harvest season—and Shamash the God of Justice was often listed as the creditor.[75] Also listed were the names of the debtor, the principal amount, the name of a witness, the year the loan was originated, and the seal of the debtor. Loan contracts were agreed to orally because most people were illiterate.[76] The creditor kept the sealed loan agreement until it was repaid, at which time the record was usually destroyed.

Though most creditors preferred to be repaid the principal plus interest, there were times when debtors just couldn't make good on the loan. Declaring personal bankruptcy wasn't an option, so there was some creative license in making repayments. When a debtor couldn't repay a silver-based loan, they offered livestock and food. The Sumerian word for interest, *máš*, or "calf," has been interpreted to mean that payments were to be made in livestock.[77] There were even instances of men giving up their wives or sons to avoid interest payments.[78] When debts outstanding amounted to levels at which the public threatened unrest, sometimes the royal court, usually with the ascension of a new king, decreed clean slates that canceled all agricultural debts.[79]

A similar practice of debt amnesty happens even in modern societies. Until recently, the first act of a new French president was to cancel all parking tickets.[80]

In Mesopotamia, the logic for setting interest rates varied based on the type of loan. Variation in seasonality was the reason that barley-based loans had higher interest rates than silver-based loans, approximately one-third of the principal versus one-fifth.[81] These rates were inscribed in the Code of Hammurabi, named after the Babylonian king who installed it as a type of governing directive, though it wasn't always followed to the letter, and as Garfinkle notes, may have also served as "royal propaganda."[82] Sometimes, however, temples acted like a modern central bank, dropping interest rates to lower the cost of borrowing for debtors.

Economic records suggest that interest rates declined through successive ancient civilizations: 20 percent in Mesopotamia, 10 percent in Greece, and just over 8 percent in Rome. Lower interest rates can be a sign of market efficiency and lower risks of lending, and could reflect increases in productivity and development between successive civilizations.[83] However, Michael Hudson, an expert in Babylonian economics, surmises that rates were based on mathematical simplicity and not so much on economic conditions.[84] In Mesopotamia, most payments, including interest payments, were measured with weights, so it was helpful to use simple fractions and round numbers. The Sumerians used a sexagesimal numeral system, a system with the number 60 as its base.[85] We even use such a system today for measuring seconds and minutes. Calculating interest rates with this system was straightforward because 60 is easily divisible: The measurement of silver, *mina*, was split into sixty shekels, and interest was typically charged at one shekel per month on a one-*mina* loan. That amounted to 12/60ths of a mina per year, or a 20 percent annual interest rate. Even today, interest rate payments for some mortgages are based on a sexagesimal system, a 360-day calendar, partly because it's easier to use. Classical Greece and Rome employed numerical systems with different bases of 10 and 12 respectively. Interest typically charged worked out to 1/10th of principal, or 10 percent in Greece, and 1/12th, or just over 8 percent, in Rome.[86]

In short, almost everyone needed credit, and interest-bearing loans have been integral to the functioning of economies both ancient and modern.

Sinister Bonds

Raju thought he had just landed himself a new job. A Burmese laborer, he journeyed to Thailand to work. He was required to pay a "brokerage fee," which he couldn't afford, so he borrowed the funds. He reasoned that his eventual income would help pay off the debt. He was then forced at gunpoint to work long hours on a Thai fishing boat. Raju said of one person who attempted to escape, "The man was tied to a post... electrocuted and tortured with cigarette butts... later shot through the head."[87] Raju courageously dove into the water, swam to safety, and lived to share his story. This isn't an ancient tale but rather a modern one detailed in the US Department of State's 2012 report on human trafficking.

Stories like these show that all too often, debt becomes not just a way to reinforce status but an instrument of oppression. Debtors' inability to repay loans can result in situations that deprive them of their freedom. Debt becomes a way to control others.

In the case of a social debt, it can be difficult to determine an acceptably equivalent way to reciprocate. Without specific prices, the value of a gift is open to interpretation and approximation. With lending and borrowing in the commercial sphere, there's no guessing because it comes with an exact price. Attaching a nominal money value to debt certainly makes clear to everyone where they stand, down to the penny. But it also provides less wiggle room when someone can't repay. In the name of debt contracts, creditors can ask a borrower to do things that they normally wouldn't in the familial sphere—forgo a visit to the doctor, sell your wife, or work as a bonded laborer—all in order to make a debt payment.

Anthropologist Alain Testart distinguishes among different types of debt bondage: (1) Slavery is when insolvent debtors lose rights and citizenship and are essentially exiled with no chance to attain freedom; (2) pawning is a type of forced labor in which a debtor serves a creditor, and eventually, but not always, attains freedom after the debt has been repaid.[88] Both deprive a debtor of freedom, and often pawns become slaves, as creditors add the cost of food and medicine to the outstanding debt as well as charging high interest rates.

In ancient Mesopotamia, pawning involved ruthless practices. Graeber's research finds that a man was disallowed to sell his wife. But the Code of Hammurabi stipulated that creditors could seize a man, his family, or his slaves if he was unable to repay a debt—and force them to work. A debt contract effectively turned a person into an object or commodity to settle an account, contorting the familial sphere into the commercial one.[89] Upholding one's creditworthiness was part of maintaining honor, apparently a virtue for which anything or anyone could be sacrificed.[90] Maintaining one's reputation is vital to the gift economy, too, but the punishments in the commercial sphere are usually more severe. In a gift economy, the benefactor risks his own reputation if he treats a debtor without compunction. In the market economy, historically, the creditor could resort to cruel measures.

The Code of Hammurabi offered borrowers some protections: A debtor was to be freed after three years of bonded labor; and if a debtor died because of abuse while a bonded laborer, the creditor was punished with the death of his son.[91] Over history, many leaders have tried to protect debtors. For example, in Athens around 600 BC, there was a real possibility of popular revolution—as bonded labor and slavery had become rampant. Solon, the archon of Athens, canceled debts and abolished debt slavery (but not all forms of pawning).[92] He, like many overlords in antiquity, recognized the disastrous effects of too much debt: If the balance of power tilts too heavily in favor of the creditor, a whole society can come crumbling down. Debt protection, then, is also creditor protection. Let's not upset the whole applecart.

Imprisonment for debt was also a common practice in ancient times. During the Roman Empire, a creditor could arrest the debtor for debt delinquency and haul him into court. If guilty, the debtor could land in a private jail, and after sixty days become a slave, bonded laborer, or even be killed. Though uncommon, creditors were allowed to cut up a debtor's body into chunks commensurate to the debt owed.[93] Yet Roman rulers, like those of Greece and Babylon, realized the importance of debtor protection. They ushered in public prisons, four-month grace periods for repayments, and eventually the abolition of debt imprisonment altogether.

But debt imprisonment endured. In eighteenth-century England, many debtors found themselves locked up in Fleet Prison in London, or Marshalsea Prison, which Charles Dickens mentions in his writings. One of these debtors in Fleet Prison was a trader who simply had had a bad financial year. He was dragged from his room and laid outside to face inclement weather. Though he was in poor health, the trader was beaten and abused with a sword by the warden. The next day the prisoner was tortured by having irons put on his legs. The prisoner pleaded that he would like a hearing before a court to protest such cruel punishment, yet he was taken to the dungeon, where even more irons were used to keep him in constant pain for three weeks, and he almost lost his ability to see. After many inhumane episodes like this, Parliament banned debt prisons with the Debtors Act of 1869.[94]

Many who fled England for America were debtors themselves, escaping the reach of creditors. However, debt prisons existed in colonial America and were a common grievance among colonists.[95] Pennsylvania's founder,

William Penn, and Revolutionary War financier Robert Morris both spent time in these prisons. My native state of Georgia actually began as a debtor's safe haven. Its founder, James Oglethorpe, developed a strong opposition to debtors' prisons because his friend died from smallpox in one. He established the Georgia Society, a debtors' refuge, which ultimately won a royal charter from King George II to set up the colony of Georgia. Despite efforts to stamp out debt imprisonment, it still lingered. In 1830, more than ten thousand people were imprisoned in New York debt prisons. Many times the debts were minimal. In Philadelphia, thirty inmates had debts outstanding of not more than a dollar.[96] There were five people imprisoned for debt delinquency for every one put away for a violent offense. Eventually, by 1833, the federal government wised up and abolished debt prisons.[97]

State-sponsored debt bondage and imprisonment has declined considerably. But according to the US Department of State, even today, millions like Raju in South Asia and in other parts of the world are laboring to repay their debts, and find themselves in difficult circumstances. Sometimes they are even working to repay the debts of their deceased ancestors.[98]

The dark side of debt isn't limited to the emerging world. Remarkably, in America, several states still allow the jailing of debtors, and more than five thousand warrants have been issued since 2010.[99] In 2011, citizens were jailed essentially for carrying outstanding debts. Collection agencies resorted to harsh measures during the global financial crisis. One lady who was pulled over because of an ineffective muffler was arrested because she had failed to show up in court to answer for $730 in unpaid medical expenses; she wasn't even aware that the collection agency had filed a lawsuit against her.[100] Though financial debt instruments have become more complex and easily tradable, the dark side of debt has lingered since before Hammurabi's times.

From Mind to Matter

The first part of this book serves as the intellectual foundation for the next section. The evolutionary investigation into money shows that *exchange* is fundamental to all organisms. Initially the instruments being exchanged were food items that served an evolutionary purpose to promote survival. But as humans gained capacity for symbolic thought, more durable commodities were exchanged. Chapter 4 is an extension of this line of thought, and it addresses the commodity form of money.

However, this anthropological investigation into money suggests that debt is our primary currency. Not every transaction is completed immediately. We do favors for each other and remember who owes us. Moreover, financial debt precedes the invention of coined money by thousands of years. Money need not be a commodity, then. We can transact in something that doesn't have intrinsic worth, since it can still be a symbol of value. Chapter 5 is an extension of this line of thought. It addresses money as a symbol of value determined by the issuer, which is usually the government.

From the Galapagos to the Trobriand Islands, my quest to understand money started with grasping the roots of an idea. Whether using money is a function of genetics, a neural stimulant, or a behavior instilled by culture, why we exchange remains a fascinating question. But now is the time to move from *why* to *what*. To move from the mind of money, to the body of it—how it looks and feels. And how despite its changing forms, it remains a symbol of value throughout.

PART II
BODY

The Material Forms of Money

CHAPTER FOUR

Hard and Heavy

A brief history of hard money

Gold is irresistible.
—*Goethe*[1]

Men agreed to employ in their dealings with each other
something intrinsically useful and easily applicable to the
purposes of life, for example, iron, silver and the like.
—*Aristotle*[2]

The possession of a gold coin is incontestably more agreeable
than the possession of goods.
—*Silvio Gesell*[3]

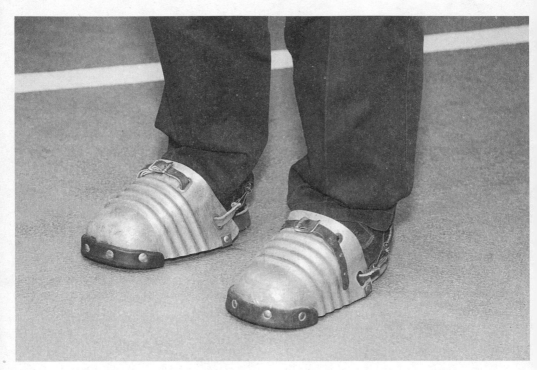

Employees in the vault at the Federal Reserve Bank of New York wear these magnesium shoe clips when moving gold bars.

When I was a kid, someone on the playground told me that if I dug far enough, eventually I would reach China. That's a myth, but here's something that isn't: If you dig deeply enough in New York City, the town in which I live, you may just strike gold.

Eighty-six feet below ground level, resting on the bedrock of Manhattan, behind a ninety-ton door, is the gold vault of the Federal Reserve Bank of New York, which is home to more gold than anywhere else in the world: 530,000 bars, weighing an aggregate of 6,700 tons.[4] I learned about this vault years ago, but I still had my suspicions: Is there *really* a vault? Why store gold in a city subject to potential terrorist attacks? And a more sweeping question: Why stockpile so much of a primitive, antiquated metal in the first place? To answer these burning questions, I signed up for a public tour and jumped on the No. 4 train down to Wall Street.

The New York Federal Reserve building is so large you almost don't see it. Inspired by the design of Renaissance palaces, the twenty-two-story building with its stonework and black iron gates conveys power and authority, yet it hides in the shadows of neighboring buildings. A guard brandishing an automatic weapon checks my name on a list. I pass through a metal detector and am greeted by a neatly groomed tour guide wearing a navy pinstripe suit and ocean-blue tie. He ushers me down via a crowded elevator to the vault. I walk by a dozen cubicles and an exhibit for tourists and there it is: yellow, bright, and heavy. Gold bars, plenty of them, tucked into several light blue holding cells that span the length of half a football field. The vault *smells* like stale, locked-up metal. Some bars are shaped like rectangular bricks, which can be seven inches long, more than three inches wide, and almost two inches thick. Bars made after 1986 are in the form of trapezoids. A bar can weigh about twenty-eight pounds, but because of its density it feels like twice that. Etched on every bar is its purity level and identification numbers. There is an old giant scale that can weigh amounts as little as one one-hundredth of an ounce up to 640 pounds. It's a reminder of the mechanical process involved in storing, weighing, and moving the gold bars. While transporting bars, workers wear protective metal casings over their shoes. In the spirit of a Jules Verne novel, I journeyed to the interior of the vault, and verified that, yes, it exists.

As for my next question about storing the gold in New York: It's here largely for historical reasons. Built in the 1920s, the vault became a popular and secure place to store the world's gold, especially during and after World War II. At the time of my visit, the value of all the gold totaled more than $350 billion and represented 25 percent of the world's whole supply. But the Federal Reserve doesn't own any of it. It belongs to other entities, like governments, foreign central banks, and international organizations.[5] And despite the prospect of calamities besetting New York City, the vault is impenetrable: There are no computers, in order to rule out cyberattacks, and the door is air- and watertight. There have been no successful robberies of the Fed except for the one staged in *Die Hard III*. Should anyone ever stage a burglary, one of the marksmen who practices on the second-floor shooting range will quickly put an end to it.

And as for my last question, about why to store gold in the first place, the easy answer is because it's valuable and there isn't a lot of it. If you put all the known gold in the world into the 555-foot Washington Monument, only one-third of the obelisk would be full.[6] But it's not just a question of scarcity; there's something special about gold. Not every metal is safeguarded under an enormous custom-designed solid vault door. To understand why, I looked for answers in another New York City institution. I jumped on the train again and took it uptown to the public library.

Since the dawn of civilization, there has been a recurring question about money: Is it hard or soft? Expanding the question, is money an item with intrinsic worth? Or is it inherently worthless and merely represents something else of value? Put in material terms: Is money a gold coin or a dollar bill? It depends on the time and the place, and what the people, or the ruling authority, deem acceptable. Alas, money can clearly be both—as long as it remains a symbol of value. Lest we forget, the brain has neuroplasticity; it is capable of learning new ideas and updating old ones. Ultimately, the social brain, the "super-brain" of society, determines what will function as currency, from cacao, used by the Aztecs, to butter, which once circulated in Norway.

While there have been many forms of money, answering "hard" or "soft" to the aforementioned question has historically been a dividing line between two economic doctrines, metallism and chartalism. They're worth exploring because they provide a straightforward framework for understanding monetary history. Early twentieth-century economist Georg Friedrich Knapp coined both terms. Though these terms aren't used widely today, they're easy to remember and accurately convey the underlying meanings. The main distinction between these two doctrines concerns the source of money's value. Metallism posits that money's value comes from its intrinsic worth, the market price of commodities, usually but not necessarily metal. Silver, gold, and other commodities like barley and grain have served as currency because they have inherent worth as determined by the market. Paper notes can also serve as money in the metallist worldview as long as they are backed by metal or some other item with intrinsic worth. For example, in an economy using a gold standard, the currency may be convertible into a fixed amount of gold. The fixed supply of hard money supposedly makes it difficult for anyone, especially the government, to create more and adjust the overall supply.

Chartalism, derived from the Latin word *charta*, or ticket, contends that money itself doesn't have intrinsic value.[7] In this doctrine, money is "soft," a noncommodity, or a token—like a dollar bill, which is merely a piece of paper with no intrinsic value. It's the state that creates money and its use value. The dollar is created by an authority, the Federal Reserve System of the United States. The state also creates a large demand for its currency by administering taxes, fines, and fees in dollars. Since payment of these items is mandatory, one must procure and deal in dollars. The state may also institute legal tender laws. For example, in the United States, the Coinage Act of 1965 states, "United States coins and currency (including Federal reserve notes and circulating notes of Federal reserve banks and national banks) are legal tender for all debts, public charges, taxes, and dues."[8] In addition, because of its minimal cost of production, soft money can easily have its supply adjusted by its issuer and, to a lesser extent, counterfeiters.

Metallists and chartalists hold different ideas regarding how money originated, evoking the divide between Adam Smith and Alfred Mitchell-Innes. Metallists contend that money replaced barter. Money, then, is a creation of the private market, and the state merely blesses what the market settles upon. Chartalists believe debt or credit systems preceded money: Evidence of interest-bearing loans appears in ancient Mesopotamia, thousands of years before coins surface in the Kingdom of Lydia around 630 BC. We become aware of the fault lines between these two doctrines: metallism versus chartalism, metal versus credit, marketplace versus state, hard versus soft. It seems as if chartalism has won the day since the current global monetary system relies on non-metal-backed soft currency. Yet the link between money and metal is a dominant one in economic theory. Many influential economic thinkers are considered to hold metallist views, including John Locke, Adam Smith, John Stuart Mill, and Karl Marx.[9]

I focus on hard money in this chapter and soft money in the next. I define "hard money" as coins made from precious metals or paper backed by it.

Indeed, there were commodities that functioned as currency before the invention of coinage, or the M in Karl Marx's formula of monetary exchange, $C \rightarrow M \rightarrow C$. Economic historians refer to the commodities in the $C \rightarrow C$ exchange as "proto-money." Proto-money, like barley or gems, can normally be used for another purpose—like nourishment or jewelry. But that's not always the case. During the nineteenth century, Western explorers found an unusual currency on the island of Yap in the Pacific Ocean. *Fei*, a bulky limestone rock found in round shapes up to four meters in diameter, functioned as money. These rocks were transported from limestone quarries more than four hundred miles away via boats made from bamboo. There's a local legend from Yap that once a very large *fei* sank to the bottom of the ocean while in transit, but it was agreed that it would continue to represent wealth for its owner and could be used for purchases despite being at the bottom of the sea.[10] *Fei* was cumbersome and rare but served as a store of value and was an instrument that facilitated exchange—even though it didn't physically change hands.

Some of the monetary words we use today originate from proto-money. *Capital* and *cattle* come from the Latin word *caput*, which means "head." The number of cattle heads that one owned was once a measure of affluence. During the Roman Republic, soldiers were paid a *salarium*, a salt ration from which the word *salary* originates.[11] Buckskins were used as currency in the American frontier during the eighteenth century, which led to the word *buck* being used as a synonym for the dollar. But proto-money is typically not issued by a state or authority, and not formally denominated with a stated value. It's a less formal instrument of exchange than coins as we know them today.

The development of coins made money easier to use. Coins were small and their value was eventually standardized by authorities. Coins helped facilitate human cooperation, or as Ofek might say, they were an output of the evolutionary force of exchange. Like Paleolithic hand axes refined over thousands of years, coins have been continually improved to make trade more convenient and efficient. Minting technologies have evolved from hammer-striking to automated presses. Starting in the seventh century BC, the coin maker would make planchets that were cast from molten metal in a relatively standard size, which were then hand-struck. In late antiquity and early medieval times, coin makers would take a sheet of metal, cut a blank piece, shape it into a round form, and then place it on a set die.[12] The blank would then be struck with a hammer. In sixteenth-century France, the screw press was adopted. A rolling mill that was powered by horses or water was used to flatten metal, which was then cut. The blank was struck with a die using a big screw. In the nineteenth century, steam-powered machines were used to make coins.[13]

As coinage technology improved, the symbols on coins became more intricate. As civilization and art developed outside the cave, we adorned coins with assorted symbols of various meaning. Authorities employed skilled artisans to design complex symbols to help create a state identity.[14] The coins also helped to spread the culture of the issuers. Invading armies couldn't carry with them buildings or temples, but they brought coins with depictions of these structures. The art on the coins told a story. In time, these symbols would represent kings and queens—and define countries and cultures.

But the progression from proto to hard money didn't happen overnight. It took thousands of years, and began in the cradle of civilization.

Silver Civilization

In Mesopotamia around 2500 BC, several commodities, like vegetables, cattle, and sheep, functioned as proto-money.[15] These valuable commodities were ultimately sources of energy that helped to increase the chances of survival for humans, and had also become instruments of exchange. Over time, more durable, nonperishable items served as proto-money. As in the Paleolithic era, hand axes functioned as currency in northern Mesopotamia, and later axes became a symbol of money itself. The shekel was originally a unit of weight in this civilization, and the concept was depicted with the sign for an axe in the Sumerian language.[16] Clay objects known as *bullae* may also have functioned as proto-money. These clay spheres were like an archaic piggy bank: Inside were clay tokens, etched with numerals, which could have been used in transactions.[17]

Silver and barley were the two most widely used proto-monies.[18] Both of these commodities, but especially silver, seemed to fit the traditional definition of money: a medium of exchange, unit of account, and store of value.

As a medium of exchange, payments to laborers were made in silver and barley. Documents that have survived since the second and first millennia BC indicate that one-quarter of a bushel of barley was the payment to a worker for a day's labor.[19] Loan and sale documents indicate prices in silver.[20] Merchants would have weighed and exchanged silver bullion.

To facilitate smaller transactions, some silver bars were made into ingots, spiral coils, or rings of similar weight. Each ring ranged in value from one shekel to ten shekels, which could be easily broken off from the larger coil.[21] One shekel of silver would have weighed about the same as a US quarter—about three-tenths of an ounce.[22]

As a unit of account, balance sheets show silver as an accounting measure: Incoming and outgoing goods were weighed and assigned a value in silver. The remaining balance was also expressed in silver. Because silver was rare, it wasn't used in many transactions for slaves, real estate, or other goods. But prices were still quoted in silver, exhibiting the existence of a silver standard.

As a store of value, silver maintained its worth. Silver was not abundantly available in Mesopotamia. It was mostly imported from neighboring areas, like the Taurus Mountains, that had more known ore deposits. Because of its scarcity, silver was seen as a prestigious item, and many squirreled it away for use at a later time.[23] In contrast, the value of barley, which grew locally, fluctuated with the harvest.

The Third Dynasty of Ur certainly had the ingredients necessary for a nascent market economy: silver and barley proto-money, a functional credit system, and merchants like Turam-ili. But instead of a highly decentralized market, kings and religious authorities played a redistributive role in the economy. They gathered food items and other goods and reallocated them to people according to status and occupation, like an archaic potlatch.[24]

They also monitored monetary affairs. Not only did the temples, palaces, and other public institutions act like ancient central banks that adjusted interest rates; they also established weights for silver. They safeguarded standard weights in the shape of ducks and lions used to determine the silver standard. And they stored large amounts of silver bullion. "Silver was a highly valued substance with strong symbolic associations with royalty, wealth and power, and the substantial surplus that was not immobilised in treasuries was potentially available for monetary use," write the curators at the British Museum.[25]

The authorities increased the demand for silver by issuing law codes. For example, from the city of Eshnunna, an ancient law code contains a price list of nine common goods by weight and volume that were equivalent to one shekel of silver, essentially outlining the exchange rates against silver.[26] A liter and a half of pig's fat was priced at one shekel of silver.[27] Fines were also assessed in silver: ten shekels for slapping someone's face, and sixty shekels, or one *mina*, for biting a man's nose.[28]

Metallists and chartalists both find supporting evidence for their philosophies in this ancient civilization. Metallists contend that the authorities merely blessed what the informal market had already determined would be used as money. Silver was valuable regardless of whether the government authorized it.[29] Chartalists assert that the state created the demand for silver by administering fines in this metal, for example. Moreover, loans were issued in the form of silver and barley, which increased the demand for these items. In other words, proto-money was an instrument to enact and repay debts.

While the debate over the origin of money continues, most agree on what circulated as currency. Precious, durable metals increasingly replaced edible commodities as the dominant proto-money. This was the case not just in the city-states of Mesopotamia but also among the villages of the Nile River.

Weigh Like an Egyptian

Around 3100 BC, civilization arose like an oasis between a desert and a mountainous area along the winding Nile. The yearly flood of the river, known as the inundation, left behind minerals, organic matter, and fertile land.[30] Crops like wheat and barley flourished and were used as proto-money to pay common laborers. These staples formed the basis of the Egyptian diet in the form of bread and beer. Beer, it should be noted, wasn't a lager-colored, smooth liquid but resembled a wholesome soup, sometimes infused with local plants. Many tomb drawings show the elaborate preparation process of making both beer and bread, suggesting they were ubiquitous items.

The Egyptians even created tokens in the shape of loaves to symbolize allotments of bread rations, which tokens could have functioned as proto-money. Tokens found in Egyptian fortresses in Nubia were about twenty centimeters in diameter, made of wood, painted, and shaped like various types of bread loaves.[31] The symbols bear hieroglyphic inscriptions that indicate the number of loaves and the amount of wheat for which they could be redeemed. Though historians don't know whether they were traded in great numbers, the carvings may be a personal tally of a ration's value, which could have served as a claim if there were a disagreement about the value of grain in the ration received. The standard ration for workers was ten loaves and a beer that measured up to two jugs. Higher-ranking officials who staffed temples and palaces were provided larger rations. Calculating rations, like dividing one hundred loaves among ten men, required the use of fractions, which Egyptians are said to have invented.[32]

Bread and beer served as payment for work completed, but as Egyptologist Rosalie David points out in her *Handbook to Life in Ancient Egypt*, wheat not only served as a medium of exchange but increasingly became a unit of account in the sixteenth century BC,[33] as did other commodities.

Egyptians traded with neighboring civilizations for silver, spices, and copper, for instance. Because of the influx of new goods, there was a need to establish a standard, first expressed in terms of wheat, against which other goods could be measured and appraised. Say there was a discrepancy between the value of two goods that were being traded. Some amount of wheat would be allocated to resolve the difference.[34]

By 1580 BC, silver, gold, and copper were also used as a standard. Egyptians made special units to measure these metals: a *deben*, which weighed ninety-one grams; and a *kite*, which was one-tenth of a *deben*.[35] These metals were used to value other goods and facilitate transactions, as the metals themselves rarely changed hands. Tomb drawings show officials using fixed weights in the form of a seated lion to measure a *deben* of metal, yet the system may not have become widespread, since Egypt's economy was still mostly informal and pastoral. Nevertheless, merchants traveled with weights so they could conduct transactions more conveniently. As was done in Mesopotamia to make dealing with gold and silver more convenient, these metals were smelted into smaller ingots or rings.[36]

The evidence that precious metal was precisely measured conveys that Egyptians believed it to have intrinsic worth. The Egyptian word for silver was *hedj*, which may have also meant "money."[37] Silver was imported from other countries, and for a time was considered more valuable than gold. The Egyptians searched their lands for more precious materials: copper, tin, and alabaster. Many pharaohs dispatched military expeditions to manage the sometimes tens of thousands of workers needed to mine in surrounding lands.[38] In approximately 2500 BC, King Sahure dispatched men to Punt, which was known as "God's Land," and they returned with vast amounts of *ntyw*, or myrrh, and various metals. During the twelfth century BC, according to surviving documents, Ramses III "constructed great transport vessels . . . loaded with limitless goods from Egypt . . . They reached the land of Punt, unaffected by (any) misfortune, safe and respected."[39] But Punt has long been a mystery to archaeologists, who have been unable to determine its location.

One region they have examined is Nubia, south of Egypt in the alluvial lands near the Nile. It's an area where Egyptians mined gold.[40] The Egyptian word for gold was *nbw* and may explain the origin of the place-name

Nubia.[41] Taxes were sometimes collected in gold and then stored in the treasury, which was part of the most important temples.[42] The pharaoh's administration carefully tracked, measured, and weighed the incoming gold before some was provided to artisans to shape into jewelry, masks, and other ornaments. Jewelry pieces made from precious metals weren't just symbols of status and wealth, but were thought to have magical qualities, protecting against evil. Pharaohs wanted to be entombed with their jewels so they could take them along and be protected in the afterlife.

The pharaohs were certainly accustomed to being surrounded by immense wealth during their earthly lives as well. Technically, Egyptian pharaohs owned everything, including all the bread, beer, and gold. The pharaoh presided over the centralized economy and granted lands to friends and relatives, who became powerful landlords. As in Mesopotamia, temples were centers of enormous wealth, like one that managed almost 100,000 commoners, 500,000 cattle, and hundreds of orchards.[43]

The middle class was composed of traders, soldiers, artisans, and, most important to the purposes of understanding the role of money, scribes. Up to 5 percent of Egyptians were literate, and many of them were scribes who created papyrus records of taxes, granary inspections, and commercial transactions in which precious metals were weighed.[44] However, Graeber says there is scant record of interest-bearing loans, perhaps because papyrus isn't as durable as coins in the archaeological register.

However, economic historians can still study later Egyptian coins to understand more about the society in which they were issued. One such gold coin exhibits a fusion of cultures: on one side, hieroglyphics, and on the other side, a horse of Greek design. It's probably from the reign of Nectanebo II, one of the last pharaohs, who came to power in 359 BC.[45] The coin shows that Egypt was influenced by Greece. But coins weren't invented in Egypt.

Coined in Lydia

Located on the Ionian coast of Asia Minor, in what used to be Anatolia and is today Turkey, the Kingdom of Lydia emerged around 700 BC under the Mermnad Dynasty. Not having left behind a copious archaeological record, it would have been a historical footnote if not for the discovery of a few hoards of coins and the writings of the Greek historian Herodotus, who wrote, "Lydia, unlike most other countries, scarcely offers any wonders for the historian to describe, except the gold-dust which is washed down from the range."[46] He is alluding to the wealth of this kingdom, the first to invent coinage in the Western world.

Lydia derived its wealth from three sources: tributes, natural resources, and eventually, coins. Lydian kings conquered several Ionian and Greek cities and received tribute, which helped them to amass substantial fortunes. Lydia was blessed with abundant amounts of natural resources. Legend has it that Phrygian king Midas bathed in the Pactolus River to rid himself of his golden touch and left the golden gift in the waters. But the mines at Tmolus, near the Pactolus and Hermus Rivers, yielded another metal, what Herodotus called "white gold."[47] It was actually an alloy of gold and silver known as electrum, which comes from the Greek word *electron*, which means "amber."[48]

Just like gold and silver, electrum was first traded as bullion. But because the amounts of gold and silver varied in electrum, its value could not be easily determined. Over time, electrum bullion was turned into smaller chunks that were easier to handle—and eventually into coins. Archaeologists discovered more than ninety electrum coins at the ruins of the temple for Artemis, a Greek goddess, at Ephesus; they are estimated to be from 630 BC.[49] The hoard includes coins of varying degrees of sophistication, from unstamped metal lumps to flatter ones bearing images of lions.[50] Just as Paleolithic hand axes were refined, humans gave coins characteristics that increased their convenience. It wasn't long until no weighing scale was needed. Electrum coins were standardized, weighing 14.15 grams and given the denomination of the stater. Coins became over time the new criterion against which to measure all other commodities.

Coins are usually assessed by collectors according to their metal composition and the symbols they bear. Many staters have a face value that is up to 20 percent more than the intrinsic value of their metal content. Electrum from western Anatolia has a gold content of 70 to 90 percent, yet Lydian coins had less gold, around 50 percent. Lydians became skilled metalworkers and diluted the amount of gold in coins as an act of seigniorage: a way to profit from the issuance of currency. The difference between the face value of issued coins and the actual market value of the precious metal leads to a profit for the issuer.[51] One justification for seigniorage is that the labor that goes into creating a coin may constitute a value-add, resulting in a higher face value.[52] Seigniorage also lays bare the historical propensity for the issuer to control the value of money through its manufacture. Minting money is a profitable business, and many governments engage in seigniorage even today.

The symbols on coins offer insight as to who issued them: merchants, bankers, aristocrats, or kings. One coin from this era has a Greek inscription, "I am the sign of Phanes." Coins that bear the words KALIL and VALVEL have also been discovered.[53] These inscriptions may reflect the name of the person or mint that issued them. During the early sixth century BC, the mint in Sardis, the capital of Lydia, probably produced the most coins.

Coins thought to be from ancient Lydia came in several hundred types, with depictions of boars, horses, dolphins, and monsters, among others. The images were a distinguishing mark of the issuer. Coins issued by the Lydian kings bore a lion's head or paw. The image was etched on a die and then placed on a chunk of electrum, on which it was hammered, leaving an impression.

The last king of Lydia was Croesus, who reigned from 560 BC to 547 BC. He introduced coins made from pure silver or gold and bearing the mark of a lion and a bull. Croesus's coins marked the inception of bimetallism, a monetary system in which two metals are accepted as money, with a fixed ratio of value between them. According to *The Oxford Handbook of Greek and Roman Coinage*, during Croesus's rule the exchange rate between gold and silver was 1 gram of gold to 13.3 grams of silver, and 1 gram of gold to 10 grams of electrum. Issued gold staters weighed 8.1 grams, less than their electrum predecessors.[54]

The spread of coinage made Lydia an even wealthier kingdom, and Croesus's wealth became legendary. We still occasionally hear the English phrase "rich as Croesus." He lavished gifts of electrum bullion and gold on oracles. He eagerly asked an oracle what would happen if he fought the Persians, which precipitated a cryptic reply that a notable empire would perish. Croesus interpreted the remark as a good omen, so he attacked the Persians, but lost badly.[55]

The Kingdom of Lydia came to an end, but coinage flourished elsewhere in the Mediterranean world and even India and China. Classics professor David Schaps says that the coins made in Lydia, India, and China look different and were made using different technologies. Indian coins were lopsided, their sides cut off to ensure they were the right weight. They also had several punch marks that indicate they were made in a mint. Chinese coins were composed of bronze and shaped like spades, disks, and knives. Some had holes in them so they could be strung together.[56]

It's difficult to know whether these civilizations conceived of coins on their own or were influenced by others through trade. Even Schaps vacillates:

Lydia, India, and China probably invented coinage independently of each other; and even if that was not the case, they surely developed the use of coins independently of each other. It is possible that these three independent events had independent causes, and that none of them has any light to shed on the others; but it is surely worthwhile to consider the possibility that there were similar conditions in these particular places that made coinage a plausible and a useful innovation.[57]

Some scholars make the case that India, for example, developed coinage on its own. They point to silver tokens marked with cuneiform found at Mohenjo-daro, an Indus Valley civilization from 2500 BC, which suggests trade with Mesopotamia. The Rigveda, an ancient Hindu text that dates to 1500 BC, mentions a gold currency, which some have interpreted as coins unique to what's now India. Yet others contend that coinage was brought to India by the Achaemenian invasion or the eastern expansion of Alexander the Great and his Greek Empire.[58]

A Democracy of Owls

The people of Lydia and Greece had strong cultural ties. Croesus formed an alliance with Sparta and peacefully incorporated many Greek cities into his kingdom. The Lydian alphabet was derived from Greek. Several artifacts recovered from Lydia, like vases and bowls, were made in a Greek design, and Greek engravers also likely designed Croesus's coins.

Most Greek coins were made from silver. Greece received silver tribute from its allies, and another rich source of silver was just twenty-five miles away in the mines of Laurion. Roughly 30,000 slaves staffed 2,000 shafts at the mine during its peak of operation.

The Greeks began producing coins in Athens around 546 BC, during the reign of Peisistratus, who needed to compensate mercenaries and finance his ambitious building plans. The unit of account for coins was the *drachm*, which comes from the Greek word meaning "to grasp" and was first used when measuring proto-money like grain or bullion. One *drachm* was made of six *obols*, which is derived from the Greek word that means "spit," as in iron spits that were used to cook meat. There is evidence from the seventh and sixth centuries BC that spits were used as items in dedication or sacrificial ceremonies. Iron spits were a valuable item that may have functioned as proto-money. The trading of iron spits harkens back to Neolithic man, who relied on food preparation and sharing for survival.[59] The *drachm* was standardized to 4.32 grams of silver, and an *obol* weighed 0.72 gram.[60] Coins of greater value were issued, too. For example, the frequently used *tetradrachm* was equivalent to four drachmas and weighed 17.28 grams. The *decadrachm*, equivalent to ten drachmas, was the largest denomination, yet issuance of this coin was limited.

Fourteen types of coins have been discovered from the reign of Peisistratus. The variety of symbols found on the coins, from horses to wheels, suggests they were made by different issuers. But the coin depicting an owl is most famous because of its staying power. It was issued almost continuously for several hundred years, until the silver mines were tapped out. In 525 BC, the image of a gorgon like Medusa, an emblem associated with Athena, was added to the front of the *tetradrachm*. After a few years, the gorgon was replaced with an image of Athena, and her bird, the owl, on the other side. Most of these owl coins were made at the Athenian mint, which was a large building adjacent to the agora, an open area used as a marketplace.

During the Peloponnesian War, Sparta blocked passage to the silver mine at Laurion, so Athens almost drained its entire silver supply. It minted coins made from the gold of the Nike statue at the Acropolis. The shortage worsened, and Athens issued owls made from bronze and coated in silver. Smaller denominations of owls were issued because there was less metal to use.

In addition to state-led debasement of its coins, there was the problem of counterfeit owls. Athens prohibited cities not fully under its control from issuing owls. The decree wasn't fully obeyed, so Athens dispatched commissioners to its distant provinces like Egypt to enforce the law and administer a penalty of ten thousand drachmas for violations.

With the kingdom of Alexander the Great the owl coins were supplanted with coins bearing images of Hercules and Zeus. Alexander's coins also replaced the gold Daric, which had been introduced by Darius the Great around 520 BC and circulated throughout the Persian Empire. The successors of Alexander the Great set up more than twenty mints from Macedonia to Egypt. His coins achieved international circulation and helped to expand his influence throughout the region. As evidence of his reach, his golden staters are among the oldest coins found in Britain.[61]

However, owl coinage was revived in Athens in the third century BC. Inscribed on them were the initials of Athenian officials administering the issue, and the month of issue. Economic historian Peter van Alfen notes that in 42 BC, after the Battle of Philippi, waged to avenge the death of Julius Caesar, the production of owl coins was halted, since Rome had become the dominant power. Rome's hard money had become the coin of the realm.[62]

In parallel with the monetary doctrines, metallists contend that owl coins were intrinsically valuable, made from precious metal. The state merely legitimized what already functioned as currency. Chartalists acknowledge the owls' intrinsic value: These coins would have little worth without their base metals. However, seigniorage shows that the coin's value derived from something more than metal. The additional value stemmed from the state, which issued owl coins and enforced their use as acceptable means of payment. Athens issued guidelines for which coins were acceptable in the agora. That it banned counterfeit owls demonstrates that the government recognized that a principal source of value was people's faith in the currency. People had to *believe* that the coins were authentic legal tender.

Widespread questions regarding the legitimacy of coins could lead to concerns in the agora, a currency crisis, or even the destabilization of power.

Moreover, state expenditure introduced an abundance of coins into circulation. It's estimated that millions of coins were issued during the fifth through third centuries BC, making coins one of the first mass-produced items in history. The mass issuance of coins coincides with Athens building its fleet to combat the Persians around 480 BC. Coins were needed to pay soldiers for several conflicts, such as the Peloponnesian War. The state also paid more than sixteen thousand drachmas for building the Parthenon temple. It paid jurors and citizens to attend the Assembly, where matters were debated. Even a couple of *obols* were paid to citizens for going to the theater for religious activities. State spending put more money in people's hands, including those of foreigners, which created the demand for more goods and services.

Over time, soldiers, workers, and citizens took these smaller coins, their movable fortunes, to the agora, which became a center of life in Athens.[63] Coins were an invitation to buy and sell at the agora. They were symbols of civic pride and represented the values of a land ruled by laws. After all, the Greek word for coin, *nomisma*, is similar to the word for law, *nomos*, which eventually led to the modern English word for coin collecting, *numismatics*. Coinage stimulated the marketplace: more money, more people, and more goods. Merchants actively monitored the supply and demand of their goods and adjusted prices accordingly. Nonmerchants and illiterate people who previously relied on brokers and other representatives were now empowered to trade for themselves. No longer was there a need for scales and weights to assess the intrinsic value of basic goods (though the agora still had scales for larger goods). Coins became the standard of value against which almost everything was measured, including other commodities like wheat and barley. But now soft, intangible items like time and labor could also be valued with the same monetary standard.

Credit abetted the adoption of coins. Scholars have debated whether banks, or *trapezai*, in Athens were more than just moneychangers and pawnbrokers. Yet banks, shops, and temples all issued loans. Classicist Edward Cohen notes that banks were given a prominent position in the agora, recognition of the vital role they played in the economy. Loans were often received in the form of coins, creating more demand for hard money. There is evidence that *trapezai* extended large amounts of credit to facilitate trade, which introduced more goods and dynamism into the marketplace. For instance, perfume vendors held large inventories and relied on bank credit to stay solvent. Banks also issued loans to help prospectors acquire mining rights and to abet military campaigns. Cohen says that the largest loans were made to finance ships, and were secured against their cargo. Despite credit flowing through Athens, it had become a coin-based economy.[64] There wasn't an easy way to transfer wealth without handling coins, and payments for tolls, custom duties, and rents were mostly made in coins.[65]

Coins were shaping not just the agora but also the larger Athenian society. Instead of a top-down redistributive system, in which people relied on the central power, aristocracy, or even onerous family relationships, coins had a democratizing effect. Money helped form a web of interdependent relationships without the lingering gratitude-induced obligations of the gift economy.[66] Anthropologist Jack Weatherford writes in *The History of Money* that coins may have even augmented democracy.[67] In addition to Solon's reforms to cancel debts, the leader broadened the criteria of those who were eligible to serve in public office. Wealth became a determining factor, not just whether someone was from a noble family.[68]

Athenians exhibited entrepreneurial qualities, but to consider Athens a bursting market economy would be to distort the past through a modern economic prism. Moreover, to consider coinage as the only catalyst for liberal reforms is too narrow. In *The Economy of the Greek Cities*, Léopold Migeotte writes that changing demographics, increasing urbanization, and better transportation routes also played roles in economic growth.[69] Nevertheless, money was a democratizing force.

Some notable Greek philosophers didn't see it that way. Plato and Aristotle were suspicious of money and the marketplace. They discussed the differing forms of money, which convinced some scholars that chartalism and metallism originated from their philosophies. Plato thought money stoked greed and corruption and wanted to ban gold and silver.[70] He thought that trade and a retail economy would lead to "deceitful habits in a man's soul that would sow seeds of distrust among the citizenry."[71] He advocated for strict market regulations. No, he doesn't appear to be a metallist.

But was he a chartalist? Economist Joseph Schumpeter seems to think so, referring to Plato as the "first known sponsor" of what was later considered chartalism.[72] But again, that might be imprudently viewing the past through a more contemporary economic prism. Yet Plato does make a distinction between token money and what he calls real money, or between what one would call soft money and hard money. He says the state issues token money and decides its form and initial value. Therefore, token money will be accepted only within the jurisdiction of the state and not the realm of other states. Real money, hard money, is the currency of the marketplace and can be exported and used in transactions with foreigners.[73] No doubt he would be surprised with the role of the US dollar, which is token money but hoarded the world over in the form of the hundred-dollar note and acceptable as official payment in other sovereign nations, such as Panama.

Plato's pupil Aristotle noted that at least historically, money was "valuable in itself, might easily be passed from hand to hand for the purposes of daily life, as iron and silver, or any thing else of the same nature."[74] Schumpeter credits Aristotle as an originator of metallism and for influencing generations of economists.[75] However, it's not clear Aristotle was a metallist.[76] He writes that money is man-made, has a use value, and "owes its existence, not to nature, but to law . . . and it is in our power to change it and make it void."[77] He acknowledges the role of the state, the law, as key in determining the form of money. If the law changes, so might the form of money. By that logic, money could be soft or hard.

Aristotle was more moderate and matter-of-fact in his analysis of the market than his teacher Plato. But they sound similar when considering the ethical implications of money. Aristotle acknowledges that money facilitates different types of exchange. He describes how eventually man entered the market only with money, looking to buy goods and sell them at higher prices, like a shrewd speculator. Aristotle discredits this type of exchange as unnatural because it was "people taking things from one another."[78] He also condemns usury, the lending of money at high rates, as "reasonably detested...the most contrary to nature."[79] Using money to make money only encourages man's insatiable desire to acquire more. They both believed greed wasn't good.

When in Rome

While coinage had a democratizing effect in Greece, it could also be used by authorities as a political tool. During the Roman Empire, to keep up the pace of exorbitant spending, rulers minted more coins and increased the supply of money. At the same time, they reduced the amount of metal within coins, which made the currency less valuable and contributed to depreciation. Roman history highlights a lesson about hard money: Issuers can manipulate the value of money to serve political ends. It's a lesson that plays out even today.

Roman coinage began around 300 BC. Early coins were inspired by the design of Greek coins, and some were even made in nearby Greek towns to facilitate trade.[80] The coins in circulation were the bronze *as*, the standard monetary unit, and the silver *didrachm*. Though the standard conversion rate was one *didrachm* for ten *asses*, the values of the component metals fluctuated in the market. Say silver appreciated considerably above the official face value stated on a coin. People would hoard it, removing it from circulation. And bronze coins, which were undervalued compared to their official face value, would be left as the circulating coins of the realm. This phenomenon is known as Gresham's law: Bad money drives out good money.[81] And it was a recurring phenomenon throughout the Roman Republic and Roman Empire.

After vanquishing Pyrrhus and the Greeks, Rome started to solidify itself as the paramount power of the region. It began to mint its own coins in mass quantities around 269 BC. The mint that produced most Roman coins was atop Capitoline Hill, a secure location to protect against enemies. The mint was adjacent to a temple for the goddess Juno Moneta, whence the words *money* and *mint* likely originated.[82] There are several myths regarding how Juno earned the name Moneta. One legend has it that a voice from the temple warned about an earthquake, and the only way to stop it was to sacrifice a pig. Another is that invaders from Gaul alarmed the geese inside the temple, alerting the Romans, who stopped the invaders. The common thread in both stories is that the goddess was a voice of warning; the Latin verb *moneo* means "to warn." In addition, it makes sense that the monetary units would be closely associated with this temple, since it's where other official weights and measurements were kept, such as the *pes monetalis*, the "monetal," or Roman foot.[83]

During the Second Punic War, fought against Carthage from 218 to 201 BC, Rome faced financial difficulties since sustaining the military required vast resources. The regime therefore minted debased silver coins, reducing the metal content from 98 percent pure silver to 36 percent. The end result: more coins to pay soldiers even though each coin was worth less. Despite winning the war and becoming the predominant regional power, much of the value of Rome's hard money had been lost, and coins of more value were hoarded.[84]

So Rome started over. Around 211 BC, Roman authorities introduced the *denarial* system of coinage, which included the silver denarius and the bronze *as*. *Denarius* comes from a Latin word that means "containing ten"; one denarius was equivalent to ten *asses*. The conversion rate eventually changed to one denarius for sixteen *asses*. The system was composed of four coins made almost completely from pure silver: (1) the denarius, which was the biggest in size, weighed 4.5 grams and had the largest value; (2) *victoriatus* (three-quarters denarius); (3) *quinarius* (half denarius); and (4) *sestertius* (quarter denarius). Many early denarial coins bore an image of the goddess Roma in a winged helmet and the inscription ROMA. Eventually, coins incorporated various other inscriptions and deities.

Julius Caesar left his stamp on Roman monetary history by using the gold treasure he pillaged from Gaul to increase the quantity of the *aureus* in circulation; they had previously not been issued extensively. These new coins helped Rome cope with a financial crisis in 49 BC during Caesar's ascension to power, since coins were needed to pay the military. By expanding the supply of money and preventing people from hoarding mass amounts of coins, Caesar's reforms helped the economy recover.

Caesar's eventual successor, Augustus, who came to power in 27 BC, faced a similar problem of an economy in need of more money, suffering from deflation, and enduring a depression. Augustus used loot captured from Egypt to spend lavishly on civil projects and enhanced welfare programs. The precious metals from distant lands were melted and paid to soldiers. He followed Caesar's monetary policy, minting more coins at a furious pace until 10 BC. In time, interest rates dropped from 12 to 4 percent, and the economy recovered. Caesar's and Augustus's economic policies were successful and instructive to future Roman leaders.[85]

One of Augustus's successors, Emperor Nero, reigned during a prolonged depression in AD 62, and a fire blazed through Rome in AD 64, causing even more damage. Classics scholar Mary Thornton sees similarities between Nero's initiatives and those of President Franklin D. Roosevelt—she suggests Nero created a "New Deal for Romans."[86] Nero increased food subsidies for the public and spending on civil projects like canals.

President Franklin Roosevelt expanded government spending during the Great Depression, but he also changed the implementation of monetary policy through his gold policies and the gold purchase plan, which was purposefully directed at devaluing the dollar.[87] Nero also took an activist approach to monetary policy and worked to expand the money supply. Nero followed the economic playbook of Caesar and Augustus; he enlarged the supply of coins and tampered with their value. He reduced the worth of the denarius by 15 percent, diminished its silver content from 97.5 percent to 93.5 percent, and lowered its weight from 3.9 grams to 3.4 grams. He reduced the *aureus* by 10 percent and lowered its weight from 8 grams to 7.2 grams.[88] His actions expanded the money supply by an estimated 7 percent. In the end, debasing hard money was a monetary policy that helped put the economy on a path to recovery.

The reign of Nero was a turning point in Roman monetary history. Money was losing its intrinsic worth, yet Romans increasingly transacted in these debased coins. However, foreign territories like India refused debased coins, so Rome exported silver, gold, or nondebased coins to facilitate trade.[89] The city of Rome didn't produce many goods. They had to import items, which created a trade deficit that had to be financed, a further drain on the state's coffers. Furthermore, Nero recognized that his coins were more than just minted metal. They were a symbol of value and an instrument of propaganda. Early Nero coins bore an image of the emperor at age sixteen, the year his reign began, alongside his mother, Agrippina, the power behind the throne. Later coins show him with a beard and crown, as he became his own man.[90]

The Roman Empire grew in influence and expanded its borders to the Middle East and North Africa, covering more than four million square miles. Its many captured treasures enhanced not only Rome's income but also its spending. Seized metals were melted and minted into coins to pay the burgeoning military. The surge in state spending also financed the hefty bureaucracy and subsidies for the poor.[91] In the second century AD, the Roman budget swelled to more than 200 million denarii per year.

However, profligate spending eventually put downward pressure on the economy. The monetary policies imposed in response to the financial crisis of AD 238 effectively made the denarius disappear, especially as the supply of silver was greatly diminished. The state needed more money, so in AD 214 it created another coin altogether, the *antoninianus*, which was named after its originator, whose name was Antoninus. Bad money forced out good money. People hoarded the denarius for its higher intrinsic value, and it was effectively removed from circulation. Hoarding contracted the supply of money, which forced Roman authorities to issue even more debased *antoniniani*. By AD 270, the *antoninianus* was minted with only 2.5 percent silver. With less "good" money in the system, there was an increase in barter and social debt transactions. To compensate for the diminished value of coins, merchants marked up the prices of goods, eventually sparking aggressive inflation. The economic malaise led to public outcries, including a strike by mint workers in AD 271.

Rome suffered from years of economic misfortune. Prices rose nearly 23 percent per year from AD 293 to 301. Emperor Diocletian followed the economic playbook of Nero in the late third century AD. He enlarged the military and built more roads. He instituted monetary reform, returning to a bimetallic system of silver and gold, with new denominations marked by their fractional weight in bullion.[92] Money was yoked back to metal with intrinsic worth. But metal prices moved north, too. Inflation remained, and bad money chased out good money. In AD 301, Diocletian issued an Edict on Maximum Prices, which capped the prices of more than one thousand goods, including wine, grain, and clothes. But it was largely ignored, and inflation became even more rampant.

Scholars have long deliberated the causes of inflation in Rome. Meddling with the supply and value of hard money certainly played a pivotal role. Rome's experience with debased money should give pause to anyone who thinks hard money is a panacea for economic problems. Yet the debasement of hard money pales in comparison to the devaluation of soft money that goes on today. The dollar isn't backed by metal, and some have called for a return to the one metal that's remained a fascination over the ages.

The Golden One

Years ago I descended into a South African gold mine, hundreds of feet belowground. There was a sign near the elevator shaft that read "205 days without an injury." Hundreds of helmet lights worn by the workers flashed across cavernous passageways. Dozens of trucks and hauling buggies motored past me. Such a laborious operation yields little precious metal. Every ton of crushed rock produces but a few grams of gold. Yet these grams are monitored closely by Wall Street research analysts who adjust their economic forecasting models based on mine production data. The amount of aboveground gold in the world was estimated at about 174,000 metric tons at the end of 2012.[93] Meanwhile, global steel production in 2012 alone was 1.5 billion metric tons.[94]

Gold isn't the only rare metal. Yet there is an obsession for it. Warren Buffett thinks gold lust is bizarre. He juxtaposes my journeys to the African mine and the New York Fed's vault when he says, "Gold gets dug out of the ground in Africa, or someplace. Then we melt it down, dig another hole, bury it again and pay people to stand around guarding it. It has no utility. Anyone watching from Mars would be scratching their head."[95]

Yet some market strategists say that "gold is money."[96] How did this idea begin? The neurons that register "gold" and "value" wired long ago. Early humans were probably attracted to its shine and luster. Only a few naturally occurring materials, like gemstones, water, and ice, would have reflected light and displayed a natural shimmer.

Even some animals like bright, shiny objects. Monkeys are quick to snatch objects like bangles and camera lenses from unsuspecting tourists. Among bowerbirds, a bird species native to Australia and New Guinea, the males construct elaborate lairs festooned with shiny and colorful natural and found objects such as fruit, stones, glass shards, bottle caps, foil bags, and hair ties. The fancy lair attracts females for mating. Colors are nature's way of advertising. The color of gold sells.[97]

Gold has long had a luring effect on humans. The Babylonians linked metals to objects in the solar system, with gold compared to the sun.[98] The link between gold and the sun appears elsewhere. The Latin word *aurora* means "dawn," when the sun appears, and it is similar to *aurum*, which means "gold"—and is abbreviated as *Au* on the periodic table. But the English word for gold comes the Old High German word *gelo* and the Old English word *geolu*, which means "yellow."

Some dig for gold. Others practice the abracadabra of alchemy. Early alchemists tried to transform base metals like copper, iron, and tin into "noble" metals like electrum, silver, and gold.[99] Because of its lofty ambitions, alchemy has been associated with the mystical and divine, referred to at times as "the knowledge" or "the art." The word *alchemy* is itself a mixture: *Al-* is of Arabic origin; *chemy* stems from a Greek word that means "melt" or "mixture."

Alchemy likely began in Egypt in the third century AD. Egyptians had already been experimenting with metalworking for thousands of years, and it was a natural home to alchemists. There are not many historical texts on alchemy from this period, because they were destroyed. Legend has it that the Roman emperor Diocletian banned alchemy because of the threat it posed to debased Roman money and his monetary reforms. Or he may have been fearful of someone financing an insurrection.[100] Nevertheless, some recipes have been discovered. One calls for adding sulfur to silver, causing a reaction that results in a golden hue.[101]

Alchemists gradually tried to make other metals take on more than a golden tinge. They wanted to transmute fully one metal into another. *Chrysopoeia* and *argyropoeia* were the names of the processes for turning materials into gold and silver, respectively.[102] Alchemists also wrestled with the issue of what constitutes matter. Alchemy required a deep knowledge of chemical properties, yet alchemists still found that making hard money was difficult.

Alchemy was practiced in many different societies. In *The Secrets of*

Alchemy, Lawrence Principe describes how Arabs became interested in alchemy. In the eighth century, a Byzantine emperor showed an Arab ambassador that copper could be melted and, with a dash of red powder, transmuted into gold. Undoubtedly impressed, the Arabs translated Greek alchemical texts.[103] Another culture's obsession for gold making continued in earnest. Just as in the Roman Empire, leaders in the Arab world criticized alchemy as unnatural and alchemists as frauds, and sought to ban the practice altogether.

During the Middle Ages in Europe, some alchemists saw themselves as practicing a divine art. Jesus Christ's life was an allegory for alchemy, as he transformed from one state to another. To practice alchemy, then, was to improve oneself.[104] Martin Luther's father was an alchemist who believed the practice was consistent with Christian teachings on self-improvement.

During the European Enlightenment, alchemy was studied as part of chemistry in educational institutions.[105] Surprisingly, a scion of scientific thought, Isaac Newton studied and practiced alchemy, proving that trying to create precious metals can attract the most "rational" of minds. Though scientists eventually dismissed alchemy, occult groups incorporated the practice and kept its lore alive.[106] Even today, the common use of the word *alchemy* and the reinterpretation of the practice in popular culture, from literature to movies, suggest that the fascination with gold making remains.

Quality to Quantity

It's not just the emperors of Rome who have manipulated money for political ends. Today it's still common practice for central banks to adjust the supply of money to abet political goals. There's no need to mine metals, since the state can just create more soft money. For example, the central bank of Japan purchases massive amounts of securities to inject money into the banking system, which leads to depreciation of the yen and helps Toyota, Nissan, and other exporters sell their products at cheaper prices in the global marketplace. More sales can spell more jobs, an aim of the Japanese government.

Such monetary strategies and currency manipulations have long been a part of the global economic system. However, the global financial crisis of

2008 sparked an era of large-scale currency adjustments as central banks tried to stimulate their respective economies by creating vast amounts of new money. The story goes that with more money flowing through the economy, prices will rise to reflect the reduced value of the currency, which will spur individuals and businesses to spend now rather than later, leading to a bump in economic activity.

Many pundits and politicians have panned the state's meddling with the supply and value of money. They reason that the historical debasement of hard money is nothing compared to the large-scale manipulation by the state of money that's not backed by metal. To return to a gold standard would institute *some* check, the overall supply of gold, on monetary expansion.

Returning to a gold standard invokes the debate between metallists and chartalists. It's also a debate between creditors and debtors. Creditors have historically tried to protect their investments, wanting to receive money owed to them that is of the same quality. Debtors, however, have historically looked to grow the money supply so they can make loan payments with money that is less valuable.[107]

But the nature of money is an ever-shifting issue. It depends not only on whom you ask, but on when you ask them. In the late nineteenth century, bankers resisted attempts to institute bimetallism that would expand the supply of money. They wanted to be paid in full with quality, valuable, hard money. Today few bankers advocate a return to hard money, because it could limit loan issuance and curb business.

The arc of monetary history bends toward soft money. Economist Glyn Davies mentions a "quality-to-quantity pendulum" in which the supply of money has increased dramatically over the centuries, at the expense of money's value.

The sheer amount of soft money in circulation is enormous, partly because it's so easy to make. Maybe the state has been practicing another type of alchemy all along.

CHAPTER FIVE

Some Like It Soft

A brief history of soft money

You must know that he has money made for him...out of the bark of trees...Of this money the Khan has such a quantity made that with it he could buy all the treasure in the world. With this currency he orders all payments to be made throughout every province and kingdom and region of his empire. And no one dares refuse it on pain of losing his life.
—*Marco Polo*[1]

Money makes money, and the more money that money makes, makes more money.
—*Benjamin Franklin*[2]

If you think writing about the fortunes of the stock market is tricky, try getting your arms around currencies.
—*Bill Gross*[3]

Kublai Khan established the Yuan Dynasty and issued paper money that circulated throughout his Asian empire.

The Bloomberg computer terminal blinked bloodred. But Jasper was seeing all green.[4] He had worked on Wall Street for only a few short years and never witnessed a day like this before. The markets were going to hell, yet his team was making more money than ever.

Jasper worked at the foreign exchange trading desk of a global investment bank in New York. With the bankruptcy of Lehman Brothers in September 2008, the dollar underwent sharp swings, initially depreciating more than 5 percent in one week and then appreciating 17 percent over the next two months.

But it wasn't the volatility that surprised him. That's the nature of the currency market. It was the volume.

Jasper was astonished with the quantity of dollars, the masses of money changing hands.

"We can't keep up with the flow," he said exasperatedly.

With global stock and bond markets under siege, money flooded into the currency market, rushing into cash, mostly dollars, like a tidal wave enveloping a coastal city—and stayed there. There was nowhere else to invest. The dollar was a safe haven, a port in the storm.

Money has historically been a means. In Athens during the fourth century BC, people converted foreign currencies into drachmas so they could buy olives at the agora. In recent times, people and institutions have converted currencies for similar reasons. A Brazilian company buys Indian rupees to pay its Indian supplier in its local currency. Or a more sophisticated but perfectly sensible transaction: A French company that generates most of its revenue from Quebec locks in a favorable exchange rate for the Canadian dollar as a hedge against wild market swings that could erase profits.

During the 2008 financial crisis, many investors kept their money *in* money, moving it from one currency to another. The crisis didn't start this practice, but it certainly accelerated it. Not wanting to convert their money into other assets, many investors held on to these symbols of value. Even though money is an abstraction from its original evolutionary purpose of helping humans obtain energy to survive, many considered cash a concrete way to protect their financial well-being.

The removal of money's metal anchor caused currencies to float, their values rippling with the market. Investors fish for beneficial fluctuations and convert them into profits. Currencies are now, in investor parlance, an *asset class*, an investable group with its own set of attributes similar to stocks, real estate, or precious metals. Instead of dividing your investment portfolio among stocks, you can invest in a basket of currencies. Let's say an investor allocates 10,000 US dollars: 50 percent in Japanese yen, 30 percent in Australian dollars, and 20 percent in New Zealand dollars. The investor expects a return on his or her basket as these currencies appreciate versus the US dollar for any number of reasons, such as surprising political news or changing expectations about where interest rates are headed.

The currency market has become the deepest, largest, most liquid market in the world. The average daily trading volume of currencies, including more esoteric products like currency derivatives, exploded from $1.5 trillion in the late 1990s to $4 trillion in 2010, which exceeds the volumes traded in the stock market. By comparison, the S&P 500 averages $150 billion in volume per day. Another reason for the currency market's liquidity is that it's almost always open: Trading begins on Sunday night in Auckland, New Zealand, and ends Friday evening in New York.

The United States dollar is the most significant currency in this market. That's because its issuer has been the world's leading economic (and some say, military) power since World War II. The US dollar is attractive to investors because it's readily convertible into other currencies through the foreign exchange market. There are more than 170 currencies in the world, but 85 percent of currency transactions involve the dollar. Prices of global commodities like oil and many other tradable goods are set and settled in dollars even if the United States isn't involved in these transactions; some 81 percent of global trade is settled in dollars.[5] Because it's the dominant global currency, the dollar gives the United States incredible monetary and economic advantages. It's what Charles de Gaulle's finance minister famously called America's "exorbitant privilege."[6] When I was in Marrakech, merchants of pouf cushions preferred payment in US dollars to Moroccan dirham. Shelling out dollars made my life easier, but the local currency exchange shop lost my business. Another advantage for the United States is that it doesn't have to sell real goods to acquire the liquid and versatile dollars. Economist Barry Eichengreen explains:

> It costs only a few cents for the Bureau of Engraving and Printing to produce a $100 bill, but other countries have to pony up $100 of actual goods and services in order to obtain one…About $500 billion of U.S. currency circulates outside the United States, for which foreigners have to provide the United States with $500 billion of actual goods and services.[7]

Another benefit of issuing the world's most dominant currency is that the United States can impact monetary systems beyond its borders. In response to the credit crisis, the Federal Reserve created more money and liquidity, which had international consequences. With so many new dollars flooding in, global asset markets started to move up again, causing other countries, notably China, to complain about inflation.

But quantity comes at the expense of quality, as measured by market value. The surge in the value of the dollar during the crisis interrupted a long-term downward trend, which has resumed. A dollar doesn't go as far as it used to: According to the Bureau of Labor Statistics, since 1971 there has been an 83 percent decline in the purchasing power of the dollar, from $1.00 to 17 cents.[8] One primary reason for the decline is supply and demand of money itself—the Fed has created more dollars than the market demands.

Certainly, the renewed weakness in the dollar isn't bad for all parties. American exporters benefit from a weaker dollar because real prices become lower for customers in foreign markets. But the dollar's outsized role in the global currency market, and its declining value, gives investors pause, especially since the 2008 financial crisis, which had roots in the US financial system and mortgage market. The United States accounts for 25 percent of the world's gross domestic product, yet almost 60 percent of foreign central banks' reserve holdings are still in US dollars. For central banks, there has been a gradual diversification into other currencies, as 70 percent of holdings were in US dollars in 1999. The crisis convinced more foreign central bankers that they need a Plan B, but in recent years good options weren't obvious because the euro and yen faced their own challenges.

Any currency that's highly reliable, liquid, and convertible can theoretically serve as the world's dominant currency. Great Britain's pound was the world's leading currency in the nineteenth and early twentieth centuries, until the dollar replaced it. Now the pound is involved in just over 10 percent of currency transactions. Already market prognosticators suggest China's renminbi is but a decade from becoming a leading if not dominant world currency that will reflect China's significant economic position in the world.

Many have suggested ways to preserve America's exorbitant privilege and maintain the dollar as the world's reserve currency, or at least slow the pace of decline in its share of global reserves. One solution is to bolster the quality of the dollar in terms of value by reducing its quantity, contracting the money supply, even returning to a gold standard. However, history shows that the creation of money has been a temptation few have been able to resist.

The dollar isn't what it used to be. It's no longer backed by any gold (and hasn't been since the early 1970s). It's soft money. I define soft money as currency that is not backed by commodities like precious metals. A dollar bill has very little intrinsic worth, but it remains a symbol of value. A dollar's worth is supposedly backed by the faith and credit of the US government. You could also say that the source of the dollar's value isn't determined by precious metals underground but reflects the underlying fundamentals of the US economy. But economist Milton Friedman explains it best: "The pieces of green paper have value because everybody thinks they have value."[9]

It's difficult to pinpoint exactly why soft money was created in the first place. But here are a few possible reasons:

First, convenience: A dollar bill is easier to handle than gold bullion and gold coins. Exchange is evolutionarily advantageous, and any tool that significantly helps us trade and cooperate more efficiently has a good chance of being widely adopted.

Second, abstraction: As the human capacity for symbolic thought improved, we no longer had to see or touch the source of value. Money today is an abstraction of its evolutionary purpose of helping us obtain the resources we need to survive. Brain scans reveal that obtaining dollars triggers activity in the nucleus accumbens, part of the reward center, so we clearly understand that pieces of green paper represent something else of value.

Third, universality: As the "super-brain" of society has become more global and interconnected, a common financial system, one supported by institutions that issue soft money, has become the standard. Just as it takes time for the brain to learn something new, it took more than a thousand years for the "super-brain" to widely adopt soft money as the prevailing form of currency.

Last, power: Issuers of soft money can easily alter the money supply to achieve political and economic goals, shaping a society as they see fit. Issuers can design soft money so that it has worth within a jurisdiction; hard money may always have value outside territorial borders, making it a flight risk. Soft money is nothing short of financial alchemy. An issuer can create money out of thin air and fund its agenda without directly taxing its citizens.

This final reason is cynical yet illuminating. Coinage had a democratizing effect in the ancient world. But once Rome's leaders started to tinker with the value of coins, they realized the political usefulness of being the issuer. The large-scale manipulation of hard money abetted their goals and helped them alter the economy to their liking. "Give me control of a nation's money supply, and I care not who makes its laws," said Mayer Amschel Rothschild, the financier who started the Rothschild banking empire.[10]

Metallists admit that hard money has historically been manipulated. But soft money, they reason, gives *more* power to the state. Nero was unable to affect uniformly his entire currency at once. When he issued a new batch of debased coins, there were still high-grade coins in circulation. The value of these high-grade coins would appreciate, yet it would take time for them to be hoarded and removed from circulation.[11] With soft money, the state affects the value of *all* its notes simultaneously. When the Fed issues notes, it adjusts the overall money supply, which impacts the value of every dollar. Soft money renders Gresham's law moot, as all good money becomes bad.

It's easier for the state to issue and alter soft money. Whereas the denarius was bounded by metal, the dollar is boundless by its absence. As of June

2013, there were 1.1 trillion in circulation, much of which is thought to be overseas.[12] Other measures of the money supply are larger: The monetary base, the sum of money in circulation and bank balances maintained at the Federal Reserve, was $3.2 trillion in June 2013, a staggering amount.[13] The arc of monetary history bends toward expansion and inflation, especially when encountering difficult economic times. Policies geared toward increasing the money and credit supply became a prescriptive doctrine to reboot the economy during and after the 2008 financial crisis, in an attempt to encourage the extension of credit, as well as to boost certain asset prices and drive investors into riskier investments, further supporting prices.

Borrowers will be less troubled by unexpected increases in inflation because it erodes the value of money over time, which means they will pay back the lender with money that is worth less than it is today.[14] Say I borrow $100 with a promise to pay you back next year with no interest. Suppose prices increase 3 percent over the year, so the purchasing power of the dollar decreases. After one year, the $100 holds only about $97 in purchasing power.[15] It may not seem like a lot, but it can amount to a huge advantage for large borrowers at the expense of creditors. Say the United States borrows $50 million for a twenty-year term at a fixed interest rate, and prices increase at a faster-than-expected rate of 3 percent each year. At the end of the twenty years (assuming simple annual compounding), the government must pay $50 million, but with money that's worth approximately $28 million, a good deal for the government.[16] Consider the opposite case, in which prices decline unexpectedly by 3 percent each year. At the end of the twenty years the government must repay the $50 million principal to its creditors with money that now represents about $90 million in purchasing power, which is onerous.[17]

Indeed, issuers that borrow heavily benefit from a system of soft money that is prone to money creation and inflation. But the nature of soft money also presents issuers a Faustian bargain. In the second part of Goethe's *Faust*, the emperor doesn't have enough money to pay his creditors and military. The devil convinces the emperor to issue paper money that is backed by gold that will be mined later. Money remains a symbol of value, but its value has become abstracted. Harvard professor Marc Shell articulates the devil's viewpoint on this shift: "If one could mine the minds of men for credit then one would not need to mine the earth for...gold." The devil realizes that the move from hard to soft money first occurs in the brain: Psychological change is antecedent to any economic adjustment. The emperor's advisers side with the devil because "they are interested not in the source of monetary wealth...but only in becoming wealthy."[18] At first the paper money engenders incredible riches. Both the emperor's creditors and military are paid. Even tailors see a boost in business activity. But eventually this wealth proves to be ephemeral, and it exacerbates the emperor's spending problems. High inflation stirs social unrest, and the emperor faces opposition.[19]

It sounds like a fanciful tale, but Goethe's story was inspired by real events. He was familiar with events in eighteenth-century France, when soft money was introduced to rescue the ailing economy. It worked for a short period, until it precipitated financial ruin. Over the course of history, and in almost every region of the world, soft money has demonstrated both great promise and peril. It remains to be seen whether *Faust* foreshadows ominous events in the United States. The Fed expanded the money supply in response to the 2008 financial crisis, which arguably helped to rescue the economy, but uncertainty remains about the long-term consequences of its actions.

Whether it leads to boom or bust, soft money is a powerful tool. It can enable issuers to pursue political goals through monetary measures. The policy decisions of issuers can also instantly affect other parts of the world through the currency markets. In a monetary system unconstrained by limited amounts of metals, soft money has become virtually limitless—supply at the discretion of the alchemists who make it. Issuers have long known what every child learns: Paper beats rock.

Dragon Money

Ts'ai Lun knew he was on to something. He was the head eunuch in Emperor Han Ho Ti's court during the Han Dynasty in China.[20] In AD 105, he informed the emperor of his creation, but he probably didn't realize how it would forever change money and how governments institute monetary policy. Ts'ai Lun removed bark from a mulberry tree and stripped its fibers, which he then battered into a flat sheet. He created paper—though some historians suggest it may have been invented as early as the second century BC and used to wrap precious bronze items.

The Chinese refined the craft of papermaking over hundreds of years, using fibers from rattan, sandalwood, bamboo, even seaweed. They also are said to have invented ink, and inkmaking was a craft of great repute practiced by artisans, scholars, and statesmen.[21] What's more, the Chinese invented block printing and movable type.[22] In place were all the ingredients for making paper money. But until its invention, bronze coins were the prevailing currency throughout.

In the early seventh century, the Tang Dynasty succeeded the brief Sui Dynasty and became, in the words of the Metropolitan Museum of Art, "one of the greatest empires in the medieval world."[23] The Tang period, which lasted through the ninth century, was characterized by relative stability and cultural ferment. Diplomats from distant lands like Persia visited. Musicians from Central Asia toured China, too. The Tang had actually categorized ten types of music, including foreign genres. It was also an environment for robust commerce and innovation. Merchants searched for better ways to serve customers. Shops stored valuable items for patrons, like a bank that rents out safe-deposit boxes, and issued paper drafts or receipts backed by the items. These drafts functioned like money, since they could be traded.[24] Elsewhere, tea merchants wanting to communicate and transmit profits between regions used drafts so they didn't have to carry heavy bronze coins.[25]

Government officials explored ways in which to make tax collection easier since they needed revenues to finance the military to combat Tur-kic nomads in the west and Koreans in the east. The state also created drafts, or "flying money," to minimize the need to lug coins long distances between far-flung provinces and the state capital.[26] They were convertible into coins and used in transactions between local and state governments, as well as among merchants. The state realized the need to regulate these notes almost right away. In 811, it prohibited private entities from making flying money, and it instituted strict measures to protect its power.[27] Listed on some notes was the penalty for counterfeiters who "shall be decapitated summarily in punishment for the crime; the first informant shall be given . . . silver."[28] The bills were used for specific transactions and didn't circulate like a general-purpose currency, yet paper was the ultimate convenience.[29]

The later Song Dynasty, which reigned from AD 960 to 1279, is often credited as the first to implement a paper-based monetary system. In AD 970, it established the "bureau of credit cash," which issued money.[30] These paper notes flourished partly because of the shortage of coins. It's estimated that more than 260 billion coins were minted during the reign of the Northern Song Dynasty from 960 to 1127, but that still wasn't enough to meet the demands of a growing number of merchants and a burgeoning military.[31] This "currency famine" was reason enough for the state to consider other options.[32] It found one in its western province of Sichuan.

Coins were made from iron in Sichuan because the province lacked abundant amounts of copper and other metals needed to make bronze coins. It also bordered rival states, and the Northern Song wanted to minimize the flow of valuable bronze money to its enemies.[33] Iron coins were left on deposit at banks, and customers were issued receipts that could be used in transactions. At the same time, Sichuan was long known for making paper from hemp, and the imperial court used it to issue decrees.[34] It was a small step to issue money via paper, which it did around AD 1000.

At first the court tolerated a fragmented monetary system, allowing sixteen banks to issue paper money. But in 1023, the state revoked this permission, realizing that some residents couldn't work out who was issuing which notes. Moreover, the state could wield more power as the sole issuer. It established the "bureau of exchange medium" and assumed full production of paper money.[35] Its notes were named *jiaozi* and later renamed *qianyin*, which was backed by iron and then silver. At the outset, the state exercised restraint by instituting an annual quota of paper money that could be made. The quota was meant to stabilize the value of the currency, curb government spending, and prevent inflation. But the limit was disregarded. The state lifted the quota 50 percent in 1072, and that was exceeded, too.[36]

Each additional issuance further demonstrated the provincial government's considerable monetary power—and its inability to control its excess.

The Southern Song, which reigned from 1127 to 1279, sought and eventually incorporated this monetary power. But since its northern lands were lost to the Jin through war, at first there was a fragmented monetary system composed of four territories in which different currencies circulated.[37] The disunited currency system diminished trade.[38] To make matters worse, the Song faced a currency famine because it didn't possess enough of the metals necessary to make bronze coins.

The Song employed another metal, silver. Already its price had appreciated considerably versus bronze because the northern regions, more abundant in copper, had been lost. The heightened value of silver also reflected the fact that the Song increasingly used it in administrative affairs: Taxes and military salaries were partly paid in silver. And eventually, silver replaced bronze as the standard store of value.[39]

In 1170, the state recognized the *huizi*, a paper currency that had started to circulate among merchants. It prohibited private entities from issuing the currency, backed it with silver, and made it the legal tender of the land. *Huizi* eventually spread throughout the provinces, with the exception of Sichuan.[40] These notes were redeemable for new notes as a way to maintain the currency's value, but this practice was abandoned in the early thirteenth century, as the state needed more money to cover expenses. As more *huizi* was issued, Gresham's law was reprised: Coins were hoarded as a store of value and ultimately removed from circulation.[41]

Huizi was already circulating as a medium of exchange. And increasingly, this paper money was becoming the unit of account. Historian Richard von Glahn points out that prices once listed in the value of coins were marked in terms of *huizi*.[42] As for serving as a store of value, the silver-backed *huizi* was a claim on a precious metal of intrinsic worth, even though in practice this promise had diminishing credibility as the state issued more notes. It would take longer still for paper money to delink completely from metal. But that time was coming, as the man who would untether paper was preparing for war.

Despite efforts to maintain *huizi*'s value, its issuance continued almost unabated, even more so as the Song economy started to decline.[43] In the early thirteenth century, the Song's sustained warfare with the Jin left them weakened. In 1231, a large fire swept across the capital, destroying many buildings, which needed to be rebuilt. The state issued more *huizi* to cover the cost, and the value of the currency subsequently declined. The value of *huizi* dropped further when the state replaced its high-quality paper made from mulberry trees in Sichuan with locally available paper of lesser quality. To be sure, the state endeavored to restore the value of its currency. It made vouchers for silver and gold to reduce the *huizi* in circulation, and even mandated that everyone had to acquire a fixed amount of notes.[44] But it couldn't resist the temptation to print more notes to cover its significant expenses, and the Song's economy deteriorated. After years of fighting, the Song were vanquished by Kublai Khan and the Mongols, who unified China under the Yuan Dynasty in 1279.

During the thirteenth century, the Mongol Empire spanned Asia to Eastern Europe, making it one of the largest in history. The empire was a loose confederation of territories that relied on the leadership of local chieftains and required great administrative oversight. The empire had started to fragment in the mid-thirteenth century because of fighting among successors to the throne. One of those heirs, Kublai Khan, sought to maintain the strength of the empire, but the question was how. He was torn between expanding and controlling his sphere of influence via nomadic military expeditions, or serving in the state capital as the chief administrator and overseeing an expansive bureaucracy.[45] He quickly learned that paper was mightier than the sword. He used money to unify the empire, promote trade among different regions, create more wealth for his court, and strengthen his grip on power.

First printed in 1260, Kublai's paper money, known as *zhongtong chao*, was issued in eleven denominations, with no expiration date for when it had to be used, and was backed by silver.[46] The selection of silver was on the advice of his financial ministers, who had experience dealing with silver-backed paper in other provinces. Moreover, the Mongols had historically benefited from an extensive tributary system in which silver was remitted from provinces to the capital, and silver was seen as a store of value.

Kublai's innovation was his diktat. He declared his currency the *only* acceptable currency of the land.[47] Counterfeiters were put to death, and whistle-blowers who knew of counterfeiters were rewarded. He forced everyone to use his money or else face punishment. The state issued small denominations to eliminate the use of bronze coins entirely. So that *chao* would be without rival, Kublai banned the use of gold and silver in trade, and seized the metals of foreign merchants who visited his lands.[48] These restrictions were later eased as *chao* reached wide circulation.

At first, the state administered a careful monetary policy. To promote the notes and reaffirm their credibility, the state occasionally redeemed them in silver. The old notes were destroyed in public so that corrupt officials couldn't pocket them. The notes spread throughout, unifying the empire under a single currency. They even circulated as far as modern-day Thailand, Myanmar (Burma), and Iran. Historians have suggested that early Western banking institutions were greatly influenced by the Yuan Dynasty's monetary system.[49]

However, from 1280 to 1350, the state endured bouts of inflation. The trouble began with the annexation of the Southern Song territories. The Song's population of 60 million dwarfed that of Jin, the seat of Kublai's initial power. Adding so many people generated giant demand for Kublai's notes, and *huizi* were converted to *chao* at a rate of fifty to one. The state issued notes at heightened levels and exhausted its silver supply. With less silver, the state printed more paper, which reduced the credibility of the currency, and its convertibility to metal came into question. Ultimately, the value of the *chao* declined 90 percent, to an unsustainable level.[50] To meet its growing expenses, the state sacrificed the value of its currency.

So Kublai started over. In 1287, the state issued a new currency, *zhiyuan chao*, which was set at five times the value of the old currency, an effort to devalue the old currency into extinction.[51] Up until this point, soft money was paper backed by metal. Kublai's new currency was declared inconvertible to hard money. Soft money had lost its anchor. It was, in the words of economists, fiat money: issued by the state, circulated on faith, and rendered worthless when people lost trust in it.

To increase adoption of the new currency, the state again banned the use of gold and silver in transactions. But that led to further depreciation of the new currency as these precious metals were hoarded, reprising

Gresham's law. The state even banned private vouchers and coupons, anything that could be a threat to the new currency.[52] Instead of the old currency vanishing, it circulated in the shadows, and eventually alongside the new currency because in theory it still was backed by silver.

People lost faith in Kublai's currencies, especially as budget deficits grew. Kublai's successors experimented with creating new currencies, but it wasn't enough to restore faith in the monetary system. In 1311, the dual monetary system was restored. Prices were listed in *zhongtong chao*, and it became the monetary standard, since it was supposedly convertible to silver. The currency of daily transactions was the *zhiyuan chao*. The reprised system helped to foster years of relative economic calm, until the power of his successors of the Yuan Dynasty eroded in the middle of the century.[53]

Chinese monetary history illustrates that the stronger the state, the more credible its institutions, the softer the money. The value of money wasn't derived from its intrinsic metal worth. People had faith in, or even feared, its issuer. A strong leader like Kublai Khan could make monetary decisions without compunction. Yet these early experiments in soft money demonstrate the Faustian bargain. Despite initially having the confidence of its people, issuers fell victim to the temptation of overproduction, which led to higher spending and rampant inflation. The rise and fall of soft money took decades in China. In another part of the world, it would take only four short years.

A Man in France

Some of what we know about Kublai Khan comes from Venetian explorer Marco Polo, who shared stories about how paper money was used in these distant lands. His discoveries may have been what inspired Europe to adopt similar monetary instruments in the fourteenth century. But the West didn't engage in its elaborate experiment of using soft money to rescue a flagging economy until much later. In one telling example, the French monetary system of the 1710s, different institutions worked together to reboot a sluggish economy. Yet, as was the case in the East, an unchecked soft monetary system precipitated a decline in the value of the currency and high inflation.

The man who orchestrated an early experiment had a colorful background. Born to a goldsmith near Edinburgh, John Law was educated at top schools, developed a fondness for gambling, and was a notorious womanizer. In 1694, at the age of twenty-three, he even killed an opponent in a duel over a woman. He was subsequently arrested, and sentenced to death.[54] But with the help of prominent friends, he escaped on a boat that was headed to continental Europe.[55]

He eventually wound up in Amsterdam, a bustling financial hub, where he learned firsthand of financial innovations like foreign exchange banking, joint stock companies, the stock market, and paper money.[56] The Amsterdamsche Wisselbank, or Exchange Bank of Amsterdam, didn't charge customers for deposits but for withdrawing coins, as much as 2.5 percent to cover the operating costs of the bank. These fees discouraged withdrawals. In 1683, the bank tried to make withdrawals easier and issued receipts against the coins a customer had on deposit. Over time, the bank prevented customers from withdrawing coins, and these receipts turned into a tradable currency. The change enabled the bank to loan money more easily to large borrowers like the Dutch East India Company.[57] The bank's decision wasn't widely questioned, as outsiders including Adam Smith thought it had a large reserve of precious metals. Already possessing a mind adept in mathematics, John Law now had an idea that he could reformulate elsewhere.[58]

In 1705, he wrote about this idea in his book *Money and Trade Considered, with a Proposal for Supplying the Nation with Money*, which he circulated in Scotland with the help of his aunt, who was a publisher. He tried to connect the dots between money and trade, arguing that more money in circulation would lead to more commercial activity. In addition, he linked the money supply with price levels by pointing out that Europe's importing of precious metals, hard money, would generate an increase in prices. He advocated for countries that were suffering from shortages of money and depressed prices to increase their supply of it. The most expedient way was to abandon hard money for soft, a new twist on alchemy, to turn paper into gold.[59] To be sure, paper money wasn't new to Europe, since its origins have been traced to medieval Italy. John Law synthesized other people's ideas and proposed the creation of a state bank, analogous to the Exchange Bank of Amsterdam, to issue paper money.[60]

But no country wanted what he had packaged and was selling. That changed with the death of Louis XIV, who left France with a monetary and financial crisis.[61] The Sun King's incessant wars and profligate spending generated heavy debt, exorbitant interest rates, and high unemployment. France faced bankruptcy and default. Moreover, it lacked enough precious metals to mint coins at levels necessary to facilitate an adequate level of trade. France was enduring a currency famine.[62]

The Duke of Orleans, who had been elevated to regent, the head of state, invited John Law to France to help resolve the monetary crisis. Law's prescriptions for France were right there in the title of his book: money and trade. He thought France needed more money, which would end the currency famine. And he believed France needed a large trading company that could absorb the national debt, promote commerce, and mitigate the financial crisis.

In 1716, he put his plan into action by founding Banque Générale, which functioned as a traditional bank in that it accepted deposits and issued loans. It had friends in high places, as the regent was also a customer. The bank was permitted to issue banknotes that were convertible to hard money. In 1717, the state allowed tax payments to be made using these notes, immediately broadening their use value, making them legal tender and a currency.[63]

In 1718, the regent took over Law's bank because of its tremendous profitability and turned it into the official state bank, Banque Royale. The new bank issued notes known as livres, the French currency at the time. Law welcomed the takeover because it strengthened his proximity to power, which would give him more leeway to implement the ideas described in his book. Law knew that the stronger the state, the more money could be governed by fiat. Just like in Kublai Khan's court, the French government prohibited the trade of gold and silver. By 1720, just four years after Law's arrival, his system had increased the money supply by a factor of four. The currency famine was over, and prices were on the rise.[64]

But there was still the concern of France's large debt and high interest rates. Law looked to absorb the national debt into another institution, a company of which he took control and modeled on a Dutch joint stock trading company. In 1717, Law became the head of Compagnie d'Occident

(Company of the West), which was financed with 100 million livres.[65] Historian Niall Ferguson explains Law's plan: "He was (not unreasonably) trying to convert a badly managed and burdensome public debt into the equity of an enormous, privatized tax-gathering and monopoly trading company."[66] The company had procured exclusive rights to commercial activity in Louisiana. In exchange, it was to assume part of the French national debt. At first, it seemed like a fair deal. The Louisiana territories at that time stretched north to Canada and held great promise of copious minerals and precious metals—future revenue with which to repay investors. The regent helped the company by giving it plum opportunities to merge with companies that operated in Africa and Asia. The resulting conglomerate was known as the Mississippi Company.[67]

Banque Royale and the Mississippi Company were intertwined in Law's system, and they even merged in 1720. Banque Royale was akin to a central bank, and issued money that people used to buy stock in the company. The Mississippi Company continued to sell shares, which were scooped up by the hungry public. The share price doubled. Law experimented with new ways to promote the shares, such as allowing deferred payment plans, as well as pricing the shares at levels affordable to the common man. Eventually, an options market appeared that provided investors opportunities to buy shares with less money up front. To keep demand strong, Law trumpeted the promise of Louisiana, even planning a city named New Orleans in honor of the regent.[68]

Meanwhile, in mid-1719, Law saw an opportunity to advance his system and oversee a broader portfolio of France's economy. The Mississippi Company, flush with investors' cash, loaned the state money to repay the debt balance. The state had lowered the interest rate on its debt issuance from 30 percent to less than 4.[69] Investors who held government debt were steered toward buying shares in the Mississippi Company, and its share price again almost doubled in just two weeks. In just two years, a share had risen in price from 150 livres to 10,000 livres. Investors had seen their holdings appreciate considerably, and the term *millionaire* was first used in 1719.[70] The prospect of getting rich quick generated a market mania in which poor and rich folks alike lined up to buy shares. In a sign of the times, a man

suffering from a hunchback condition made 35,000 livres by charging traders to use his back as a table, and subsequently bought shares for himself.[71]

Law's system was firing on all cylinders: The money supply had expanded,
and the share price of his company had exploded. The monetary stimulus
worked, in four short years. The renewed confidence in the state spilled over
to the French private sector, which was becoming a leader in international
trade and commerce. For having turned around France's economic fortunes,
Law was bestowed the title Duke of Arkansas. He converted to Catholicism
because he was to become a public official, the Contrôlleur Générale des
Finances, similar to the US Treasury secretary, in charge of tax collection
and the nation's finances.[72] This Scottish man set an example that inspired
others as the British South Sea Company followed a similar course of action,
converting state debt for corporate equity.

Everything that goes up must come down, and the markets began to feel
the gravitational force of reality. Because the money supply had expanded
drastically, there was runaway spending and high inflation, and the value
of the French currency depreciated considerably. The faith in fiat money
had started to wobble, and more people began to return to dealing in hard
money. To make matters worse, Law's zigzagging policy of whether to allow
or ban the use of hard money led to uncertainty. The share price of the
Mississippi Company also declined as more people realized that the area
resembled more of a muggy swamp than a Promised Land of minerals and
precious metals. Louisiana, at that point, was a risky, subprime asset. It
wasn't generating the income to support the high stock price.

Investors panicked. Law tried to slow the decline of the share price,
using the bank's capital to support price levels. But the market had tipped
from bull to bear, and the stock price halved. The state issued an edict that
steadily lessened the value of paper money and shares, like letting the air
out of a balloon. But that only angered investors and quickened the selling.[73]
Investors wanted out, and the public demanded Law be jailed. To stop the
selling, he oversaw open bonfires in which paper money was burned to
reduce the money supply and jack up the currency's value. But it was too
late. Law fled France, and left it with a financial mess that slowed its future
economic progress.[74]

Law is the real-life devil who presents the Faustian bargain of soft money to the regent. His system was short-lived, but the interconnectedness of institutions and reliance on paper money provided a glimmer of what was to come.

All About the Benjamins

Born in Boston, Benjamin Franklin moved to Philadelphia at the spry age of seventeen, in 1723. Coincidentally, it was the same year that the Pennsylvania Provincial Assembly first issued paper money. There was a shortage of coins because the colonies didn't have abundant deposits of precious metals. The British also prohibited the minting of coins in the colonies. To procure coins, the colonies traded goods with nearby Spanish territories for silver coins known as pesos, or Spanish dollars.[75]

The shortage of money dampened trade and business activity in Philadelphia. The Pennsylvania Assembly decided to experiment with paper money to see if it could help ameliorate the economic situation. But it realized the perils of soft money, which could generate rapid inflation. In order to prevent overissuance of paper notes, the state backed its notes with future taxes and the land of citizens who borrowed notes from it.[76] It also put an expiration date on them. The paper money helped to revive the economy as it stimulated manufacturing, construction, and trade. Though he didn't play an active role in the adoption of these notes, young Benjamin Franklin recognized how paper money was instrumental in reinvigorating the local economy.

As the expiration date of these notes approached, wealthy Philadelphians didn't want the state to renew them. They recognized the potential dangers of soft money: Overissuance of notes could lead to spending, high inflation, and a depreciated currency.[77] Benjamin Franklin defended paper money in a 1729 pamphlet that he wrote, anonymously titled *A Modest Enquiry into the Nature and Necessity of a Paper Currency*.[78] He echoes the viewpoint found in John Law's book—paper money abets trade. Franklin writes:

As we have already experienced how much the Increase of our Currency by what Paper Money has been made, has encouraged our

Trade...And since a Plentiful Currency will be so great a Cause of advancing this Province in Trade and Riches, and increasing the Number of its People...Upon the Whole it may be observed, That it is the highest Interest of a Trading Country in general to make Money plentiful.[79]

Not only did Franklin believe that paper currency spurred commerce; he also thought it could be more stable than precious metals. Economist Farley Grubb notes that Franklin understood the risks of soft money. It wasn't enough for money to be backed by something abstract, like faith in government. Because Philadelphia notes were backed by land, he believed that a land bank could ensure that it didn't issue too many.[80] Franklin's pamphlet helped to convince the legislature to issue more paper money of this kind. Franklin also benefited personally since his printer was selected to make the notes. Over the years, he even helped to improve the notes by inventing new printing technologies and methods.

Franklin thought that paper currency could help all the colonies, not just Pennsylvania. He suggested a common colonial currency backed by land. Yet he recommended that the British operate the land bank and use the accrued interest to finance the British efforts in the French and Indian War. The colonists didn't want the British to meddle with local monetary affairs, and his plan was not adopted. Grubb points out that Franklin's proposal was the first to advocate a "national" paper currency across all the colonies.

In the mid-eighteenth century, some colonies, for example New Jersey, were already using paper money or "bills of credit" that weren't convertible to hard money or backed by land. Facing currency shortages, more colonies like Virginia introduced these types of bills. Many notes were denominated in British units such as pounds, but various colonies had different standards for what constituted a pound.[81] The colonies increasingly relied on these bills to finance their debts, like those that arose from military campaigns of the French and Indian War.

The colonies were exhibiting more independence in terms of monetary affairs. But what was happening in the colonial courts irritated British merchants, as well as Adam Smith, who accused colonists of cheating creditors.

The courts began to enforce legal tender laws during debt cases. This meant that colonial money could be used for payments to British creditors, with amounts calculated on the basis of the face value of the notes, even though the current market value was lower than the face value.[82] The British didn't want to be ripped off.

The British usurped the monetary power of the colonies. Parliament enacted a series of Currency Acts to prohibit the use of these legal tender laws, which prevented colonists from paying British merchants in these notes. In addition, the British Board of Trade prevented colonies from issuing paper money backed by land. This type of system allowed colonies to use the accrued interest to pay for various administration costs.[83] But when it was banned, the colonies had to raise money by direct taxation. The colonists grew angry at these British measures, as well as the prohibitions of trade with other territories.[84] In time, these economic grievances added up, and some were listed in the Declaration of Independence, such as "For cutting off our Trade with all parts of the world."[85]

Franklin's vision of a unified currency was soon realized, but it wasn't exactly as he imagined. American financiers wanted a common currency to unite the colonies and finance the military during the Revolutionary War. The Continental Congress authorized the creation of Continental currency, or "continentals," which were theoretically convertible in terms of Spanish dollars on certain dates: They were structured like zero-coupon US savings bonds with the full face value realized only at a set future date, so they traded for less than their face value.[86] Colonists had transacted in Spanish dollars and were familiar with their consistent and reliable value. The plates used to mint the money were designed in part by Benjamin Franklin.[87] However, continentals weren't backed by land but by the future taxing power of the government—but that future was in doubt.

The British engaged in economic warfare by issuing counterfeit continentals to increase the money supply and erode the currency's value. In total, the American colonists issued $200 million in continentals in four years.[88] All these factors supposedly led to the considerable depreciation of continentals. In 1777, according to the Massachusetts Historical Society, $1.25 of continentals bought $1 of hard money; by 1781 it required $100 in continentals.[89] But Grubb maintains that the value of continentals cratered after 1779 because Congress instituted high taxes for the redemption of the notes.[90]

The poor performance of continentals wasn't lost on the country's founders. In 1783, Alexander Hamilton, who would serve as the nation's first Treasury secretary, wrote about the hazards of soft money:

> Indeed, in authorizing Congress at all, to emit an *unfunded* paper as the sign of value, a resource, which, though useful in the infancy of this country, and indispensable in the commencement of the revolution, ought not to continue a formal part of the Constitution, nor ever, hereafter, to be employed, being, in its nature, pregnant with abuses, and liable to be made the engine of imposition and fraud; holding out temptations equally pernicious to the integrity of Government and to the morals of the people.[91]

Congress stopped issuing continentals in 1779. But states continued to issue their own money using British nomenclature, which led to confusion among merchants. In 1785, at the urging of Thomas Jefferson, the government adopted the dollar as the standard unit of account. The word *dollar* came from *thaler*, a coin minted from silver in Joachimsthal, Bohemia, Germany (modern-day Jáchymov, Czech Republic). The dollar was to be parsed using a decimal system, instead of the Spanish system, which was divided into eighths. One holdover from the Spanish-American peso was its symbol, as "$" became the symbol for the American dollar.[92] The Coinage Act of 1792 established the dollar as a coin that was fixed at a certain ratio of silver and gold.[93] The founding fathers thought the new nation should rely on a more sound currency—hard money. They prohibited the states from making their own money but permitted the use of gold and silver as legal tender in Article I, Section 10 of the Constitution:[94]

> No State shall enter into any Treaty, Alliance, or Confederation; grant Letters of Marque and Reprisal; coin Money; emit Bills of Credit; make any Thing but gold and silver Coin a Tender in Payment of Debts.[95]

By restricting the powers of the states, this clause solidified the monetary authority of the federal government.[96] In addition, in Article I, Section 8 of the Constitution, the framers gave the federal government the authority to regulate the value of hard, coined money, and to borrow money, which would serve as a basis for the creation of soft money later.[97] Though the dollar began as hard money, it didn't remain that way for long. Benjamin Franklin's vision for a unified paper currency would eventually be realized, albeit not as money backed by land. It's only fitting that since 1914 his portrait has graced the one-hundred-dollar bill, the largest denomination of paper money circulating today in the United States.

Getting Softer: The Civil War

Abraham Lincoln made a difficult but necessary decision. During the Civil War, the United States desperately needed funds to finance Union troops. The nation's finances were meager, with few sources of revenue. He supported the creation of money not backed by land or convertible into precious metals. However, like the nation's founding fathers, Lincoln understood the perils of soft money. Left unchecked, it could lead to runaway spending, raging inflation, and financial ruin. Though he wanted hard money, he needed soft money. In his annual message to Congress in 1862, Lincoln praised the suspension of convertibility but cautioned there would be a need to return to it:

> In no other way could the payment of the troops, and the satisfaction of other just demands, be so economically, or so well provided for...A return to specie payments, however, at the earliest period... should ever be kept in view. Fluctuations in the value of currency are always injurious...Convertibility, prompt and certain convertibility into coin, is generally acknowledged to be the best and surest safeguard against them.[98]

Lincoln signed the Legal Tender Act of 1862, which authorized the federal government to emit nonconvertible paper money. These "greenbacks," printed with green ink, were mandated to be used for all debts public and private. Some $150 million of greenbacks increased the money supply and helped the government cover its expenses. Lincoln found what Law and Franklin had experienced: Paper money spurred trade and commerce.

But as in Kublai Khan's court and Law's Banque Royale, the Union needed more money to cover its yawning costs: The army had swelled from sixteen thousand soldiers at the beginning of the war to one million at the conclusion, and the nation's debt had grown to more than $2 billion. Other methods of raising capital, such as issuing war bonds and Treasury notes, helped but weren't enough. Lincoln signed a Second Legal Tender Act and Third Legal Tender Act, which approved the issuance of $450 million in greenbacks.[99] The value of this currency fluctuated with the success of Union troops. Meanwhile, the Confederacy had seen a considerable depreciation in the value of its paper notes. The Civil War was being fought with cannons, gunpowder, and paper.

It was a difficult decision for Lincoln to sign the act, and not just because of the dangers of soft money. He risked angering a powerful constituency: bankers. Before the war, there hadn't been a unified national paper currency. Instead, state-chartered banks issued notes backed by coins, which generated handsome profits.[100] Yet these notes were risky since they depended on the credibility of the issuing bank. If a bank failed, so did its currency, thus notes typically traded below their denominated value. These "wildcat" banks were thought to be taking advantage of the public by issuing unstable, worthless notes. The term may have come from a failed bank in Michigan that had images of wildcats on its bills. Upon learning about the government's plan for a national currency, northern banks lost even more credibility when they suspended the convertibility of notes to hard money. Without a metal anchor, the volatility of these notes spiked, and the public demanded a change. Realizing the inevitable, bankers successfully lobbied Congress to ensure that gold would still be used in interest payments owed to them. Republican congressman Thaddeus Stevens noted, "A doleful sound came up from the caverns of bullion brokers, and from the saloons of the associated banks."[101]

Despite the protests of bankers, Lincoln and the Republicans largely prevailed in reshaping the US monetary and banking system. Lincoln signed the National Bank Acts of 1863 and 1864, which instituted a tax on state bank–issued notes, resulting in banks ceasing the creation of these notes, and which gave the federal government the power to charter banks. The measures also permitted the federal government to keep its reserves in federal bonds, not just in hard money.[102] State banknotes were eventually removed, but several state banks survived by creating checking accounts, which became popular.[103]

With the Union victory, many bankers and creditors thought that the government would retire the greenbacks. The notes were, after all, an emergency measure, and the crisis was over. As we saw above, Lincoln had remarked on the need to return to hard money when he implemented the greenbacks. Creditors and businesses also wanted to retire the notes so that they could be repaid in more valuable hard money. But debtors wanted to keep greenbacks in circulation because of their inflationary effect. The purchasing power of the money they used to repay loans would be less.

The creditors achieved victory in 1875 with the Specie Resumption Act, which restored convertibility of greenbacks to metal in 1879 and retired $300 million worth of greenbacks. Opposition forces organized, even creating the political Greenback Party, which sought to repeal the legislation.[104] The government eventually instituted provisions that kept the greenback in circulation but backed it with hard money. In 1879, the Treasury bulked up on metal reserves in anticipation of massive redemptions, but the tidal wave of people looking to convert soft into hard money didn't materialize. The people had come to rely on the convenience of paper money, whether it was or wasn't backed by metal. Many had faith in paper money.

The monetary debate evolved from *whether* paper money should be backed by hard money to *which* type of metal. Debtors, including farmers and populists, advocated for bimetallism, silver and gold, because it would increase the money supply: more metal, more money, more spending, more inflation. Creditors, including businesspeople and bankers, desired the gold standard: fewer types of metal, more valuable money. In 1900, Congress passed the Gold Standard Act, which established gold as the only metal backing paper money. It would take another emergency to sever the link between precious metals and paper money again.

Getting Softer: The Great Depression

That emergency was the Great Depression, and it showed that the harder the times, the softer the money. During the Great Depression, 25 percent of American workers became unemployed, and many suffered drought and hunger. Trade and GDP declined almost 30 percent. This wasn't just an American phenomenon; it was a global one. But before we examine the monetary decisions during this period, a bit of history is needed.

From 1880 to 1914, many industrializing countries were in the "classical gold standard," what economist Murray Rothbard calls the "literal and metaphorical Golden Age."[105] It was an era of robust international trade, price stability, economic growth, and political harmony. The United States experienced a paltry 0.1 percent inflation every year during this period. Great Britain's exports constituted a higher percentage of GDP then, about 30 percent, versus now, 19.3 percent.[106] The gold standard is straightforward and best defined by economist Michael David Bordo:

> The gold standard essentially was a commitment by participating countries to fix prices of their domestic currencies in terms of a specified amount of gold. The countries maintained these fixed prices by being willing to buy or sell gold to anyone at that price.[107]

However, World War I abruptly ended this era. Several European countries left the gold standard so that they could print money to finance their military efforts. After the war, many countries returned to gold because of its prewar success.[108] Yet it was a modified system known as the "gold-exchange standard," which Rothbard explains:

> The gold-exchange standard worked as follows: The United States remained on the classical gold standard, redeeming dollars in gold. Britain and the other countries of the West, however, returned to a pseudo-gold standard, Britain in 1926 and the other countries around the same time. British pounds and other currencies were not payable in gold coins, but only in large-sized bars, suitable only for international transactions. This prevented the ordinary

citizens of Britain and other European countries from using gold in their daily life, and thus permitted a wider degree of paper and bank inflation.[109]

Great Britain introduced this standard at the behest of Chancellor of the Exchequer Winston Churchill. The same exchange rate that was used in leaving the gold standard was used in returning to the gold-exchange standard. But the rate didn't account for the inflation that had occurred during the war, which overvalued the pound. Rothbard writes, "[The British] did so for reasons of... national 'prestige,' and in a vain attempt to re-establish London as the 'hard money' financial center of the world."[110] Prices plummeted some 50 percent, British exports remained uncompetitive in the global market, and unemployment skyrocketed. Churchill later regretted his decision.[111]

During World War I, many European leaders realized what Abraham Lincoln understood decades before: Often during an economic emergency, a country needs more money than it has in its reserves of precious metals or cash. Officials also grasped that gold can be restrictive: When an economy bends, gold doesn't and neither does the exchange rate. In 1929, the US market crashed and the economy spiraled downward. Several countries, including Great Britain, at first remained committed to the gold-exchange standard. These countries raised interest rates to attract investor capital, creating a more restrictive climate for borrowers and global markets. Scholars contend that they should have cut rates to make borrowing and trading easier during these difficult times.[112] A gold standard, however, keeps currency exchange rates constant and forces the country to endure price deflation.[113]

This doesn't happen today. Because the dollar isn't moored to metal, it floats against other currencies. Instead of deflation, the dollar can devalue, making exports from the United States cheaper and more competitive in the global market. Policy makers today prefer currency devaluation to price deflation. But a gold standard provides only one option in a contracting economy: deflation.

Mired in depression, Great Britain raised rates to maintain the value of the pound, the world's reserve currency at the time. But it reluctantly bowed to political realism: The public didn't want to endure the bitter golden pill of deflation. Great Britain therefore abandoned the gold-exchange standard in September 1931.[114] The pound lost its luster as the world's reserve currency. Soon after, twenty-five countries also left the gold-exchange standard. Investors looked to the United States to see whether it would be next.[115]

In 1933, when President Franklin D. Roosevelt took office, he realized the restrictiveness of a gold standard. He thought it was partly responsible for bank runs, as people sought to convert paper dollars into hard money, causing banks to fail.[116] He instituted policies that sound as if they came from Kublai Khan's economic playbook. He authorized Executive Order 6102, which mandated that all gold coins, bullion, and certificates (with some exceptions like jewelry and rare coins) be turned over to the government at a rate of $20.67 per ounce. The US Treasury built a bullion depository in Fort Knox, Kentucky, to house the seized gold. Gold hoarding was banned and made punishable by ten years in jail. The government also prohibited gold exports and mandated that gold mining companies sell their gold to the government.

The Gold Reserve Act of 1934 canceled contract clauses that stipulated terms could be settled in gold. The Supreme Court upheld the cancellation of the gold clause by one vote. The act also allowed the government to adjust the exchange rate between the dollar and gold. Roosevelt increased the gold-exchange rate to $35, devaluing the dollar in an effort to kick-start inflation. There wasn't exactly a scientific method in adjusting the gold price upward. Roosevelt once suggested on a whim that the price be increased by twenty-one cents. His adviser stated, "If anybody ever knew how we really set the gold price through a combination of lucky numbers . . . I think they would be frightened."[117]

During the Great Depression, the US government exercised more control over the monetary system, making it less restrictive and more flexible than under the gold standard, but at the same time bounding closer toward soft money, like the emperor in *Faust*. It would take one final shock to cut the metal anchor completely.

The Final Shock

In 1944, with World War II coming to a close, officials from forty-four nations assembled at the beautiful Mount Washington Hotel in Bretton Woods, New Hampshire, to hash out an international monetary system. The United States obtained beneficial terms in the new system since it was emerging from the war as the leading world power. One outcome of Bretton Woods was that other countries fixed their currencies to the dollar, which was fixed to gold at $35 per ounce.[118] Similar to how other countries set their clocks in relation to Greenwich, England, now they had to set their currencies to the US dollar.

The dollar was the world's reserve currency: Other countries would hold securities denominated in dollars, and the United States paid interest for these holdings. The United States held gold. In a sense, the dollar became the new gold. However, despite having largely authored the Bretton Woods system, the United States eventually abandoned it.[119]

A range of factors caused the United States to desert Bretton Woods: growing costs, burgeoning inflation, and a constraining system. During the 1960s, President Lyndon Johnson's "guns and butter" policies—the Vietnam War and the Great Society domestic programs—required significant amounts of money. The butter, programs to help the poor, children, and elderly, saw an increase in annual spending from $6 billion in 1965 to $12 billion in 1968.[120] But these numbers were nothing compared to what was needed to finance the Vietnam War. Instead of instituting an onerous tax on the people, the US government borrowed funds to pay for the nearly two million members of the armed services involved in war efforts. More than 9 percent of America's GDP was allocated for defense spending, and more than $100 billion (over $700 billion in today's dollars) was spent.[121] The surge in spending negatively impacted America's fiscal situation, and deficit spending continued.[122] President Johnson bemoaned, "That bitch of a war killed the lady I really loved—the Great Society."[123] It would also help to end the Bretton Woods system.

From 1965 to 1971, the money supply increased at an average annual rate of 7.4 percent. In time, with more money came more spending and inflation. Consumer price inflation swelled from just over 1 percent at the beginning of 1965 to more than 13 percent in 1980.[124] Economists debate the origin of this period known as the Great Inflation. Some contend that politicians were more concerned with achieving a target unemployment rate of 4 percent and thus used stimulative measures like deficit spending and tax cuts to boost economic activity.[125] Economist Benjamin Klein contends that moving from hard money to soft helped to stoke inflation during the 1960s.[126] Economist Allan Meltzer, an expert on the Federal Reserve System, asserts that because inflation is a monetary phenomenon, fault lies with those responsible for monetary policy. The Fed dithered in order to build consensus, and it finally raised rates in 1965 to tame inflation.[127] But as the economy slowed down, the Fed reversed course and eased rates in 1968, which further stoked inflation.

With more inflation came more questions. Would the United States honor its commitment to keep the dollar pegged to the price of gold at $35 per ounce? Foreign governments that held dollar reserves were increasingly doubtful about America's ability to convert dollars into gold. In 1965, France and Spain redeemed millions of dollars for gold. In just over a decade, America's gold reserves had dropped by half. The global economy was expanding briskly, yet the global gold supply couldn't grow quickly enough.

A gap emerged between the high market price of gold and the low mandated peg of $35 per ounce. In 1961, a group of central banks formed the London Gold Pool, which was intended to defend the Bretton Woods peg mostly by selling gold. But the gap became unsustainable, and the pool eventually collapsed in 1968. The United States provided most of the gold and didn't want to sell it at such a low price level.[128] The dollar needed to devalue, but it couldn't be accomplished without jeopardizing the entire currency exchange rate regime of Bretton Woods; thus the dollar became increasingly overvalued and a contentious issue globally. For example, the strength of the dollar displeased European officials, since it enabled US corporations to more easily acquire European firms and assets.

Other countries started to detach themselves from the system by revaluing, devaluing, and floating their currencies. For example, the German deutschmark and Dutch guilder were floated against other currencies. The

United Kingdom needed to devalue the pound to try to boost exports. There were many attempts to keep the pound strong, but in 1967 it finally devalued more than 14 percent, a large drop during a time of relative currency stability. Investors asked: If the pound could devalue, why not the dollar? They bought gold in anticipation of a dollar collapse.

President Richard Nixon took office in 1969 and was confronted with deficit spending, high inflation, and a constrained monetary system. To make matters worse, in 1970 the economy started to dip into recession, and the market anticipated an imminent devaluation in the dollar, despite denials by the Nixon administration.[129] In 1971, he holed up with his economic advisers at a secret meeting at Camp David. Some of these advisers would become luminaries in their own right, including George Shultz, a future Treasury secretary and secretary of state; and Paul Volcker, future head of the Fed. The question facing his team: Should the United States honor an international agreement at the expense of national interest? Bretton Woods had become a monetary noose for the United States, and it became evident that it needed to be chopped and the dollar devalued. Secretary of the Treasury John Connally proposed "closing the gold window" by suspending convertibility of the dollar into gold. Even Congress issued a report that suggested the suspension of the gold standard.

After a vigorous debate, Nixon determined his course of action. On August 15, 1971, he delivered a twenty-two-minute televised speech (on NBC it was just before the start of the hit show *Bonanza*) in which he blamed international speculators for creating monetary crises and targeting the dollar. He also unveiled his "New Economic Policy," which called for a ninety-day wage freeze to limit inflation, a 10 percent surcharge on imports that would make foreign products less competitive in the United States, and a temporary suspension of the convertibility of dollars into gold. He translated his plan to the masses by appealing to patriotism:

> If you want to buy a foreign car or take a trip abroad, market conditions may cause your dollar to buy slightly less. But if you are among the overwhelming majority of Americans who buy American-made products in America, your dollar will be worth just as much

tomorrow as it is today. The effect of this action, in other words, will be to stabilize the dollar.[130]

His policies became known as the "Nixon Shock" among international trading partners who were surprised by US protectionism. The onerous 10 percent tax acted like an immediate devaluation of the dollar. In response, Japan floated the yen, which appreciated 7 percent versus the dollar, resulting in a dramatic 17 percent increase in the price of Japanese goods sold in the United States, factoring in Nixon's 10 percent tax.[131] In America, the stock market surged and the press applauded Nixon's measures: "We unhesitatingly applaud the boldness with which the President has moved," stated an editorial in the *New York Times*.[132]

Despite the creation in December 1971 of a new international monetary system known as the Smithsonian Agreement, which reprised a system of fixed exchange rates, it didn't last, as the United States and other countries wanted more monetary policy flexibility when confronting domestic issues. By 1973, many currencies of the industrialized economies started to float against each other. Bretton Woods was dead. Gold was gone for good. The dollar was and remains soft. Economist Benn Steil notes the significance of these events:

> Though the bond between money and gold had been fraying for nearly sixty years, it had throughout most of the world and two and a half millennia of history been one that had only been severed as a temporary expedient in times of crisis. This time was different. The dollar was in essence the last ship moored to gold, with all the rest of the world's currencies on board, and the United States was cutting the anchor and sailing off for good.[133]

Central banks now steer this ship. They preside over a vast web of interlocking institutions that alchemize money. Henry Ford, who believed the dollar shouldn't be manipulated by bankers, wrote in his 1922 autobiography, "It is a serious question how [the people] would regard the [monetary] system under which they live, if they once knew what the initiated can do with it."[134] It's important to understand how our modern monetary system works so its complexity doesn't obscure the Faustian bargain of soft money.

Centralized Alchemy

The world's first central banker was sentenced to death. Johan Palmstruch, whose story predates and eerily anticipates that of John Law, was a foreigner who moved to another country to set up a banking system. Born in Latvia, trained in Amsterdam, he moved to Sweden and convinced King Karl X Gustav to charter Stockholms Banco in 1656. It was one of the earliest European banks to issue paper money. But like Law's system, it overheated, and Palmstruch was imprisoned and banished to die. Yet he was eventually freed. Despite the bank's demise, the Swedes weren't ready to abandon the idea of having a central financial institution. After all, the bank had helped several companies secure financing, and paper money had proven popular with the public because it was convenient to use. The Swedes created Sveriges Riksbank, the world's first central bank, which is still in operation today.

Central banking has evolved from its wobbly start in Sweden into a central pillar of today's financial system. Central banks have become the primary alchemists in the modern system of finance. In a monetary system not reliant on metals underground, they proverbially create money out of thin air. This newfangled alchemy doesn't evoke images of chemists who mix metals but a complex diagram of the interlocking system of banks and government institutions: fewer funnels and more organizational flowcharts.

In the United States, the alchemy of money creation involves the Federal Reserve System, the banking sector, and the Treasury. The Fed was established in 1913 by the Federal Reserve Act in response to the financial panic of 1907, which had led to several bank runs and bankruptcies. At that time, the banker J. P. Morgan came to the rescue of the American financial system. Officials realized that the United States needed a permanent institution to monitor, regulate, and even control monetary issues. The Fed's role has expanded over the decades to cover several areas, from supervising the banking system to facilitating international payments.[135]

The Fed is best known for setting interest rates, the price of money. Technically, the Fed sets a target for the "federal funds rate," the rate at which banks lend to one another. It intervenes in the market to achieve this target rate. If the Fed wants to lower rates, it buys securities in the market, which serves to expand the money supply: more money, lower rates. If the Fed wants to raise rates, it sells some of its securities in an act to contract the money supply: less money, higher rates. Let's say the Fed wants to lower rates. It buys $1 million of US Treasury bonds from a bank like Citigroup with new money that it creates out of thin air. The $1 million of bonds are added to the Fed's balance sheet. Citigroup, like all large banks, has an account at the Fed, and its account is credited with the $1 million it received for selling the bonds.

For this new money to circulate more widely through the economy, Citigroup can loan some but not all of it to borrowers. Banks are required to keep a fraction of their deposits, about 10 percent, in the vault or as a deposit with the Fed. Citigroup must keep $100,000 of the $1 million in reserves. It can lend out the remaining $900,000. Let's say someone borrows the $900,000 and deposits it in her account at Wells Fargo. Then $90,000 must be kept on reserve, and $810,000 can be lent. In this way, the "fractional reserve system" enables a multiple expansion of money, as the initial $1 million can be expanded up to ten times: A little money generates a lot of credit. And that's how money is made.

Because banks keep only a fraction of deposits on hand, they face the prospect of bank runs if depositors demand more cash than is held in reserves. It's like when George Bailey confronts panicked customers in *It's a Wonderful Life* and explains, "The money is not here...your money is in Joe's house...and a hundred others." In modern times, to increase the confidence of depositors, the government insures deposits up to $250,000.

In its monetary operations, the Fed can buy assets from organizations that aren't banks, such as insurance companies, but in this case new money might not remain in the banking system and would have a lower impact on the economy. The Fed can also use its invented money to buy securities like Treasury bonds directly from the US Treasury in a process known as "monetizing the debt," an incestuous process whereby the government can raise funds by means other than raising taxes or selling bonds. In this way, increasing the money supply helps the borrower, the government, since the value of the dollar will likely be less in the future. That's why governments have historically resorted to creating more money; it's easier than raising taxes. But because more money can lead to inflation, the value of everybody's money declines, acting as a covert tax on everyone.

As for the movement of tangible money, the Fed acts as the distributor. The Bureau of Engraving and Printing creates paper notes, and the US Mint makes coins. Both are part of the US Treasury. When, say, SunTrust Bank in Atlanta anticipates an increase in cash demand during the holiday season, it asks the Fed for more money. SunTrust has an account at the Federal Reserve Bank of Atlanta, one of twelve regional Federal Reserve banks. The Atlanta Fed has a cash inventory; it debits SunTrust's account and provides it cash. In 2012, the Fed processed 31.7 billion notes through its twenty-eight processing centers across the United States.

It's a big operation. Several institutions make up America's expansive monetary system, and it's fair to say modern alchemy is contemporary bureaucracy. Despite the complexity and apparent sophistication of the system, the Faustian bargain of soft money still lurks, and it's incumbent upon the monetary authorities to use their powers wisely and cautiously.

To Invisible and Beyond

Kublai Khan, Johan Palmstruch, John Law, Benjamin Franklin, Abraham Lincoln, Franklin Roosevelt, Richard Nixon, and countless others recognized the benefits of soft money and controlling its levers. It can support a struggling economy by stimulating trade and commerce. It also helps avoid unpopular policy decisions such as raising taxes or reducing spending. But all monetary officials must be alert to the risks of soft money. During the 1970s, the move from hard to soft money likely played a role in generating "stagflation," characterized by low growth and persistent inflation, which reached 13.5 percent in 1981. To tame inflation, Paul Volcker, who was now head of the Federal Reserve Board, instituted tough measures, raising the federal funds rate during a period of high unemployment.

In the wake of the 2008 financial crisis, the Fed dramatically increased the money supply, yet high inflation hasn't materialized. Nevertheless, one thousand years of monetary history teaches a convincing lesson: As societies move from hard money to soft money, as the "super-brain" forms new ideas about currencies, those economies risk failure. All of us, not just central bankers, must recognize the perils of the Faustian bargain— especially as money evolves in the digital age. Money is becoming more electronic and invisible. It has become so abstract that we risk forgetting the concrete lessons of history. As long as money remains a symbol of value, some will seek to control it.

CHAPTER SIX

Back to the Future

The future of money

Gold is a way of going along on fear... But you really have
to hope people become more afraid in the year or two years
than they are now.
—*Warren Buffett*[1]

When you're using the iPad, the iPad disappears, it goes away.
You're reading a book. You're viewing a website, you're touching
a website... The technology goes away... And the same is true
with Square. We want the technology to fade away so that you
can focus on enjoying the cappuccino that you just purchased.
—*Jack Dorsey*[2]

In our abundant future, the dollar goes further... This happens
because of the dematerialization and demonetization... because
each step up prosperity's ladder saves time; because those extra
hours add up to additional gains.
—*Peter H. Diamandis and Steven Kotler*[3]

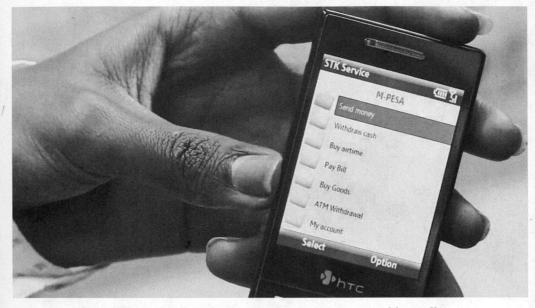

A mobile phone–based payment system, M-Pesa enables millions of Kenyans to transfer money.

A fortune cookie once advised me, "The more things change, the more they stay the same." Not much of a prophecy. But it may describe how fortunes will be made in the future.

Years from now, there will no doubt be new types of money and payment methods. But thousands of years of monetary history can be a guide for what to expect. The more money changes, the more it might stay the same, retaining properties—like being hard or soft—that we've already seen. It may also become increasingly digital, invisible, and intangible.

The form of money will depend on how the "super-brain" of society changes. Let's consider three possibilities of how the world may fare in the future: (1) a "bear case," in which the world deteriorates because of several disquieting events, from financial crises to devastating terrorist attacks or natural disasters; (2) a "bull case," in which the world progresses at a brisk pace as technology is developed and incorporated rapidly and broadly, much like it is right now; and (3) a "dream case," many years in the future, in which the lines are blurred between man and machine.

In the bear case, one could envision that money will return to being hard and intrinsically valuable. Financial writer Nathan Lewis advocates for hard, stable money in his book *Gold: The Once and Future Money*. During difficult times, people lack confidence in fiat money because they are concerned about the stability of institutions that issue and back it. They return to proto or hard money, like gold, with intrinsic worth and exchange value. Even though dollars still circulated, Americans hoarded gold during the Great Depression until the government prohibited it, largely because they thought it was a better store of value than dollars backed by the US government. What's more, in periods of monetary uncertainty, people also resort to bartering and even create alternative currencies.

In the bull case, technologists like Jack Dorsey conjecture that money will be increasingly digital, intangible, and invisible. In times of monetary stability, people go about their lives and don't think twice about the paper, plastic, or electronic forms of payment. They have confidence in the technologies that facilitate transactions, the institutions that issue money, and don't resort to hoarding or bartering. In this case, people adopt new technologies to make exchanges seamless. It's a future in which technology enables millions more people to join the global marketplace.

In the dream case, inspired by science fiction, futurists imagine a range of mind-bending possibilities.[4] Maybe it's a future in which new metals and materials are discovered on distant planets, replacing earthly metals like gold as hard money. Perhaps man and machine merge in some capacity: If one can embed a pacemaker in the body, why not a payment device? The blurring of man and money could spawn amazing new markets, currencies, and monetary systems. However, if these technologies are used in malicious ways, such a dream could turn into a nightmare.

Let's look into the crystal ball.

The Bear Case

Say there's an asteroid strike or a nuclear world war that renders much of civilization dysfunctional, from roads and telecommunication systems to bank networks and government institutions that oversee the financial and monetary systems. In the bear case, there is hoarding of all valuables and a return to commodity money. With no official entity to issue soft money or mint coins, people revert to a system in which items are evaluated on intrinsic worth, as metallists have always insisted. Other proto-monies like food and furs may circulate, as they did in the earlier civilizations. Money would return to its evolutionary purpose, helping us survive, an immediate source of energy and shelter. It wouldn't be an abstraction like it is today because we could no longer rely on the "super-brain" of society and institutions to issue and verify money. We would have to depend on ourselves.

"I'm so embarrassed. I feel like one of those end-of-the-world crazies who stock up on toilet paper and canned goods," said my friend, a portfolio manager who manages billions of dollars. "I just bought gold bars and hid them under my bed," he explained.

Civilization didn't crumble during the global financial crisis of 2008, but I glimpsed how people react during an economic crisis. When I heard that my friend lacked confidence in the global monetary system, I feared the worst. He's not exactly the type of guy you imagine appearing on National

Geographic Channel's *Doomsday Preppers,* a show about people preparing for the apocalypse.

My friend viewed gold as a safe haven. It doesn't generate income or dividends, but gold has historically maintained its value in volatile economic and political conditions. It doesn't depreciate over time like a floating currency with a growing supply. It's rare, precious, and in high demand. After the fall of Lehman Brothers in 2008, the price of gold soared almost 125 percent, to more than $1,800 an ounce in 2010. The CEO of Bullion Management, Nick Barisheff, boldly predicts the future price in the title of his book *$10,000 Gold: Why Gold's Inevitable Rise Is the Investor's Safe Haven.*[5] He points out that after two decades of selling gold, central banks are buying gold to preserve the value of their currencies, balancing the value destruction wrought by printing so much new money. Central banks accounted for 12 percent of aggregate gold demand in 2012, up from the average over the preceding five years of 4 percent. The largest gold producer, China, also imported 209.7 tons of gold in 2010, a yearly increase of 500 percent. China is reportedly trying to exceed the United States' holdings of gold. It's not just these global superpowers: Sri Lanka, Ukraine, and Kazakhstan have also increased their gold holdings.[6] Market strategists have debated why investors buy gold in such large amounts; maybe it's an expectation of rising inflation or fear of a market meltdown. Ben Bernanke offered one explanation. While testifying before Congress as chairman of the Federal Reserve in 2011, he said the Fed holds gold because of tradition.[7] Whatever the reason, in times of economic turbulence, we trust in gold.

However, it would take an extreme disaster for a commodity with intrinsic value like gold to eclipse the dollar as the primary circulating currency. Even as people amassed hard money during the global financial crisis, they also hoarded soft money. "I keep a roll of twenties in my underwear drawer, just in case," said another friend during the crisis.

During the crisis, there was more money to go around: The Fed took actions to dramatically increase the money supply and stimulate the economy. The amount of cash in circulation increased 45 percent from 2007 to 2013. After the fall of Lehman Brothers, there was a 10 percent increase in the amount of $100 bills being held by the public.[8] Presumably, these $100 bills were "hoarded" because they were still seen as a store of value.

Paradoxically, people lost faith in the banking system but still wanted the money that it created. Maybe my friend hoarded cash because he expected that dollars would always be accepted. US legal tender laws curb Gresham's law and explicitly state that dollars are acceptable for all debts private and public no matter how much of their value has been lost. My friend could use his underwear money in the United States despite how soiled it was.

Cash is dirty, low-tech, useful for small transactions, and anonymous. Researchers found three thousand types of bacteria on dollar bills: microbes that can cause acne, pneumonia, and staph infections. Dollar bills they obtained from a Manhattan bank had 1.2 billion markers of DNA, only about 50 percent of which came from humans. The rest were from viruses, fungi, horses, dogs, and possibly even white rhinoceroses. Some bills had small remnants of anthrax. In another study, British researchers examined a batch of their country's notes and found that 6 percent had amounts of *E. coli* similar to what is in toilets.[9]

It is also difficult for the government to track cash transactions and collect taxes on them. Many people in the $2 trillion "underground economy" who don't have full-time jobs, from nannies and construction workers to drug dealers and prostitutes, prefer dealing in cash. The Internal Revenue Service reports the US government lost more than $500 billion in uncollected taxes in 2012 due to undisclosed income.[10] Then there are investors who prefer keeping at least a portion of their wealth in cash, particularly the dollar, because it's liquid and a relative safe haven—remember Jasper's foreign exchange desk, which helped investors diversify their holdings.

Hoarding gold, and sometimes even cash, is a reminder of money's role as a store of value. As we have seen, hard money has historically held exchange value in that it can be traded for other necessary items like food and water. In times of monetary uncertainty, when a national currency is under threat or has vanished altogether, people realize the exchange value of hard money by trading and bartering. In the bear case, an informal network of exchange, a barter community, could replace the monetary system. Transactions would be demonetized. Social capital, social debt, gifts, doing favors for each other could become the primary currency. The gift economy, like that found among the Maori or Kwakiutl people, could replace the market. We would resort to new currencies since exchange is likely part of our evolutionary algorithm.

One doesn't have to look to our ancient past for examples of barter in times of economic hardship. During the recession of 2008 and 2009, small business owner Anne Phyfe Palmer resorted to bartering. She grew up in a middle-class family, and frugality wasn't foreign to her. In 1996, at the tender age of twenty-six, she opened 8 Limbs Yoga Centers in Seattle. Low on cash, she was flush with another currency: yoga lessons. Though she traded classes for other services like haircuts and massages from the start, in 2004 she stumbled upon BizXchange (BizX.com), an online barter network that operates in cities such as Seattle, Oakland, and even Dubai. The website smooths some of the friction found in bartering. For instance, bartering is subject to taxes, so BizX manages record keeping and account details for its customers.

At first, she found plenty of people wanting yoga lessons, but she couldn't find items that she wanted. This illustrates the "double coincidence of wants" issue in bartering: In order for bartering to work, both parties must want exactly what the other is offering. The probability of two parties wanting the same thing is low. Let's say Anne Phyfe has a plumbing emergency, but the plumber doesn't want yoga lessons. No deal. Hence, some economic historians say money was invented to facilitate exchange and solve the problem of the double coincidence of wants.

With more participants in a barter system, there is a higher chance of a double coincidence of wants occurring. The BizX community grew over the years and now boasts 8,000 individual users and 2,000 business users. Eventually Anne Phyfe's yoga lessons became a hit, garnering $20,000 in trade value, which she exchanged for things like business signage and bulk mailing. There was also the added benefit that each exchange could generate recurring business. It was a win-win solution: more customers with little cash outlay. And BizX benefits to the tune of $10 million in revenue for facilitating $60 million in trades per year.[11]

During the global financial crisis in 2008, when business slowed and money was tight, Anne Phyfe put her amassed credit toward a new ceramic tile floor for her kitchen. At the same time as the remodeling, her husband shifted from freelance design to overseeing the construction, so they lost one source of income. The downtown location of Anne Phyfe's yoga studio revenue declined, too. In sum, their income halved, and they were living on credit. In hard times, she resorted to exchange in a rudimentary form—she bartered.

During the euro crisis in 2010, which was an economic downturn, debt crisis, and currency panic, some European countries saw the rise of barter communities. In Spain, many bartered because they lacked incomes as unemployment reached 26 percent, and 55 percent among young workers.[12] Those who had cash savings tried to preserve it. For example, as Spain's economy flagged, Sabino Liebana, a Spanish online retailer of computer equipment, tried to preserve his company's cash flow. He got creative with his office rent, paying not in cash but in kind—with printers and computers. Bartering helped him conserve his cash for other important expenditures.

"Because of liquidity problems I think [bartering] is something that will be used by more and more firms, especially in the service industry," Liebana explains.[13]

Anne Phyfe initially encountered limited liquidity in the barter economy, but Sabino praised it as an alternative to cash in economic downturns. Liquidity, the ease with which one can buy or sell a good, depends on many factors, from the number of people in the barter network who are able to fulfill the double coincidence of wants, to the viability of other types of currency. In Sabino's case, there was an economic downturn and debt crisis that was calling into question the viability of the euro. When people lose faith in a soft currency and the institutions that back it, they often take matters into their own hands. Not trusting the issuer, they trust themselves. They barter to survive.

Besides the economic reasons, the creation of barter networks can also be an act of "solidarity through the rough times."[14] Many who barter see the benefits of a "Do it yourself" economic system, instead of one administered by technocrats hundreds of miles away. "I felt liberated, I felt free for the first time...I instinctively reached into my pocket, but there was no need to," said a man who started a barter network in Greece.[15] When national institutions fail, people rely on their communities and neighborhoods. The marketplace becomes local.

Bartering can be an informal exchange without written contracts, and thus difficult to track, so metrics of its use during the eurozone crisis are limited. But some regional numbers exist. During the crisis, in Catalonia, Spain, several dozen barter communities emerged.[16] There's also a small but growing market: One Spanish online barter network grew quickly and facilitated bartered trades with a value of nearly 10 million euros. In 2012, the International Reciprocal Trade Association, a global barter exchange, helped more than 400,000 member companies make $12 billion in revenues by trading excess business capacity.[17]

For a broad study of bartering during and after economic troubles, consider Russia after the fall of the Soviet Union. Russians had to adjust to free markets and a new price system. But they couldn't always afford a given good, so they bartered. In free markets, the prices of goods adjust according to supply and demand. But the Russian government prohibited many companies from dropping prices if it meant selling goods at below production costs—even though those costs were too high in the first place. The effects of bartering were felt throughout the Russian economy as businesses took in less cash, and in turn didn't have enough to pay workers and vendors. It was a bear case, and there wasn't a viable alternative.

Bartering was a vestige of the old Soviet economic system. For example, in 1991 researchers examined the business practices of a successful Soviet furniture retailer. All the store's wall units had sold quickly because of their high barter value. There was a significant demand for wall units because every apartment required one. Customers considered furniture as proto-money that could be exchanged for other necessary items. Even the managers of the furniture retailer engaged in bartering.[18] Researcher David Woodruff of the Massachusetts Institute of Technology estimates that bartering made up 50 to 70 percent of business transactions in Russia in 1998.[19] In Bulgaria, once a satellite state of the Soviet Union, bartering became prevalent as the nation endured an economic crisis. "You can buy almost anything with potatoes," observed the mayor of a Bulgarian village in 1996.[20]

Indeed, the bear case may result in an increase in hoarding and bartering. But it could generate a rise in sharing, which seems counterintuitive. During the 2008 crisis, the US government rescued the banks because it needs them. Government allows the banking system to create money, and the banking system allows governments to borrow massively. This partnership has historically led to unchecked spending, inflation, and the destruction of the currency's value—telltale signs of the Faustian bargain of soft money. Social scientist Mary Mellor says that in the current system money has been partly privatized, administered by a cartel of banks and government, not just in the United States but in most countries. Because banking officials decide who should receive loans, money is not being appropriated like a public resource. Banks distribute money to certain individuals and enterprises through loans, which have interest rates. In other words, the banks *make* money from the dissemination of money. However, Mellor argues that money should be seen as a public resource, a commons—like water and air.[21] During the crisis, it was the public's money, tax revenue, after all, that was used to save failing institutions. The interdependence of governments and banks, laid bare during the 2008 financial crisis, has eroded people's faith in financial and governmental institutions. A Gallup poll found that since the 2008 financial crisis, only about 25 percent of Americans have a "great deal" or "quite a lot of" confidence in the banks, down from 53 percent in 2004. This was still a better showing than "big business," which received 22 percent, and Congress at a dismal 10 percent.[22]

Even now, after the financial crisis, the public isn't demanding an immediate reform of the monetary system as we know it, unscrambling the eggs of government and banks. It's hard to imagine government officials and bankers relinquishing control of the monetary system, let alone playing a diminished role. But let's say there were an impetus for reform and the bear case realized: After a series of terrible economic crises, an enraged public demands reform of the monetary system. What would such a system look like?

Mellor envisions restoring money as a public utility. The financial and monetary systems could be combined, removed from the auspices of central banks and put under the aegis of elected representatives, or even the people themselves. For example, in Porto Alegre, Brazil, tens of thousands of citizens are involved in a participatory budgeting process, and the World Bank has credited the system for improving the standard of living for the community: The number of households with sewer connections jumped from 75 percent to 98 percent in a decade.[23] Mellor proposes that the government could issue money to local communities, cooperatives, or directly to citizens—instead of it flowing first through the banking system. To prevent elected politicians from abusing their monetary authority, another entity staffed with a group of elected officials would determine whether to enlarge or contract the overall money supply. This reformed system, Mellor argues, would likely reduce the amount of money, leverage, and power in the financial system. The electorate would gain power and the ability to prioritize spending for better or worse. Mellor's ideas may seem counterintuitive for the bear case: Sharing money more democratically is the opposite of hoarding. Yet perhaps a future crisis will generate a rise in neosocialist communities that would try an experiment like this.

Already some communities have taken matters into their own hands and introduced alternative currencies, like BerkShares in the Berkshires region of Massachusetts; Equal Dollars in Philadelphia; and WIR in Switzerland. It's not illegal to create alternative currencies in the United States, but there are two stipulations: (1) New currencies can't resemble dollars, to minimize confusion and counterfeiting; and (2) one must pay taxes just as if one were transacting in dollars.

One of the best-known alternative currencies is Ithaca HOURS, which were created by community organizer Paul Glover in Ithaca, New York, during the 1991 recession. He wanted to lessen the impact of the declining national economy on his community and promote local commerce. Glover explains:

> In 1991, a lot of people in Ithaca who had talent and time were not being used by the formal economy, and [Ithaca HOURS] . . . created a network that welcomed their skill. People were either unemployed, underemployed or malemployed. They had skills and passions they wanted to convert into livelihood, and while the classified ads and major employers didn't care about their special skills and passions, the Ithaca HOURS network celebrated them.[24]

HOURS are exchanged like dollars for goods and services, such as groceries and doctor's appointments, and are accepted only within twenty miles of Ithaca. HOURS are printed on paper notes that feature community members. The fronts of some notes read "ITHACA HOURS are backed by real capital: our skills, our time, our tools, forests, fields, and rivers." The backs of some notes read "ITHACA HOURS stimulate local business by recycling our wealth locally, and they help fund new job creation."[25] HOURS come in six denominations. One HOUR is equivalent to ten dollars, a half HOUR is worth five dollars. More than $130,000 worth of HOURS are in circulation, and more than five hundred businesses accept the currency. Most noteworthy, loans made in HOURS are made with no interest charge. Debtors don't have to borrow even more in order to cover interest rate payments. In contrast, banks create money by issuing loans that carry interest rates. Debtors who borrow in dollars often must take out even more loans to cover the interest rate charges.

Alternative currencies circulated widely in antebellum America when state banks issued notes during the "wildcat" banking era. Some eight thousand currencies circulated, and the US government oversaw a paltry 4 percent of the money supply.[26] The public grew wary of bankers and their dubious banknotes, and as we saw earlier, eventually the greenback was adopted. Another period of wildcat banking, in which subprime loans were issued to those who could ill afford them, led to the 2008 financial crisis. This time the public was irate not just with banks but later with the government for bailing them out.

Unlike the mid-nineteenth century, alternative currencies now may be part of the solution. In his book *The End of Money and the Future of Civilization,* noted economist and community activist Thomas Greco carefully considers alternative currencies. He readily admits that these currencies often start with much fanfare but eventually lose their novelty and ultimately decline in terms of usage. It's difficult to predict what currency will catch on in the bear case, but he outlines the properties of a successful alternative currency system. Most important is that any vendor in the marketplace can issue currency, putting monetary power in the hands of its users.

To some degree, this is already happening. Loyalty programs like frequent-flier miles are corporate-issued currencies. In 2005, the *Economist* determined there were more unspent miles than dollars in circulation.[27] Starbucks customers earn Starbucks Star points by paying for items with the Starbucks card or mobile application. In the United States, there are already seven million active cards that are used for 30 percent of Starbucks' daily transactions.[28] These loyalty currencies are issued by nonfinancial institutions. Advertising executive Paul Kemp-Robertson believes that corporations can leverage their trusted brands into creating more dominant currencies, especially at a time when so few people trust banks.[29] Right now these currencies have limited use and liquidity. But what if they were more flexible and fungible? You could use Starbucks Star points to pay for a plane ticket to Tokyo and a taxi ride to Koishikawa Botanical Gardens. Starbucks points could be exchanged with Amazon points, just like dollars are swapped for euros. There are already websites where you can convert one corporate currency into another.

Greco believes that a new era is here, one in which technology provides the tools for a digital, alternative currency, combining all the existing corporate currencies or creating a system that links all the regional barter communities or credit-clearing exchanges. These exchanges are business groups that extend credit to each other to facilitate transactions among the community. It's not unlike what happens today with digital transactions: Money isn't physically changing hands, but the record of who owns it gets constantly updated.

Looking for a precedent, Greco points out that the US Postal Service monopoly in letter carrying didn't prevent the rise of email and text messages. He highlights several technologies that may be a threat to the government and banking monetary monopoly: social networking, peer-to-peer credit clearing, systems that evaluate counterparty reputations, and encrypted and secure systems.[30] Already start-ups like Lending Club, an online peer-to-peer lending company, have originated more than $2 billion in loans, with only a 3 percent default rate.[31] These are loans determined not by bankers but by the community. Greco makes the case that technology can scale monetary networks like never before:

> Will eBay or Amazon be able to exploit this opportunity . . . ? The past three decades have seen great progress in the development of private commercial "barter" or trade exchanges that provide direct credit clearing among their business members. Optimizing their design, putting all the pieces together, and taking these networks to scale are

the remaining tasks that will revolutionize money and banking and enable the evolution of civilization toward greater peace, prosperity, and sustainability.[32]

One of the most visible examples of how technology is redefining money is the digital currency Bitcoin. Created in the wake of the 2008 financial crisis by a person or persons with the pseudonym Satoshi Nakamoto, Bitcoin is a decentralized currency that leverages peer-to-peer connectivity. In order to make bitcoins, one must "mine" them. Mining is a process in which computing power is used to solve math problems, and to verify and validate transactions on a public ledger.[33] It is unprofitable and untenable to use personal computers for mining anymore because they use up too much electricity without generating commensurate amounts of Bitcoin.[34] Instead, many buy specialized mining hardware, and then they download software to start the mining process. Many join pools of other miners, thereby combining computing power and increasing the speed in which they attain bitcoins. Finally, one sets up a Bitcoin wallet to receive the Bitcoin that one has earned. Instead of mining bitcoins, one can also buy and sell bitcoins on several online secondary markets. There is a fixed amount of 21 million total bitcoins that can ever be created, and this won't be achieved until 2140. The currency doesn't rely on central banks but rather cryptography, mathematics, and decentralized authentication.

Bitcoin has seen early success. According to Bitcoin.org, the value of bitcoins in circulation exceeded $1.5 billion in 2013.[35] Wall Street banks have written favorably about the currency. The foreign exchange strategy team at Bank of America Merrill Lynch writes, "We believe Bitcoin can become a major means of payment for e-commerce and may emerge as a serious competitor to traditional money transfer providers. As a medium of exchange, Bitcoin has clear potential for growth, in our view."[36] Even Ben Bernanke, then head of the Fed, seems to have given a nod to Bitcoin. In a November 2013 letter to the US Senate, he writes:

While these types of innovations may pose risks related to law enforcement and supervisory matters, there are also areas in which they may hold long-term promise, particularly if the innovations promote a faster, more secure and more efficient payment system. Although the Federal Reserve generally monitors developments in virtual currencies and other payments system innovations, it does not necessarily have authority to directly supervise or regulate these innovations or the entities that provide them to the market.[37]

However, it remains to be seen whether Bitcoin will have lasting power as a currency or fade away like other alternative currencies. It has experienced volatility in its price. In 2013, it seesawed from $20 to $266 and then $130 in just a couple of months. Nobel Prize–winning economist Paul Krugman cites this instability, saying that Bitcoin isn't a firm store of value, something that money needs to be.[38] Detractors say Bitcoin, like gold, is deflationary, unable to expand with growth, and could lead to currency famines in times of economic turbulence if it became a leading global currency.

Bitcoin also has a PR problem. In March 2014, Mt. Gox, a leading Bitcoin exchange, was hacked. It lost almost half a billion dollars' worth of Bitcoin, which amounted to nearly 850,000 Bitcoin, or 7 percent of the entire circulation.[39] In October 2013, the government seized 144,336 bitcoins valued at $28.5 million found on computer hardware operated by the creators of Silk Road, an online marketplace that accepted only bitcoins for various goods like books and illegal drugs. The former vice chairman of the Bitcoin Foundation, an organization that purports to safeguard the currency, was indicted for laundering $1 million in bitcoins on Silk Road.[40] Already, the FBI possesses more than 3 percent of bitcoins in circulation.[41]

The government is the greatest impediment to the widespread adoption of Bitcoin. Thousands of years of monetary history show that issuers want *more* control over the money supply, not less. Only a few months after Ben Bernanke's letter, in March 2014, the IRS stipulated that, in terms of taxes, Bitcoin will be treated as property and not currency. According to Bloomberg, "Purchasing a $2 cup of coffee with bitcoins bought for $1 would trigger $1 in capital gains for the coffee drinker and $2 of gross income for the coffee shop."[42] Keeping track of the capital gains is inconvenient and an impediment to the adoption of Bitcoin. Dollars are fungible in that one

$10 note can be used in place of another. But the IRS limited the fungibility of Bitcoin because you have to consider the tax implications of using every bitcoin.

The point is that the United States is asserting its monetary power—curbing and controlling the use of Bitcoin. And so are other countries. At first, Chinese monetary officials tepidly supported the participation of its citizens in the Bitcoin marketplace.[43] BTC China was one of the largest Bitcoin exchanges in the world. However, in December 2013, the Chinese central bank cautioned payment processors not to use Bitcoin. It threatened to reprimand banks that were involved in Bitcoin transactions.[44] As a consequence, BTC China's Bitcoin trading volume declined 80 percent.[45] The failure of traditional monetary institutions would likely happen only during an emergency. Only then, during the bear case, could Bitcoin spread in an unimpeded manner. And even then, electricity and digital networks are needed for Bitcoin to flourish.

But all this discussion of Bitcoin as a *currency* misses the greater point of recognizing it as a *technology*. On a recent trip to San Francisco, I met with a friend who runs a company that trades Bitcoin. He put it to me simply: "Even if Bitcoin fails, it can be a success." He then geeked out on me: "Bitcoin isn't just a currency, it's a protocol," he stated. A protocol is a set of rules that guide how data should be exchanged among computers. For example, the "http" at the beginning of a website address stands for "hypertext transfer protocol," which lets your Web browser, for example, Google Chrome, talk to a Web server located in California.

Historically, digital currencies have been plagued by the double spending problem: Digital currencies can be easily duplicated, which leads to fraudulent transactions. The Bitcoin protocol, in the words of an economist at the Chicago Federal Reserve, is an "elegant solution" to this problem.[46] In short, the Bitcoin protocol enables a digital item, like money or a music file, or any item that can be represented digitally, to be *transferred*, not copied. Venture capitalist Marc Andreessen explains the significance of this:

> Bitcoin gives us, for the first time, a way for one Internet user to transfer a unique piece of digital property to another Internet user, such that the transfer is guaranteed to be safe and secure, everyone

knows that the transfer has taken place, and nobody can challenge the legitimacy of the transfer... What kinds of digital property might be transferred in this way? Think about digital signatures, digital contracts, digital kcys (to physical locks, or to online lockers), digital ownership of physical assets such as cars and houses, digital stocks and bonds... and digital money.[47]

He provides a thought experiment in which you own a car, and a key that opens it that is activated by your mobile phone. Let's say that you sell the car. Immediately the ownership of it is transferred to the person who bought it, and the key on your mobile phone no longer can open the car, as it has been updated to reflect the new owner.[48]

The way this verification process works is that all Bitcoin transactions are stored in an Internet-wide public ledger known as a blockchain, which, once edited, cannot be amended again. There's more to this technology, but, in essence, this decentralized network authenticates all Bitcoin transactions.[49] The implication is that you don't need a centralized party like a bank or brokerage to validate the legitimacy of whatever is being transferred.

Instead of diving deeper into the technology, let's look at the big picture—where Bitcoin and digital currencies fit in the evolution of money. It is worth recognizing how digital technology facilitates both hard and soft monetary systems. Lest we forget, the US dollar is also a digital currency that can be traded without being converted into physical form, although electronic transactions in dollars will be cleared through the banking system. But now modern metallists have something to cheer as Bitcoin's parameters prevent unlimited currency expansion—even if Bitcoin doesn't have intrinsic worth. Admittedly, the currency is still in its infancy, but metallists need not decry virtual currencies, even if they find themselves bizarrely aligned with "anarcho-technologists who distrust the government authority and believe in the power of distributed networks."[50]

Alternative digital currencies may be the future of money. But it's hard to see widespread adoption in a way that threatens the major fiat currencies, because the US government can decree what is or isn't considered legal tender within its borders, just like President Roosevelt did when he banned the hoarding and use of gold. It's more likely that Bitcoin will prevail *as a technology* that enables the transfer of anything of value such as deeds, titles, or even the movement of other currencies like dollars.

Even if the bear case was realized and global monetary institutions failed, another of the five ideas that I discussed may be adopted: a return to metal money, increased usage of cash, bartering, money as a public resource, and alternative currencies. Or it might be something else entirely.

The Bull Case

I don't like coffee. I much prefer tea: Darjeeling blended with Assam. That's why on my recent trip to San Francisco I initially resisted my friend's suggestion, more like a demand, that we visit Blue Bottle Coffee. We arrived at the café, located in Mint Plaza, and joined a scattered line of customers waiting to be served. The café has a trendy, bare aesthetic with vintage equipment, like a San Marco lever espresso maker. Customers sip their slow-dripped coffees while they read *TechCrunch* on their iPads and calmly debate recent trends in typography. One of the mustachioed baristas asked for our order.

"Two New Orleans iced coffees, please," requested my friend.

Mmmmm. The coffee was soft, chilled, and hit the spot on a temperate summer day. Further adding to my enjoyment (and convenience): Neither of us had to take out our wallets. My friend used Square, the digital payment system that lets small merchants accept credit card payments and enables customers to buy products by using their mobile devices. Sounds like something out of the future. But the future is already here. The technology is simple and revolutionary, something one of the company's founders, Jack Dorsey, a cofounder of Twitter, has a knack for. But it has also proven to be ephemeral, as Square has since shuttered its "Wallet" application, which enables people to pay using their mobile phones, due to lack of adoption.[51]

Nevertheless, convenience has proven to be an impetus of monetary innovation: from silver bullion, silver coins, silver-backed paper, to silver-colored phones. Square seemingly demonetized the transaction and removed the friction of cash and the experience of paying altogether. Not seeing money probably minimizes brain activity and the fear of spending (or losing) money. Indeed, some technology companies have gotten into trouble for making it too easy to buy items. Apple settled a class action lawsuit of up to $100 million brought against it by parents whose kids had racked up huge fees while playing games on iPads. For example, one girl bought $200 worth of virtual items without being asked for a password, since her parents' credit card information was on file.[52]

It's difficult to know whether Square, or one of its competitors like PayPal, Google, or Apple, will be the dominant mobile payment company in five or fifteen years. For example, in the early 2000s, there were hundreds of payment start-up companies, and arguably only PayPal has survived and reached mass consumer adoption. Nowadays, however, while the companies themselves may be in doubt, the technology they are leveraging is not likely to be. Square and its competitors are revolutionary because they turn the mobile phone, pervasive from Union Square to Tahrir Square, into a payment device, and expand the number of buyers and sellers in the global marketplace.

But before examining how mobile telephones are reshaping commerce, it's important to recognize the distinction among money, payment device, and payment network. My coffee was paid for *in* dollars (as the currency) *using* Square Wallet (as the mobile application) through the Visa credit card payment network.[53] To better understand the bull case, let's focus on the payment technologies that are crucial now and will also be integral to the future of money especially in the developing world: the credit card and the payment networks.

Looking to the future by revisiting the past is exactly the opposite approach taken by Edward Bellamy, author of the science-fiction book *Looking Backward: 2000–1887* published in 1887, the third-bestselling book of the nineteenth century, after *Ben-Hur* and *Uncle Tom's Cabin*. The plot concerns a man named Julian West, who falls asleep and wakes up more than one hundred years later in 2000. He encounters America as a socialist utopia in which people work fewer hours and retire at age forty-five. People use "credit cards," which are more like debit cards linked to someone else's bank account, to purchase items at a local store.[54] The cards draw upon a share of the government's wealth, which is distributed to each citizen. Money has become, as Mellor envisioned, a public good.

The creation of the credit card is a case of real life imitating fiction. It wasn't until the 1920s that cards were introduced by oil companies and hotel operators to facilitate customer transactions, but they couldn't be used elsewhere. In 1946, more widely accepted cards were introduced by Flatbush National Bank in Brooklyn, with its "Charge-It" card.[55] In 1950, a better-known card, the Diners Club card, was an outgrowth of an embarrassing experience of its creator, Frank McNamara, who didn't have enough cash to pay for dinner one night. In just two short years, there were twenty thousand cardholders. American Express and Bank of America followed suit by introducing cards in 1958. American Express garnered more than one million cardholders in its first five years. By introducing its card in California with its massive population, Bank of America obtained a sizable user base, and other banks joined their credit card network, which was later renamed Visa. In the late 1960s, the card that eventually became known as MasterCard was created by a group of banks to compete with Bank of America. The competitor card received a major lift when First National City Bank, later renamed Citibank, merged its card and joined MasterCard.[56]

Credit cards are convenient, widely used, and vital to the future of money in the bull case. Instead of carrying and counting cash, swiping a credit card (or entering its number for an online transaction) has proven incredibly expedient. In 2013, there were more than 160 million cardholders in the United States, with 1.1 billion cards, purchasing more than $3 trillion in volume, which translates to about 19 percent of GDP.[57] Visa alone processes nearly 50 billion transactions each year.[58] Purchasing volume jumps to $15 trillion when adding debit and prepaid card transactions.[59] The people have spoken and spent.

The prevalence of credit card usage can be explained by several factors. In short, people like the benefits of increased and immediate spending power, even if that means borrowing against their future income. Credit cards present every user a Faustian bargain, as millions have racked up high amounts of debt they were unable to pay off. Of course, it didn't start off this way. The credit card was one of the many instruments that democratized debt during the twentieth century. Policy makers crafted laws that helped low-income Americans access affordable housing loans, for example. The Equal Credit Opportunity Act of 1974 banned discriminatory lending practices, and the Community Reinvestment Act of 1977 directed banks to extend credit, in a prudent manner, to those in low-income areas.

In 1978 the Supreme Court ruled unanimously in *Marquette National Bank of Minneapolis v. First of Omaha Service Corp.* that state interest rate laws couldn't be applied to banks that were chartered in other states. The deregulation of interest rates helped to spread credit cards to people with lower incomes. The governor of South Dakota, Bill Janklow, realized that states could export their rates: "If South Dakota had a 25 percent ceiling, then you could charge 25 percent, even to a loan in Florida."[60] Losing money with their credit card businesses, many large banks opened divisions in South Dakota, and later Delaware, because these states had lifted or eliminated interest rate ceilings. In exchange, these states benefited from thousands of new jobs. Banks determined their own credit card interest rates and applied them across the country. Because they could charge higher rates and spread the risk, banks issued credit cards to lower-income individuals. The credit card business became very profitable, and issuers continue to spend billions in advertising to attract new customers.[61] Credit card companies have certainly engaged in unfair and harmful practices, charging sky-high rates and onerous fees. Nevertheless, the policy objective of democratizing debt helped to make this payment device, the credit card, ubiquitous in the United States.

But it's not available everywhere. While the United States is saturated with credit cards, penetration levels are low in other parts of the world, and still 85 percent of global retail transactions are conducted in cash.[62] For example, China, with a population of 1.3 billion, has only 67 million cards. The Chinese have high savings and have been reluctant to take on debts. That is likely because, according to the IMF, the Chinese government hasn't historically provided an ample social safety net for its citizens.[63] Economists have even found that high saving rates may be the result of households trying to make men appear more attractive in a skewed marriage market, with more males than females reaching adulthood. In one study, the savings of households with sons exceeded that of households with daughters in China. The researchers also found that the saving rate increased in regions that had a higher imbalance between men and women, in other words, a more competitive marriage market.[64] Credit card penetration levels are even low in more developed countries like Germany, which has a population of 82 million but only 10 million cards. Like the Chinese, Germans have been historically averse to debt. Even the German word for debt, *schuld*, translates to "guilt."[65] Credit card companies have taken notice and beefed up their international efforts. If a handful of developed countries reached penetration levels like those found in the United States, it would mean an estimated $2 trillion more in volume for Visa and MasterCard.[66] The future of money for hundreds of millions of people around the world is simply to use credit cards and their payment networks.

There are many economic reasons for governments and businesses to encourage credit card adoption. There are positive correlations among credit card penetration, growth, and exports. Moody's found that electronic transactions added almost $1 trillion in global growth across fifty-six countries from 2008 to 2012.[67] Scott Schmith of the US Department of Commerce contends that more credit card users means a larger consumer market. He found that consumer spending grows 0.5 percent when the share of credit card payments increases 10 percent. In 2008, he estimated that if China grew its credit card penetration from 20 percent to 22 percent, based on 2005 levels, that would generate $4.3 billion in new consumer spending.[68] Already, consumer spending in China and India is growing faster than in the United States, and developing countries are rapidly coming to represent a larger percentage of global consumption.[69] Credit cards also reduce costs. Economists found that electronic transactions cost 30 to 50 percent less than paper transactions (for example, there's less physical labor involved in an electronic transaction). They estimate that a country could save 1 percent of its annual GDP especially if its banks used credit and electronic payments instead of paper payments.[70]

But getting all vendors to accept credit card payments has proven difficult. In the United States there are more than 30 million merchants that don't accept credit cards, usually because of fees and the lag of a few days that it takes for the vendor to receive the money. Even those that accept cards may prefer cash to avoid fees, like taxi drivers in New York City who grunt disapprovingly when customers swipe their cards. Yet small merchants stand to benefit from accepting credit card payments because nearly 30 percent of consumers say that convenience is the most important attribute of a transaction, and 70 percent of consumers ages eighteen to thirty-four say they will shop only at stores that accept multiple types of payments.[71] Fortunately, convincing small merchants to accept cards is getting easier.[72]

In the bull case, the future of money will involve mobile phones and other mobile devices, like tablets, in developed and developing nations alike. That's because mobile phones have far greater penetration than credit cards. The International Telecommunication Union observes that there are almost as many mobile phone subscriptions, 6.8 billion, as there are folks in the world, 7.0 billion, with 128 percent penetration (many own more than one phone) in developed countries and 89 percent in developing nations.[73]

Recognizing the pervasiveness of mobile devices, entrepreneurs are building mobile payment systems to get a piece of the $900 billion in revenue that the payment industry generated in 2011, or even to grow this number substantially. Already research company Gartner has found that there are more than 140 million mobile payment users globally.[74] Though mobile payment volume is less than 5 percent of that which is physically swiped on cards, McKinsey estimates brisk growth rates ranging from 62 to more than 100 percent in the coming years.[75] The future for mobile payments is bright.

The growth of these systems won't initially come at the expense of the major credit card companies. Just as Facebook and Twitter rely on an existing network, the Internet, so, too, will mobile technologies like Square, PayPal, and Apple Pay depend on the established credit card (or debit card) payment networks administered by Visa, MasterCard, and American Express. Card networks route transactions between banks and help with authorization and settlements. Merchants, even those who don't accept cards, rarely complain about the reliability, effectiveness, and security of payment networks. To replace a credit card network means building a new network and convincing customers to provide sensitive personal information and bank account details—a tall order.

Instead, new mobile systems will likely facilitate and improve the point of transaction, when the customer buys the product. To better understand the mobile payment space, it's helpful to divide the technologies among three groups: (1) mobile readers; (2) mobile wallets; and (3) mobile commerce.[76]

Mobile readers enable mobile devices to accept credit cards. Every day for lunch in New York, several food trucks line up outside my office. While they offer a range of delectable foods, from spicy burritos to tangy meatballs, I rarely frequent them because they don't accept credit cards, and I seldom have cash. In contrast, whenever I'm in Austin, Texas, a town that is known for its tech savviness, I order lunch from one of many food trucks because they accept credit cards, using a card reader that plugs into any mobile device. The food is tasty and the payment process is painless.

Like Diners Club founder Frank McNamara, who was annoyed by not having enough cash, Square cofounder Jim McKelvey's frustration was the genesis of the Square reader. A software engineer and glassblower, he lost a $2,500 order for a handblown glass faucet because he was unable to accept credit cards. He turned his disappointment into a company that adds 100,000 merchants per month and completes $15 billion in purchase volume annually.[77] Millions of merchants use Square because of its simplicity, transparent pricing, and quick settlement times.[78] While Square is the most widely used reader, PayPal's Here and Intuit's GoPayment have also made inroads into this market.

Mobile wallets allow customers to use their phone like a payment device. At Blue Bottle Coffee, my friend used the now-defunct Square Wallet to buy our coffees.[79] When my friend walked into the coffee shop, the barista's Square terminal detected my friend's mobile phone and a picture of him appeared on the register screen. The barista identified my friend based on his picture, confirmed the transaction, billed his credit card, and emailed him the receipt. However, this method of identification is non-anonymous and isn't as ubiquitous as other technologies, like waving your phone next to a merchant's payment reader. That technology is known as near-field communication (NFC), and it's used by Google Wallet. Another type of payment system is text message–based and is widely used in Europe and developing nations. Each mobile wallet is different, but they all replace the need to carry a bunch of cards, and they all rely on the payment networks.

Already the competition is fierce. Apple Pay leverages NFC technology and Apple's enormous customer base with its Passbook application for iPhones, which stores coupons, gift cards, and credit card details. PayPal's mobile wallet enables users to order ahead, skip the line, and pick up goods in person from retailers like Radio Shack and Foot Locker.[80] Starbucks' mobile application also helps users to order ahead their Americanos and Macchiatos.[81] Even the major credit card companies Visa and MasterCard are leveraging their trusted brands with the creation of their own mobile wallets, V.me and PayPass. Many merchants and banks already count on these credit card companies for their networks and other services. Competition is global as companies in countries with low Internet penetration are building their own mobile payment systems. In Japan, already 20 million people use mobile wallets. Japanese company NTT DoCoMo has partnered with MasterCard to make its mobile wallet technology available in more than forty countries.[82] Whichever mobile wallet becomes the industry standard, consumers and merchants stand to win because mobile wallets shave seconds from transaction times, which means shorter lines, increased worker productivity, and potentially more customers. But most of these companies are discovering that consumer behavior is difficult to shift. For example, many folks still swipe their credit cards, even though their mobile phones have NFC chips that enable them to wave their devices and "tap and pay." But maybe because of the prevalence of the iPhone, Apple Pay will change consumer behavior.

Mobile commerce encompasses a broad range of transactions that happen on a mobile device, from mobile banking to mobile shopping. Though mobile commerce accounts for only about 10 percent of all e-commerce sales, US consumers spend more time shopping (but not yet buying) on their mobile devices than on desktop computers. The gap between time spent and sales is due to the fact that consumers use their mobile phones to locate stores, research products, and find deals. Mobile sales among top merchants are growing quickly, more than 60 percent, to $34.2 billion in 2013.[83] Leading online retailers like Wal-Mart, Target, and Amazon have optimized their mobile websites, streamlining the payment process for the surge of mobile users.

Most exciting is how mobile commerce and payments are positively impacting citizens in developing nations. The *Economist* observes that "paying for a taxi ride using your mobile phone is easier in Nairobi than it is in New York."[84] Kenya has M-Pesa, a mobile payment transfer system started by Safaricom. People deposit and collect money at Safaricom outlets found at shops or gas stations, and their M-Pesa accounts are updated. More than 60 percent of adults in Kenya, 17 million people, use the system.

People transfer money to friends, family members, and vendors using SMS messages. That a developing nation has leapfrogged developed ones, in terms of mobile payments, shows that lasting and meaningful monetary innovation doesn't require the most sophisticated technology but needs only to make easier the most basic of transactions—like paying for a taxi.

"I don't need to go to the bank when I have the bank in my phone," says a Kenyan businessman who runs a transportation company.[85] Rather than trekking to a bank that might be many miles away, he can instantly pay his employees with a tap on his phone.

In the bull case, money disappears, and everyone, from Nairobi to New York, is connected in the global marketplace. Thanks to technologies like M-Pesa, PayPal, Apple Pay, and Square, which transform mobile devices into payment systems, money will become increasingly digital, intangible, and invisible. People can exchange money without touching or seeing it. Money becomes more abstract from its evolutionary purpose of helping us procure resources to survive. In so doing, the transaction seems more pure, like a familial exchange without the formality of a monetary instrument found in the marketplace. The mobile phone can remove the friction of payments and optimize cooperation. It encourages faster transactions and more exchanges, and helps grow a larger, global consumer base.

New payment systems will lead to new goods and services. Just as coins altered the agora in ancient Greece, turning more people into buyers and sellers, new mobile payment systems will transform the agora of the future.

However, there are some impediments and risks in the bull scenario. Before a mobile payment technology can be adopted universally, it helps if there is standardization. Right now, various mobile wallets are being used in the United States. It may be easy to access whatever emerges as an industry standard, since one can simply download that app. Yet a new industry standard mobile reader or wallet may require one to buy a new mobile device with a special chip or technology. What's more, there is also the risk that governments and banks will try to block these technologies if they see them as a threat to their interests.

Most worrying are the security implications. Mobile security company Lookout analyzed data from 50 million customers and found that chargeware, adware, and malware were significant threats. Chargeware is an application that charges customers who haven't given consent, a mobile pickpocket. In 2011, for example, GGTracker, a chargeware app, signed up people for fake services and made fraudulent charges. Lookout calculates a 0.22 percent probability that a user in the United States will encounter a chargeware app during a one-week period. There is a 1.6 percent probability of experiencing adware—obtrusive and unexpected ads.[86] These threats are only growing in terms of frequency and potential impact. Also of concern are malware apps that collect a victim's personal information. In one study, 56 percent of US consumers were concerned about identity theft when using mobile payments.[87] The bull case presents great promise, but it also affords new ways for criminals to take financial advantage of others.

The Dream Case

Now for some fun. It's time to dream about money. No, not what life would be like with more of it, but what money will look like many years, say hundreds of years, from now. To spark the imagination, consider how money is depicted in science fiction. There's no better place to start than . . .

A long time ago, in a galaxy far, far away. In *Star Wars*, a currency known as the "Galactic Credit Standard" or "credit" functioned as money.[88] According to Wookieepedia, a website devoted to all things *Star Wars*, credit was created on Sojourn, a moon on which the InterGalactic Business Clan (IGBC) vacationed. The IGBC was a business group of bankers and lawyers that controlled many assets—yes, even in this distant galaxy, bankers were integral to the monetary system. Credits came in bills, coins, and chips. They were backed by copious minerals found on Muunilinst, also known as "Moneylend," a planet that was the headquarters of the IGBC.[89]

Different galaxy, same problems. In *Star Wars*, there was monetary confusion and competition. Despite being backed by metals, credits were refused by planets during periods of uncertainty, such as the Clone Wars. The credit was later known as the "Imperial Credit" and was used by Luke Skywalker to pay Han Solo for transport to the planet Alderaan. Yet smugglers avoided using state-sanctioned money and opted for precious metals like platinum. Those in the Ferengi Alliance traded gold-pressed latinum, a material that could not be reproduced.[90]

Even though *Star Wars* is set in a galaxy "a long time ago," the idea of a "space currency" is futuristic, and it may be achieved sooner than you think. Virgin Galactic is booking space tourists for its commercial space journeys, and a Russian company is planning on launching a space hotel in the coming years.[91] Keen to be part of the conversation, PayPal and the Search for Extraterrestrial Intelligence (SETI) Institute have launched PayPal Galactic—an initiative to create a space currency. It's mostly an effort to spark dialogue regarding how commerce will happen in space. Perhaps yen or dollars could be put into orbit pods so that space tourists could withdraw money. But a researcher from the University of Leicester says that money we use on earth wouldn't work in space. Cosmic radiation would damage the magnetic strips on credit cards, and coins or anything sharp would be a risk to the safety of space tourists. Instead, scientists at the United Kingdom's National Space Centre and other researchers have proposed and built prototypes of "Quasi Universal Intergalactic Denomination," or "Quid," to function as a space currency. Quids are spherical in shape, made from polymers, and won't cut anything while they float in space.[92]

These proposals may be hype, but space writer Brian Dodson raises a real concern: time. On earth, we are used to quick transactions that are facilitated by a global communications network. In space, there would be a delay in transactions because the distances are far greater. For example, it took six years for the orbiter Galileo to reach Jupiter. Transmission also takes significant time: It would take too long for information to be relayed to earth for each transaction, and such a delay could even be exploited by criminals. A distributed "peer-to-peer" network might have to be built throughout the galaxy, and it's unclear who would pay for this.[93]

In 1978, Paul Krugman, who besides being an economist and *New York Times* columnist is also a science-fiction lover, published "The Theory of Interstellar Trade," which highlights the same problem. He realized that the theory of relativity would be in effect, as time would be experienced differently by those on different planets and those transporting goods between the planets. Because the time and distance would be great, any space trade would require a heavy amount of investment.[94] The *Economist* summarizes his two theorems of space trade:

1. Interest costs on travelling goods should be calculated using clocks on planets, not ships. This is because the opportunity cost of trade . . . is calculated using planet-bound clocks, regardless of what relativity does to a businessman travelling alongside his cargo.
2. Though long travel times mean prices on trading planets will never reach parity, interest rates will. If they differed, then investors could buy bonds on the more attractive planet, driving its rates back to parity with those on its trading partner.[95]

Coming down to earth, in New York City I once arrived at a restaurant and learned that they had flubbed my reservation. I had started to text my friend that he could take his time, when the host looked at me aghast: "Sir, please don't write a bad review on Yelp. I will seat you right away," he said. The restaurateur realized that one bad review could turn away hundreds of potential customers. He knew that reputation drives business. It is a type of currency.

Strategists at companies like American Airlines are trying to leverage our digital interconnectedness to burnish their corporate reputation. The company encourages and rewards customers with large social media followings—in hopes for some positive buzz in return. It occasionally permits those with a high Klout score into the first-class airport lounge.[96] Klout is an application that measures a user's social media influence and assigns a score of 1 to 100. It factors in several social media indicators, for example, the number of Twitter retweets and Facebook likes that you generate. The higher your reputation, the more you profit. This isn't a dream world. This is our world.

Science-fiction writer Cory Doctorow takes a reputation-based currency further in his *Down and Out in the Magic Kingdom*. He imagines a twenty-second-century world in which "Whuffie" is the prevailing currency. A person gains or losses Whuffie by doing something that positively or negatively impacts their reputation. Each person has a brain chip that makes them a node in the greater human network, so everyone knows each other's Whuffie balance. While implanting brain chips seems like a drastic step, it may be a sign of what's to come.

In a dream case, it isn't just reputation that could function as a currency but thoughts, emotions, experiences, dreams, ideas—any mental content. Remember that brain scans show that money elicits neural activity in many regions of the brain, such as the nucleus accumbens and insula. As long as future forms of currency activate these regions in a similar manner, we will likely continue to perceive it as a symbol of value. As technology advances, from credit cards to mobile payment systems, money becomes increasingly invisible and abstract. One day, maybe man and machine will merge, as to eliminate the "middleman" of physical money altogether, turning neural activity into a currency itself. Surely, if we can embed pacemakers, we could implant payment systems into the body. Instead of a mobile wallet, we may have neural wallets.

Whether made possible by brain chips, as in Doctorow's book, or by a linked cloud of all our brains that stores mental content, people could exchange, trade, buy, and sell almost any neural activity—and it could all be authenticated by a decentralized Bitcoin-type protocol. If you were traveling to Paris and wanted to learn French, you could "buy" the knowledge of French from your friend by "selling" her your experience as an Olympic archer. If you wanted a frightening Halloween, you could "buy" the nightmare of a friend; or you could "sell" something she desires, like the memory of a romantic walk on a beach for Valentine's Day. Maybe instead of trading these memories with others, vendors could create and sell custom experiences that they insert into your mind as memories, like when you kicked the winning goal of the World Cup. This type of currency could radically change how we deal with one another and how we think about our self-identity.

The neural wallet may even facilitate energy transfers. We could all be "plugged" into a shared grid of energy. If you were hungry, you could buy calories from someone else in exchange for your surplus vitamin D, and your body could be instantly infused with energy. This bears resemblance to the energy currency of the natural world, discussed in the first chapter. When a plant absorbs sunlight or a monkey eats a banana, there is a transfer of energy. Similarly, in this dream case, "money" may simply be what we call neural, chemical, and biological transfers that we've always valued and desired—a symbol of value. Exchange would be more "direct," triggering the same receptors in the nervous system as things we value like money or food. The more money changes, the more it stays the same.

Obviously, a neural wallet raises concerns, ranging from hacking into someone's mind, like in the movie *Inception*, to losing one's identity. The dream case, without the right safeguards, could devolve into a dystopian nightmare. That's what happens in the film *In Time*, in which time becomes the dominant currency. Everyone is born with a digital clock on their arm. After they reach twenty-five, the clock counts down to zero, at which point the person dies. Folks can use their time to pay for daily living expenses like a bus fare or trade it with other people. The rich people hoard their time at the expense of the poor. The richer you are, the longer you live.

While brain chips and arm clocks seem like they are decades if not centuries away, Ray Kurzweil, an expert in artificial intelligence, believes the blurring of man and machine is already under way: "But when it comes to actually putting computers in your body and brain, nobody protests. We seem to relish merging with machines. We use them all the time. We created this technology to overcome our limitations."[97] When it comes to money, Kurzweil recognizes its universality: "So even though we may radically disagree on some things—like let's say the US government and Al Qaeda—they both respect money. So it's remarkable how we have this universal respect for this very esoteric virtual construct."[98] Because everyone uses and respects it, a drastic change to money is sure to have profound effects on humanity. As much as we try to alter money, it may end up shaping us.

You May Say I'm a Dreamer

Besides being an amusing thought experiment, imagining the future of money may have real economic consequences. For example, researchers studied why people don't save enough money for retirement, and found a unique solution to the problem. Many "discount" the future, opting for short- versus long-term gains. With life expectancy among Americans increasing, many are in for a rude awakening and will have to adjust to a lower standard of living in retirement. Researchers discovered a way to prevent such severe discounting—by helping people imagine their future. Using virtual reality, subjects dealt with realistic renderings of themselves in which they appeared many years older. Subjects encountered their future vulnerability: gray hair, wrinkles, and other signs of aging. When asked to allocate $1,000, subjects who interacted with their aged avatar placed twice as much money into savings as those who hadn't dealt with their aged avatar. In fact, researchers found that in several studies, when people see a future version of themselves, it impacts their behavior, and they don't discount the future as much as they once did.[99]

Imagination leads to implementation. Even if it's just a short-term effect, saving an incremental ten dollars by cooking at home is a positive outcome for the eventual retiree. These findings leave one wondering whether virtual simulations can be incorporated into financial literacy educational programs to promote saving for retirement.

There's been no shortage of imagination when it comes to money throughout history. From iron spits and grains to silver coins and paper notes, money is always evolving yet remaining a symbol of value throughout. Whether it's a bear, bull, dream, or another case, money will reflect our ever-changing needs and desires.

In thinking about the future of money, my friend suggested that something might be invented to make us "better" with it: spendthrifts more responsible and misers more charitable. But we don't have to wait for new technologies to induce these modifications in behavior. While the instrument of money is continually changing, the way in which we use it may remain constant—as long as we remember that money can be a symbol of our values.

PART III

SOUL

A Symbol of Values

CHAPTER SEVEN

Angel Investors

Religion and money

For the love of money is a root of all sorts of evil, and some by longing for it have wandered away from the faith, and pierced themselves with many a pang.
—*1 Timothy 6:10*[1]

Ben Zoma said...Who is rich? One who is happy with what one has, as it says: "When you eat what your hands have provided, you shall be happy and good will be yours" (Ps 128:2).
—*Mishnah,* Pirke Avot[2]

O Bhagavati—who resides amidst lotuses, holds the lotus bloom in her hands, wears white resplendent garments, adorned with fragrant garlands, [Lakshmi], pleasing to the mind, and blessing the three worlds with plenty—shower your benefaction to me.
—Kanakadhara Stotram, *verse 15*[3]

Lakshmi, the Hindu goddess of wealth and auspiciousness.

I had never met a leper before. But here I was surrounded by several of them at Nirmal Hriday, or "Home of the Pure Heart." It's also known as Mother Teresa's Home for the Dying & Destitute in Kolkata, India. Established in 1952, it is a small hospice for thousands of poor people who are found languishing in the streets. Someone dies there almost every day.

I arrived on an overcast autumn evening. The sick men and women had been gathered into separate areas for supper. The men were dressed in teal shirts, pants, and short-sleeved black sweaters. They were seated close to each other on benches. Near me was a man without legs, quivering on the ground while yellow foam formed underneath his lips. His eyes were fixed in a thousand-yard stare. Another man in a wheelchair began to cough violently, spitting bits of *idli sambar*, rice cakes and vegetable stew, onto the floor. One of the eight volunteers rushed to remove the food from his mouth so he wouldn't choke. He put his finger in the man's mouth, only to have it bitten.

Seated among the sick was an eighteen-year-old volunteer from Toulouse, France. With a brown mop top, he looked like a young Mick Jagger. Hailing from a middle-class background, he recently finished high school, read about Nirmal Hriday on the Internet, booked a one-way ticket to Kolkata, and committed to be a volunteer at the hospice.

He swung his arm over the shoulder of an old man who was suffering from an enormous stomach tumor, as if they were old buddies.

"Time to eat," he said in French to the man, who probably only spoke Bengali but smiled anyway. Kindness is a common language.

The presence of this vibrant young adult in a room full of old, frail men was curious to me. He was so different not only from them, but also from me. When I was his age, I was burnishing my college application so that I could attend a first-class university. Admission to a good school can mean an opportunity to land a great job. And now that I had a proverbial great job on Wall Street, I continued working at a frenetic pace in order to accumulate more money, which would supposedly take me to higher ground.

This young man wasn't thinking about any of this. He was unsure when or whether he would attend college at all. It led me to ask: What leads a healthy young man to live among the old and sick, to forgo riches for rags?

"I do as my religion teaches," he explained. He was raised as a Catholic and his parents regularly read to him the Gospels when he was a child. He then said something I'll always remember, a paradoxical yet universal insight: "Though everybody here is poor, they are rich in spirit." His response made me consider another question that has stayed with me: How is it that those who had nothing—at the edge of death—were nevertheless at peace?

Since its creation, money hasn't been just a measure of wealth; at times it's been a symbol of our values and a test of our morality. How one handles money has many implications beyond saving and spending, and can demonstrate whether someone honors the moral code of a society: A rich woman who never donates to those in need is judged as stingy, and a poor woman who gives what she can is considered generous. It seems as if the poor person is acting in the "right," or at least, in a more humane manner. The way in which one uses money may build or destroy one's reputation and standing in a community, and it certainly demonstrates one's character. Because money is an expression of value, it matters *how* it's expressed.

The manner in which money is expressed depends on one's motivations. Consider a simple, clarifying way in which to think about our intentions. In the first case, someone wants more money. This view is predicated on the economic logic that *more is better*. In the second case, someone doesn't strive for more money, because they have detached from it in search of something else. This view is based on the spiritual logic that *less is more* or *enough is enough*, because they are embracing the paradoxical premise that renouncing material wealth will yield spiritual growth and contentment.

Using economic logic, we desire more money because it helps us obtain the resources necessary to survive. Up until this point, this entire book has been predicated on the logic that *more is better*. Whether it's our evolutionary algorithm or our reward circuitry in the brain, we are constantly in search of more money, which has come to symbolize attributes like success, status, and privilege. It follows that financial success has become an almost universal goal, and many work diligently in pursuit of this end. A

Pew Research Center poll finds that 77 percent of Americans believe that hard work leads to success.[4]

But wanting more money and status is about "external success," which shapes and defines many who are engulfed in the competitive "rat race" culture. Yet the pursuit of external success doesn't always engender personal contentment.[5] Gallup measured the job satisfaction of 25 million people across almost two hundred countries and found that only 13 percent were "engaged" or "emotionally invested" in their job. They found twice as many "disengaged" workers, who exhibited negative or harmful feelings, as they did engaged workers.[6] The obsession of making money can have deleterious consequences. In Japan, they even have a word for someone who dies from too much work: *karōshi*.

When external success becomes a singular focus, one may begin to evaluate everything with economic logic—the more, the better, even the *right*. Gallup found that those who believe hard work leads to financial success are more supportive of capitalism. Though support among Americans for free markets dropped from 80 percent to 59 percent in 2010 after the financial crisis, trusting the market has been a mainstay of mainstream US economic thought.[7] Alan Greenspan and many leading economists long believed that the market is inherently right and self-correcting. The belief that the market is "right" even pervades American literature. In a study conducted by the Library of Congress, Ayn Rand's *Atlas Shrugged* was described as "the most influential book on American lives after the Bible."[8] The book supports libertarian views, notes the supremacy of the free market, and maintains that business and markets should be deregulated. Financial writer Justin Fox traces the belief that the market is "right" to the Middle Ages:

> Hints of the same attitude could be found in the work of early economists like Adam Smith—and even religious thinkers of the Middle Ages. While some medieval scholars argued that lawgivers should set a "just price" for every good...St. Thomas Aquinas among them, held that the just price was set by the market.[9]

The first person to reference the invisible hand wasn't Adam Smith; it was John Calvin, notes Columbia University humanities professor Mark C.

Taylor.[10] Calvin believed that God's hand brought order to an otherwise chaotic world. By using this terminology, Smith changed the "source of order" from "God, to internal relations among individual human actors. From this point of view, the market is a self-organizing system that regulates itself," writes Taylor.[11]

However, when market values reign supreme, the line between "right" and "wrong" can be blurred. The profitable can be confused for the "right." These days almost everything has a price. You can pay someone to write your entire doctoral dissertation. You can even pay someone for their virginity. In one public incident, a Brazilian woman auctioned her virginity for $780,000 to a Japanese man. But is it right? She explained it away: "If you only do it once in your life then you are not a prostitute."[12] The deal fell through, and she tried to auction it again. Even Judas sells the sacred and betrays Jesus for thirty silver coins, demonstrating that even the messiah's life had a price.

Harvard professor Michael Sandel writes that when everything is for sale, anything can be bought and subject to corruption.[13] Putting a price on what was once priceless degrades it. These outrageous acts introduce a market norm into a previously nonmarket arena, similar to the example in chapter 3 in which a Mesopotamian man couldn't sell his wife unless he was settling a debt.

Ironically, yearning for more external success can leave one with less time, satisfaction, and serenity. The economic logic can yield suboptimal results. This prompts the question, is there another way? Invoking the spiritual logic of *less is more* may yield superior results. If money symbolizes strength and power, then the lack of it represents the opposite: weakness and impotence. Why would someone *want* these things? Indeed, the spiritual logic is counterintuitive, yet it is the means to a different end, not financial treasure, but heavenly riches. It's in experiencing vulnerability that one creates the space and need for faith. If money is a sign of external success, then the detachment from it is about attaining inner peace—where the shadow of money ends and the sunlight of God shines.

When it comes to money, many religious leaders champion the spiritual logic of *less is more* and the paradoxical wisdom that detachment from material treasures can yield spiritual riches. During different periods, as civilization and markets developed, various religious leaders, like Laozi, Buddha, Jesus, and Muhammad, embraced this paradoxical wisdom. They steered their followers away from coveting material things like money and toward a more ascetic path. These religious leaders sought to enlighten man regarding the outsized power of money. They warned their followers about being enveloped by greed. Considered a deity among some Taoists, Laozi once cautioned that "he who is attached to things will suffer much."[14] That so many religious leaders admonished the worship of money and advocated this paradoxical wisdom deserves further attention.

Anthropologist David Graeber points out that influential religious leaders like Pythagoras, Buddha, and Confucius all lived during the sixth century BC in areas where coinage was invented—Greece, India, and China.[15] He suggests that it's not a coincidence that from 800 BC to AD 600 both money and several lasting religions were created. It's plausible that some organized religions spread as a response to the rising importance of the marketplace. Many of Jesus's earliest followers, for example, were poor and receptive to his paradoxical, liberating wisdom regarding material wealth.

Here we explore the paradoxical wisdom embodied by the teenager I met in the hospice, but through the lens of the three Abrahamic religions and Hinduism. There are countless interpretations of religious texts from these faiths regarding money. But one can surely make a case that elements of this spiritual logic can be found in each.

No Two Masters

As Jesus traveled through Galilee, he taught and healed the sick. He reserved his most famous teaching for when he came upon a throng of followers and delivered the "Sermon on the Mount," a meditation on *how* to live. Most biblical scholars consider it to be a template for life as a Christian. It's a comprehensive instruction, as Jesus spoke about a range of topics from adultery and divorce to fasting and prayer.

When it comes to money, Jesus's paradoxical wisdom shines through when he says, "Do not store up for yourselves treasures on earth ... But store up for yourselves treasures in heaven."[16] He points out that earthly treasures erode and can lose their value, and are meaningless in the afterlife. What's the point of being the richest man in a cemetery? Most important, your treasure reveals your priorities, allegiances, and values. Jesus says as much: "For where your treasure is, there your heart will be also."[17] He summarizes his views on money with lucidity: "No one can serve two masters. Either you will hate the one and love the other, or you will be devoted to the one and despise the other. You cannot serve both God and money."[18] His instruction is clear: Reject the pursuit of money; treasure and cherish God.

Jesus doesn't qualify his instruction. In the Gospel of Matthew, Jesus urges his followers to detach from money entirely—to *renounce* it. A rich man asks Jesus about achieving the heavenly treasure of eternal life. At first, Jesus advises the man to follow the commandments, yet the rich man insists that he has. Jesus ups the ante and urges the man to embrace the paradoxical wisdom of *less is more* or even *nothing is everything* by advising him to "sell your possessions and give to the poor, and you will have treasure in heaven."[19] Upon hearing this, the rich man grows sad because it wasn't the answer for which he had hoped.

Turning to his disciples, Jesus emphasizes his point: "Truly I tell you, it is hard for someone who is rich to enter the kingdom of heaven. Again I tell you, it is easier for a camel to go through the eye of a needle than for someone who is rich to enter the kingdom of God."[20]

Jesus's remarks undoubtedly surprised the disciples, since the threshold to achieve heavenly treasure is high—*to forgo completely earthly riches*.[21] Because the disciples had given up their earthly treasures and filled their hearts with God's message, Jesus promises that they will sit "on twelve thrones" and "receive a hundred times as much and will inherit eternal life."[22]

There must also be a place in heaven for a certain teenager from Toulouse. By giving up his material well-being and serving lepers, he took to heart the words of Jesus in the Sermon on the Mount: "Blessed are the poor in spirit, for theirs is the kingdom of heaven."[23] To be *poor in spirit* means that one humbly realizes the need for God, the treasure above all others. This young man subscribed to the spiritual logic that *less is more*, and that *nothing is everything*. He believed in the paradoxical wisdom of detaching from earthly treasure in order to receive heavenly riches.

But many find the ethical standard for Christians to be unattainable—the renunciation of material items and external success. We desire more money, status, and material success through the economic reasoning of *more is better.* In some cases, we even pray for more money. Christian author Bruce Wilkinson wrote a bestselling and controversial book, *The Prayer of Jabez,* which made famous two sentences in 1 Chronicles:

> Jabez cried out to the God of Israel, "Oh, that you would bless me and enlarge my territory! Let your hand be with me, and keep me from harm so that I will be free from pain." And God granted his request.[24]

This prayer suggests that it's okay to ask God for material goods. Wilkinson explains one application of the prayer: "I think God doesn't want you praying for a pink Cadillac, but he may not say no if you say, 'I need a new car.' "[25] Putting the prayer in historical context, Chronicles was written after the Jews had returned from exile to the last remaining province of Israel. Professor Alan Cooper of the Union Theological Seminary says that the prayer makes sense considering the times, as Jews wanted to expand their territories.[26]

Jabez's prayer has served as one of the bases of the "prosperity gospel," which teaches that Christians are rewarded with economic prosperity because of their faith in God. The prosperity gospel is controversial because of the messengers and the message. Many televangelists, some of whom have been implicated in financial scandals, have trumpeted it. The prosperity gospel also runs counter to the teachings of Jesus, who was crystal clear in his call to renounce material wealth.

Jabez's prayer seems to sanction greed, which, according to the scriptures, is a sin. Paul says that those who practice "jealousy...selfish ambition... envy...will not inherit the kingdom of God."[27] Rev. Daniel Gard, a dean at Concordia Theological Seminary, takes issue with Wilkinson's book, saying, "American culture is very oriented toward paychecks and big houses. This basically [let's you] feel good as a religious person and at the same time go after all the stuff in the world."[28] This prayer, this instance of greed, is easy to spot. But the economic logic of wanting more money can also blind us from recognizing greed in ourselves. The blinding nature of greed is a topic that Jesus returns to frequently during his meditations. In the middle of his commentary on money in the Sermon on the Mount, he summons this subject:

> The eye is the lamp of the body. If your eyes are healthy, your whole body will be full of light. But if your eyes are unhealthy, your whole body will be full of darkness. If then the light within you is darkness, how great is that darkness![29]

Jesus is warning about the blinding nature of greed, according to Pastor Timothy Keller of the Redeemer Presbyterian Church in New York City. Jesus is saying that if you value the right things, and your eyes are working and healthy, you won't stumble. But if your eye isn't working, and you treasure the wrong things, you will "darken" your entire body. It's vital that one's eye takes in light and works because greed is a sin that's difficult to spot.

Pastor Keller remembers when he was giving monthly talks on each of the seven deadly sins, such as lust and pride. His wife predicted that his talk on greed would attract a smaller audience. Sure enough, she was right. He concluded that many in the audience thought that greed simply did not apply to them: They couldn't see their own greed. In his many years of advising church members, he can't remember a time in which someone confessed the sin of being too greedy or materialistic.[30] That's because, as Jesus indicates, greed has the power to blind us.

When most people think of greed, they envision someone who is wealthier than them. I think of a private equity billionaire I once met who drives a Bentley Continental and owns a Gulfstream V plane. In contrast, I'm a guy in the lower rungs of an investment bank who works hard and saves money for retirement. But it's all relative. Some friends of mine who don't earn as much may think of me as greedy or too showy with money.

We infrequently compare ourselves to those who have less. We rarely face the man in the mirror and recognize our own greed and materialism for what it is. In her book *The Overspent American*, Juliet Schor writes that "the comparisons we make are no longer restricted to those in our own general earnings category, or even to those one rung above us on the ladder. Today a person is more likely to be making comparisons with, or choose as a 'reference group,' people whose incomes are three, four, or five times his or her own."[31] As a result, she discovers that many Americans are dissatisfied with their status and financial well-being. The Internet has exacerbated these comparisons. In a study of six hundred Facebook users, almost one-third reported feeling envy because of making upward social comparisons.[32] What the researchers call "rampant envy" exposes what can result with economic logic. If we are always comparing ourselves to those with more and chasing external success, is there room for an inner life or any peace?

What is equally troubling is that greed can prevent us from recognizing "right" from "wrong." Greed can blind us from the problems around us. One of my acquaintances worked at a hedge fund that was accused of insider trading. He told me that he wasn't personally involved in the alleged crime and frankly didn't want to know what happened or who was involved. He preferred to turn a blind eye to the suspected crimes in his midst. He's not alone. When a company engages in improper or illegal activities, an employee who asks unwelcome questions may be committing career suicide. Instead, the employee closes his eye, which darkens the body. In other words, it pays to remain silent, but at a terrible spiritual cost from the Christian perspective.

Many of us subscribe to the blinding economic logic of *more is better*, and we live in a world in which external success is celebrated widely, but money and greed can still be uncomfortable and unwelcome topics. Jesus didn't shy away from talking about them. Brigham Young University finds that eight of ten parables in Matthew and nine of twelve parables in Luke reference money in some manner.[33] Some of these parables are well-known, like the Prodigal Son, the Good Samaritan, and the Sower.

In the parable of the Sower, Jesus returns to the theme of blinding greed. He describes a man who scatters seeds in various places. Seeds are strewn in fertile areas, rocky regions, and among the thorns. Seeds in fertile areas yield an abundant harvest, as much as a hundred times over. Seeds in the rocky regions grow quickly but don't have deep roots. Seeds in the thorns don't flourish.

Jesus interprets the story for his disciples. The seed is "the word of

God," or message of Jesus.[34] The identity of the sower is unclear, but one can infer that it's Jesus who spreads the word of God. In another parable, Jesus refers to the sower as the "Son of Man," a term he uses to describe himself.[35] Each seed has a different outcome, which depends on the conditions. Because Jesus speaks of his message being "sown in their heart," the soil likely represents the heart. In the case of the fertile soil, the heart treasures the message, which yields heavenly fruit. In the case of the soil in the rocky regions, the heart welcomes the message, but the person lacks commitment and vanishes at the first sign of persecution. Regarding the seed that is thrown in the thorny areas, Jesus says that it represents "someone who hears the word, but the worries of this life and the deceitfulness of wealth choke the word, making it unfruitful."[36]

Jesus is again warning of greed's blinding nature. The worries of the world, such as money, status, and reputation, make blind the eye to the word of God. They darken the body to the message of Jesus so that it cannot be let in. The message is that a mind or heart caught up with earthly treasures is empty of heavenly ones. Money has the power to deceive one from the true path of eternal life and impair recognition of the paradoxical wisdom that renouncing money leads to spiritual wealth.

This paradoxical wisdom is difficult to accept. Yet Jesus doesn't advocate the easy path; he urges the righteous one. To buck the buck and renounce money would be a significant change to life as most of us know it. Detaching from money even seems unnatural and anachronistic, guidance that may have been easier to implement in earlier, less complicated times. Yet human greed stands the test of time. In one of his first apostolic exhortations in late 2013, Pope Francis took aim at the idolatry of money found in modern society:

> We have created new idols...The worship of the ancient golden calf...has returned in a new and ruthless guise in the idolatry of money and the dictatorship of an impersonal economy lacking a truly human purpose.[37]

He reasons that it's greed that leads to an "economy of exclusion" in which the poor suffer. The pope is aghast that many focus more on the daily fluctuations of the stock market than on the plight of the poor. The pope makes the same prevailing point as Jesus, who asks a piercing and paradoxical question that shakes the foundation of a society in which market values reign supreme:

> For whosoever will save his life shall lose it; but whosoever shall lose his life for my sake and the gospel's, the same shall save it. For what shall it profit a man, if he shall gain the whole world, and lose his own soul?[38]

In order to retain one's own soul, Jesus says, we must subscribe to the spiritual logic of *less is more* and *nothing is everything*. For the promise of this paradoxical wisdom is great—heavenly treasure. Though it seems counterintuitive, in the end we must have faith.

I was impressed with the scale of the operation at the Kolkata hospice: copious staff, food, and medicine. All of these things require money, so I asked one of the sisters how they raise funds.

"Providence," she replied, beaming. I must have looked incredulous, so she further explained, "God's will. Faith."

I took out five hundred rupees, about nine dollars, and gave it to her.

"You see, God sent you here. That is the work of Providence. Would you like a receipt?" she asked.

As much as I admire the work of the sisters, relying on "Providence" struck me as an unrealistic way to cover the costs of daily life, from taxes to taxis. Pastor Ben Witherington III notes that Jesus recognized that money and material items were necessary for daily life on earth. This is exactly what Jesus prays for in the Lord's Prayer when he asks for *daily* bread, not supplies that last a year.[39] Jesus instructs us to ask for that which we *need*, not what we *want*. When it comes to material needs, he advises us to consider the present over the future:

> So do not worry, saying, "What shall we eat?" or "What shall we drink?" or "What shall we wear?" For the pagans run after all these things, and your heavenly Father knows that you need them. But seek first his kingdom and his righteousness, and all these things will

be given to you as well. Therefore do not worry about tomorrow, for tomorrow will worry about itself. Each day has enough trouble of its own.[40]

In raising these questions, Jesus acknowledges the material needs of daily life—food, water, clothes. Before he began his ministry, Jesus was a woodworker or artisan and was probably remunerated for his work, so he understood the links among labor, money, and sustenance.

Indeed, Jesus promised heavenly treasure while also recognizing the necessity of some material things. He was mindful that money was a powerful force in the human world, and being from a small town, he was aware of the agrarian economy around him. The weather greatly impacted the harvest and the economic well-being of farmers, fishermen, traders, and merchants. Galilee and Judea weren't societies with an incredible amount of specialization or division of labor. People were self-reliant, having to weave their own clothes and grow their own food. It followed that many prayed for the weather to cooperate. That so many of Jesus's parables involve farming suggests that he understood that it was the economic lifeblood of the people.

Even the beginning and end of Jesus's life were marked with monetary exchanges: A wise man offered Jesus material wealth, and a foolish one sold him for some. There were many types of money circulating throughout Judea that are mentioned throughout the New Testament: the Tyrian shekel that bore an image of Hercules; the lepta, a coin of low value made from copper; "procurator" coins that were typically made from bronze and were issued by Roman governors like Pontius Pilate.[41] Because Galilee was part of the Roman Empire, Jesus came in contact with Roman money. Jews had to pay various taxes, some of which were passed on to their Roman rulers. An amount of one denarius per year was collected for each boy older than fourteen and each girl older than twelve.[42] One type of denarius coin circulating in the first century had the inscription "Nero Caesar the divine son of Augustus." Each letter was given a corresponding numerical value that added up to 666, or the "number of the beast."[43] According to Rev. George Edmunson, it is "a generally accepted solution" that Nero was the beast mentioned in the book of Revelation.[44] Devout Christians would later refuse to carry or transact in coins bearing this image.

The denarius is of special interest because Jesus comments directly about it in the Gospels. One of the large Jewish groups known as the Pharisees repeatedly challenged and tested Jesus. Once they tried to trap Jesus by asking him questions about taxes: "Is it right for us to pay taxes to Caesar or not?"[45] It was a loaded, "no win" question. If Jesus opposed paying taxes, they would turn him over to the Roman authorities for sedition. If Jesus answered yes, then he would anger fellow Jews who loathed paying taxes to Roman overlords. First, Jesus calls out their deception. Next, he asks for them to show him the coin in which taxes are to be paid, since he isn't carrying any money on him. They show him a denarius that has an image of Caesar. Jesus responds:

> Render therefore unto Caesar the things which be Caesar's, and unto God the things which be God's.[46]

By sidestepping the question, he provides a politically astute response and again draws a distinction between the secular and the sacred, between earthly and heavenly treasure. The Pharisees can't blame him for subversion, and the Jewish revolutionaries can't accuse him of total deference to the Romans. However, by suggesting one should pay Caesar's taxes, Jesus implicitly recognizes that money is a man-made construct that is difficult to avoid in this world. His answer presents the "spheres of exchange" that were discussed in chapter 3. Just as you don't pay your aunt cash for cooking Thanksgiving dinner, you can't buy your way to righteousness. It's the same line between secular and sacred that Jesus tries to draw when he overturns the benches of moneychangers in the temple courts: " 'My house will be called a house of prayer,' but you are making it 'a den of robbers.' "[47] In his comment about paying taxes, Jesus notes the limits of Roman money: The currency of Caesar's empire doesn't circulate in God's Kingdom. Each coin has an image of Caesar, but each person is made in the image of God.

Though it's the wrong currency for the afterlife, we still need money for earthly life. It is also written in the scriptures that the *love* of money—not money itself—is the root of all sorts of evil. Money is like blood. You need it to live but it isn't the point of life. Just as one donates blood, the scriptures instruct believers to share their wealth. Jesus mentions to whom one should give—those in need and even one's enemies: "Love your enemies . . . lend to them without expecting to get anything back."[48] His message got through to his followers, who understood that material wealth was to be shared:

> All the believers were together and had everything in common. They sold property and possessions to give to anyone who had need. Every day they continued to meet together in the temple courts. They broke bread in their homes and ate together with glad and sincere hearts, praising God and enjoying the favor of all the people. And the Lord added to their number daily those who were being saved.[49]

Jesus holds up a poor widow as an example of how to share one's wealth. She gave two coins of low value to the temple. The wealthy people gave larger amounts. Jesus says that the widow gave more than the wealthy: "They all gave out of their wealth; but she, out of her poverty, put in everything—all she had to live on."[50] The poor widow gave *all* her wealth. She renounced it, which is in line with the ethical standard of total detachment from money for Christians. She embraced the paradoxical wisdom of faith.

Most of us aren't willing to donate all of our wealth. But maybe we can interpret her actions in a different light—that she sacrificed her financial well-being. Pastor Keller construes sacrificial giving to mean that one should give in a way that sacrifices one's lifestyle. Perhaps we should follow the guideline of tithing (10 percent), according to the scriptures. Yet Pastor Keller contends it's important how we answer the question, "Is there a cross in your economic life?"[51] Author and Christian theologian C. S. Lewis further describes sacrificial giving:

> I am afraid the only safe rule is to give more than we can spare. In other words, if our expenditure on comforts, luxuries, amusements, etc. is up to the standard common among those with the same

income as our own, we are probably giving away too little. If our charities do not at all pinch or hamper us, I should say they are too small. There ought to be things we should like to do and cannot do because our charities expenditure excludes them. I am speaking now of "charities" in the common way. Particular cases of distress among your own relatives, friends, neighbors or employees, which God, as it were, forces upon your notice, may demand much more: even to the crippling and endangering of your own position.[52]

Sacrificial giving would lead to reflection upon how we spend our money and whether it adequately reflects our values. By sacrificing financial well-being, we could move away from money, detach from it, and bound toward a life of freedom from material wealth. By subscribing to the spiritual logic that *less is more* and *nothing is everything*, the promise of heavenly treasures could be closer at hand.

God's Abundance

The Torah begins with God creating the world. "And God saw everything that he had made, and behold, it was very good."[53] Everything that God made, from the birds and the bees, to man and minerals, belongs to God, and he bestows these things as blessings. There is clear instruction on how to receive more of these blessings, too. Moses advises his people that if they obey the Lord, follow his commandments, and live in a righteous manner, they will receive prosperity and abundance: "He will give the rain for your land in its season, the early rain and the later rain, that you may gather in your grain and your wine and your oil."[54]

But all too often, humans begin to worship the gift and not the giver, forgetting that we are only temporary custodians for God's abundance: "As he came from his mother's womb he shall go again, naked as he came, and shall take nothing for his toil."[55] And as such, we shouldn't confuse fleeting wealth, hoarding or worshipping it, as an everlasting one. When Moses ascends Mount Sinai, he receives the Ten Commandments, which explicitly cast idolatry, including the worship of wealth, as a sin.

You shall not make for yourself a graven image, or any likeness of anything that is in heaven above, or that is in the earth beneath, or that is in the water under the earth.[56]

However, while Moses is receiving these instructions, his people are violating them. They gather gold earrings, which Aaron fashions into an idol of a calf, a graven image. The people worship the golden calf as a god, burning offerings next to it. God demands that Moses return to his people, who have been corrupted. Moses admonishes his people for their "great sin" of making "gods of gold," but he pleads with God to forgive them.[57] Instead, God strikes them with a plague.

Not only did they worship false gods, they exhibited greed, which, according to the Ten Commandments, is also a sin. This commandment goes even further than others, since it prescribes not only how someone should act but also how they should think:

You shall not covet your neighbor's house; you shall not covet your neighbor's wife, or his manservant, or his maidservant, or his ox, or his ass, or anything that is your neighbor's.[58]

As if the commandments weren't clear enough, the Hebrew Scriptures detail the many problems that result from economic logic, such as arrogance: "But the rich answer roughly."[59] Moreover, material wealth is illusory, as one will always want more: "He who loves money will not be satisfied with money; nor he who loves wealth, with gain: this also is vanity."[60] Most troubling is that greed blinds people from realizing that it's God who blesses us with abundance. The benefactor is forgotten:

And when your herds and flocks multiply, and your silver and gold is multiplied, and all that you have is multiplied, then your heart be lifted up, and you forget the Lord your God, who brought you out of the land of Egypt, out of the house of bondage . . . Beware lest you say in your heart, "My power and the might of my hand have gotten me this wealth." You shall remember the Lord your God, for it is he who gives you power to get wealth.[61]

The blinding nature of greed is also addressed in the Talmud, an important text of Judaism, which was compiled between the third and the fifth centuries AD. It tells the story of Alexander the Great, who once asked a group of rabbis to present him a gift in order to honor him. The rabbis gave him an eyeball. Alexander weighed it against gold and silver, but the eyeball couldn't be outweighed. The rabbis explained: "It is the eyeball of a human being, which is never satisfied."[62] The rabbis then covered the eyeball with dust and the precious metals outweighed it.

In this story, dust allays greed, but elsewhere in the Hebrew Scriptures, it's recommended that we see material wealth as dust. During the trials of Job, in which he is deprived of his wealth, it is said to him to "lay gold in the dust."[63] His material possessions are fleeting, like dust, and in the end amount to nothing.[64] Instead Job must realize, "the Almighty is your gold, and your precious silver."[65] This instruction is a rejection of the economic logic that *more is better.* King Solomon recommends this same path of not chasing riches: "Do not toil to acquire wealth; be wise enough to desist. When your eyes light upon it, it is gone; for suddenly it takes to itself wings, flying like an eagle toward heaven."[66] According to Rabbeinu Bachya, a thirteenth-century Spanish scholar of Hebrew Scriptures, the writings of Solomon discourage those who are consumed with the desire to accumulate riches. One's ability to acquire riches isn't dependent on one's wisdom. Even if one obtains wealth, one may not be able to keep it, as it may depart, like a bird that takes flight.[67]

But according to Larry Kahaner, author of *Values, Prosperity, and the Talmud*, the spiritual logic of *less is more* doesn't capture what the Hebrew Scriptures state about material wealth. A more accurate description, he says, is *enough is enough*, or personal contentment. He writes, "What is important is to be satisfied with the money you have and use it for the good of your family and community."[68] One who is content will enjoy the everlasting treasure of God; as it says in Proverbs, "A cheerful heart has a continual feast."[69] According to Meir Tamari, author of *The Challenge of Wealth*, God will bestow abundance on those who have faith.

For those who have faith and are blessed with wealth, King Solomon urges charity and decries blinding selfishness: "He who gives to the poor will not want, but he who hides his eyes will get many a curse."[70] For what one reaps, he will also sow: "One man gives freely, yet grows all the richer."[71] Because wealth is seen as God's blessings, and the Torah says poverty is an everlasting problem, wealthy people must act as virtuous custodians, using their resources to help those in need:

> For the poor will never cease out of the land; therefore I command you, You shall open wide your hand to your brother, to the needy and to the poor, in the land.[72]

God instructs his people on charity: how much to give and to whom. A tithe or one-tenth should be given to those in need, especially widows and orphans. A tithe is the first biblical vow that man makes to God. Jacob promises to provide God a tenth of everything he has—if he can escape his brother, Esau, who is trying to kill him.[73] In an agrarian economy, God's instructions on charity pertain to the harvest. For example, one should not reap the corners of the fields, so that there will be some crops for the poor. God also commands that his people should be charitable with money-lending. They should not engage in usury or charge interest rates on loans to fellow Israelites: "Take no interest from him or increase, but fear your God; that your brother may live beside you."[74] Usury is later called an "abomina-tion" in the book of Ezekiel.[75]

Charity is one of the highest virtues in Judaism. The Talmud states that "charity is equal in importance to all the other commandments combined."[76] *Tsedakah* is the Hebrew word for charity, which originates from the root for justice.[77] The emphasis on charity found in Judaism is exemplified with the *tikkun olam*, which originates from early rabbinical texts and means "repairing the world."[78] It is the call for Jews to be responsible not just for themselves but for the greater community. *Tikkun olam* is a strong part of modern liberal Judaism, and has inspired many Jews to donate vast sums of money to charity—to lay their treasure to the dust.

A Test of Man

The deprivation of wealth is one of Job's trials, but within the Koran, the inverse of this test is emphasized. The abundance of *māl*, which means "wealth" or "property" is a test in itself.[79] For Muslims, life is a test—to live in a virtuous manner, according to the principles of the Koran, and to submit to God.[80] Material wealth is part of this *fitnah*, or "test of faith," since it reveals the true nature of a person's heart.

The Koran portrays this test with a parable of two men, a wealthy man and a poor man. The wealthy man's gardens bear many fruits. He boasts to the poor man, "I am greater than you in wealth." He dupes himself into thinking that his garden will never perish. The poor man questions and shames the rich man, asking whether he's forgotten the power of God: "Although you see me less than you in wealth…It may be that my Lord will give me [something] better than your garden." Then the gardens are destroyed, and the rich man regrets his folly.[81] The poor man understood the spiritual logic of *less is more* in terms of material wealth. By believing the economic logic of *more is better*, the wealthy man failed the *fitnah*. The Koran makes it clear that wealth is indeed a *fitnah*:

> And know that your properties and your children are but a trial and that Allah has with Him a great reward.[82]

Not only does the Koran openly declare that material wealth is a *fitnah*, but it gives clear guidance on how to pass it—to remember to keep one's faith in God and not be blinded by greed:

> O you who have believed, let not your wealth and your children divert you from remembrance of Allah. And whoever does that—then those are the losers.[83]

If a person passes the test and submits to God, acting according to his will, then the person will reap the bounty of spiritual riches. Similar to the scriptures already discussed, the Koran uses agrarian terms to portray God's blessings:

> The example of those who spend their wealth in the way of Allah is like a seed [of grain] which grows seven spikes; in each spike is a hundred grains. And Allah multiplies [His reward] for whom He wills. And Allah is all-Encompassing and Knowing.[84]

But if a person fails this test, and lusts after the earthly treasure of *māl*, then there will be dire consequences on Judgment Day, even banishment to hell:

> If your fathers, your sons, your brothers, your wives, your rela-
> tives, wealth which you have obtained, commerce wherein you fear
> decline, and dwellings with which you are pleased are more beloved
> to you than Allah...then wait until Allah executes His command.
> And Allah does not guide the defiantly disobedient people[85]...
>
> And you love wealth with immense love. No! When the earth has
> been leveled pounded and crushed—And your Lord has come and
> the angels, rank upon rank, And brought [within view] that Day, is
> Hell—that Day, man will remember, but what good to him will be the
> remembrance?[86]

Despite being warned about this *fitnah*, humans are easily susceptible to failing it. The Koran explains people's obsession of *māl* in various ways, from wanting to solidify one's social status to trying to attain immortality:

> Woe to every scorner and mocker. Who collects wealth and [continu-
> ously] counts it. He thinks that his wealth will make him immortal.[87]

The temptation of material wealth has always been great. In the seventh century AD, at the time of the Koranic revelations, status in the community was determined by one's wealth and number of children. Professor of Islamic studies Colin Turner finds eighty-six passages in the Koran that mention *māl* or the plural *amwāl*.[88] According to Monzer Kahf, a scholar of Islamic finance, the Koran doesn't prohibit *māl*. He explains, "[Muslims] don't condemn wealth and riches."[89] After all, two of Muhammad's associates were very wealthy, and Muhammad didn't condemn them.

Some Koranic passages specify how not to misuse *māl*, as in giving to charity and then reminding others of one's generosity. Yet several passages caution against obsession with *māl*.[90] That so many passages warn against greed suggests that the community at the time was preoccupied with earthly treasures. The obsession of *māl* prevented some from recognizing

Muhammad, an orphan and once a shepherd, as a prophet. Such a man, devoid of earthly riches, would have difficulty commanding respect in a society that venerates wealth.

Above all, the Koran's teachings about *māl* maintain that one must see the clear distinction between earthly and heavenly treasure. The paradoxical wisdom is made clear: Earthly treasure is ephemeral; God's is eternal:

> And do not extend your eyes toward that by which We have given enjoyment to [some] categories of them, [its being but] the splendor of worldly life by which We test them. And the provision of your Lord is better and more enduring.[91]

Jesus makes a similar distinction in the Sermon on the Mount. Muslims see the Koran as the continuation and conclusion of God's message that was revealed to prophets like Moses, Job, and Jesus. Many of the Koran's teachings on how to handle wealth are akin to those found in other Abrahamic faiths. For example, the Koran forbids the worship of graven images. It also recounts the story of the golden calf to illustrate the consequences of idolatry: "Indeed, those who took the calf [for worship] will obtain anger from their Lord."[92] The Koran also maintains that everything belongs to God, as he created the world:

> To Him belongs what is in the heavens and what is on the earth and what is between them and what is under the soil.[93]

God's gift creates a gratitude-induced obligation for humans, who must serve as the temporary and righteous trustee of God's abundance. The relationship between God and humans is that of *amanah*, or trust to do the right thing and fulfill God's will. Devout Muslims see their blessings, from money to children, as belonging to God, so they try to act in line with the principles established in the Koran. A paramount principle is to "do thou good," according to the Koran:

> But seek, with the (wealth) which Allah has bestowed on thee, the Home of the Hereafter, nor forget thy portion in this world: but do

thou good, as Allah has been good to thee, and seek not (occasions for) mischief in the land: for Allah loves not those who do mischief.[94]

One of the ways to "do thou good" is charity. One of the pillars of Islam is almsgiving, or *zakat*, which is mentioned in more than thirty passages in the Koran. Every Muslim who has the resources must give to the poor. The root of *zakat* means "purify" and "growth." In giving *zakat*, one cleanses wealth of greed—circulating God's gift to others, thereby sustaining this spiritual gift economy. The Koran doesn't denote how much, but tradition set by Muhammad suggests 2.5 percent of one's income per year. The Koran specifies various groups that should receive these donations, from *fuqara*, or the poor, to the *al-gharimin*, those who can't repay their debts.[95]

Another way to "do thou good" is not to make someone *al-gharimin* in the first place. The Koran forbids *riba*, which has a literal translation of "excess" or "increase" but has come to mean "interest" or any increment over the principal of a debt.[96] The Koran describes usury as "consuming of the people's wealth unjustly" and says that those who engage in it will experience a "painful punishment."[97] At the time of the Koranic revelations, *riba* was considered to sever the link between labor and capital, since one could make money without producing value for society. Over the centuries, Islamic scholars have debated the translations and meaning of *riba*.[98] If it means zero interest rates on loans, then the standard banking practice of lending with interest goes out the window. In order to comply with strictures on *riba*, Islamic banks have created at least twenty-one different types of business models, from levying service charges to structuring payment installments.[99]

Let Go

Indra, the Hindu god of the heavens, was supposed to defend the world against evil spirits known as *asuras*. He had largely succeeded because Lakshmi, the goddess of wealth and good fortune, was by his side. One day, a wise man named Durvasa came across Indra, who was riding on an elephant. Durvasa gave Indra a garland of holy flowers, which Indra placed on his elephant's head. The elephant threw the garland to the ground.

Durvasa was alarmed to see his gift treated so poorly, and he cursed Indra to lose his powers and good fortune. Lakshmi grew angry at Indra's arrogance and greed, and she descended into the milky ocean.[100] The gods were subsequently defeated in battles against the *asuras*. The gods reached a rapprochement with the *asuras* by promising to share the *amrita*, or nectar of immortality from the ocean. Together they spent a thousand years churning the waters by using a mountain as a pole and a serpent as the rope—which eventually poisoned the *asuras*.

Finally, Lakshmi emerged standing on a lotus flower and with lotus flowers in her hands. A sacred elephant showered her with holy water from the golden jug it held in its trunk. A renowned craftsman gave her the most exquisite jewelry. All the other deities sang hymns of praise to welcome her. After accepting the gifts, Lakshmi joined Vishnu, one of the primary gods, as his consort. Her presence ushered in an era of prosperity in which the gods reigned supreme.[101]

This story is laden with symbolism. The milky waters indicate the pastoral, agrarian economy of ancient times, in which milk was an important sustainer of life. The milk also represents the maternal, nurturing aspects of Lakshmi. The lotus flower blooms in the mud, its petals above the water, and it therefore symbolizes beauty and hope. It also represents, according to R. Mahalakshmi, a professor of Indian history, a "womb floating on the primordial waters."[102] The elephants signify royalty and confer regality to Lakshmi.

Over the thousands of years in which stories have been retold about this goddess, there have been various depictions of her. In one familiar portrait, she holds a banana and sugarcane to represent a rich harvest. In another, she has a child in her lap who embodies potential wealth for a family. And in others, she has golden-hued skin, is festooned with golden jewelry and ornaments, and is spraying gold coins from her palms into golden pots.

Hindu mythology is replete with stories of Lakshmi and her various incarnations, because she represents auspiciousness, wealth, and beauty. She is praised as a devout consort to Vishnu, and their relationship represents marital stability. One common depiction is of Lakshmi massaging Vishnu's feet. In years past, she was held up as an ideal for Indian women, but that is slowly changing.[103] Nevertheless, in Bollywood movies, several famous female characters are named after her, and a new baby girl is supposedly the arrival of Lakshmi into one's family.[104] New daughters-in-law also symbolize Lakshmi, and the amount of gold she wears on her wedding day is an indication of how much wealth she will bring to the new family.[105] To pray to Lakshmi doesn't mean that one is a money-grubber. Remember that it was Lakshmi who protested Indra's greed. Many respect Lakshmi for her virtuousness.

In India, she has inspired some of the biggest festivals and largest temples. Every autumn brings the five-day festival of Diwali, or the "festival of lights." In some regions, the first day is known as Dhanteras, which involves prayers known as Lakshmi *puja*. Villagers decorate their cows, the source of their earnings. Families clean their homes and light lamps to welcome Lakshmi and repel evil spirits. Businesses reset their accounting ledgers and ask for blessings in the New Year. Little footprints are drawn on the floor in preparation of Lakshmi's arrival.[106] Many buy gold coins and metal utensils. They also gamble: Every year at this time, my taxi driver in Kolkata plays cards with his five friends. They believe that whoever wins will have good fortunes for the upcoming year. He blamed the card game he lost as the reason why he failed to get a better job as a driver at a top hotel.

In Delhi, I visited the iconic Laxminarayan Temple, which is dedicated to Vishnu and Lakshmi. While I examined one of the wall etchings, a priest put a red *tika*, or mark, on my forehead.

"Lakshmi will bless you with good fortune," he said.

A bit surprised, I managed to say, "Thank you."

He stared at me. I stared back. Then I got the message. I gave him a few rupees and he disappeared.

Lakshmi has long been part of India's monetary history, too. During the Gupta Empire in the fourth and fifth centuries AD, the kings issued coins with images of Lakshmi on them, in hopes that Vishnu would bless their kingdom.[107] In the eleventh century, the Chauhan kings, who ruled much of what is modern-day Rajasthan, India, made silver coins with impressions of Lakshmi.[108] During the eighteenth century, French colonists in Pondicherry, India, issued coins with images of Lakshmi. Even today, because of the association of Lakshmi and money, many regard money as a gift from the divine. Some will even apologize if they desecrate money by accidentally dropping it on the floor.

In the Hindu pantheon, Lakshmi serves as a focal point for comprehending the nexus of Hinduism and wealth. But this goddess shouldn't be the only topic of study. Hinduism is an ancient amalgamation of copious myths and contradictory philosophies that lack a central leader or commandments. Two of these incongruous beliefs, *artha* and *moksha*, relate to money and deserve further attention.

According to the Vedas, ancient Hindu texts that date back to 1500 BC, there are four aims of life, known as *puruṣārtha*, or "that which ought to be sought": (1) *dharma*, duty; (2) *artha*, wealth; (3) *karma*, pleasure; and the ultimate goal, (4) *moksha*, liberation.[109] *Artha* is the accumulation of external successes and earthly treasures like money, image, and status. *Moksha* is partly about the renunciation of these things and embracing the paradoxical wisdom of spiritual riches. These two aims blur the lines between what is supposedly secular and sacred.[110] But the lines *must* be blurred. Instead of shunning the pursuit of material wealth, Hinduism arguably embraces it: An understanding of *artha* is that humans need material items like money to live. The economic logic of *more is better* is necessary up to a point, since nobody wants compulsory poverty. Praying to Lakshmi, a mythological manifestation of *artha*, should be to avoid suffering wrought by poverty and misfortune. The same can be said for several other regional wealth deities, like the Buddhist goddess Vasudhārā, who is supposed to help alleviate poverty, bestowing material and spiritual abundance.

The larger point is that the *puruṣārtha* balance each other and are interdependent. It's not okay to pursue *artha* while violating *dharma*—one's duty to do what's morally right. However, without experiencing the limitations of earthly treasure, one is unlikely to recognize the need to renounce it: You need *artha* to attain the awareness of *moksha*.[111] Without the emptiness that results from the economic logic of *more is better,* you'll never realize the need for the spiritual logic of *less is more.* It's a gradual process that one undergoes through life. The *puruṣārtha* correspond to the four stages life, which are (1) *brahmacharya*, student; (2) *grihastha*, householder; (3) *vanaprastha*, hermit; and (4) *sannyasi*, renouncer.[112] In the first two phases of life, one needs and pursues *artha*, making money to live. After fulfilling one's material duties to family, for instance, one seeks *moksha* in the two final stages of life. Scholars have even suggested that the *puruṣārtha* correspond to times of the day: Remembering one's *dharma* should be part of morning rituals, and *artha* should be reserved for the daytime.[113] It's this lesson of interdependence, of *artha* preparing the way for *moksha*, that Lord Krishna provides his pupil Arjuna in the Bhagavad Gita, a central text of Hinduism:

> Pleasures from external objects are wombs of suffering, Arjuna. They have their beginnings and their ends; no wise man seeks joy among them.[114]

This suffering is the realization that earthly riches like money are, as Jesus said in the Sermon on the Mount, fleeting and perishable. In Buddhism, suffering is the first of the Four Noble Truths: Life is full of *dukkha*, which means "pain" or "anxiety." Money is part of this suffering. It is *maya*, or an illusion. If you define yourself according to wealth or the lack thereof, you can easily lose your self-worth. It's this sorrow that leads one to look for something richer. Just as Lakshmi protested and inhibited Indra's greed, *moksha* extinguishes *artha*.

It's the wise person who seeks *moksha*. According to the Hindu tradition, humans are caught in a cycle of reincarnation, in which one is reborn as a different being that experiences human emotions and desires—like lusting after money. How one lives in the current life determines the circumstances of the next life. Living righteously, as by donating money to charity, elevates one to a higher plane until one can break free from the *maya* of the material world—to a place devoid of money, markets, and mankind. This is liberation, or *moksha*, when a person's soul merges with the supreme. In Buddhism, *moksha* is known as nirvana, which means "to extinguish," as, for example, all desires and material needs.

The Bhagavad Gita mentions various paths to achieve *moksha*. But the theme that keeps coming up is the paradoxical wisdom of detachment, renunciation, and letting go—only then will humans be liberated and achieve the everlasting:

A man unattached to sensations, who finds fulfillment in the Self, whose mind has become pure freedom, attains an imperishable joy... He who controls his mind and has cut off desire and anger realizes the Self; he knows that God's bliss is nearer than near... when desire, fear, and anger have left him, that man is forever free.[115]

In other words, there should come a time in one's life when one renounces money, external success, and indeed all worldly things, like belongings, status, and image. Renunciation can happen only if one abandons all desires and fears.

Adopting the spiritual logic of *less is more* is very much an internal mental battle. Neuroscientist Andrew Newberg of the University of Pennsylvania examined the brain activity of Buddhist monks while they meditated, moving toward nirvana, and found that the prefrontal regions activate.[116] This brain region is the seat of reason, gives rise to our consciousness, and makes us human. These studies seem to reinforce what spiritual leaders have long known: It's in forgetting money that we remember ourselves.

Symbolic Attachment

In a world in which almost everything is valued in terms of money, faith can be a refuge, a spiritual dam to the flood of money flowing through the rest of the world. In the humanities, such as religion and art, there is arguably less focus on the accumulation of wealth and more on how one lives—whether one is kind, generous, and content.[117] By revisiting ancient religious texts and the teachings of the spiritual masters, we glean rich guidance on *how* to live with money.

Across these faiths, the spiritual logic of *less is more* (or *enough is enough*) is presented as a powerful instruction. It's this lesson that the teenager at the Kolkata hospice took to heart when he detached from his material possessions and served among lepers. His faith helped him remember what's important. The lepers, those on the edge of death, showed that those with nothing can be grateful and content. My trip to the hospice helped me see how the economic logic of *more is better* was shaping and driving me. My research into different religious traditions reveals that the attachment to money can lead to a life devoid of personal contentment. But used in the right way, money is an instrument to be shared, and can promote human flourishing. Paradoxically, the purpose of making money seems to be to share it with others.

But some people have come to see money, the object itself, in a different way. The art on money can tell the story of our shared past. The symbols stamped and printed are a reflection not only of value but of what we have valued, across different societies, cultures, and the entire sweep of modern human civilization. My quest led me to folks all around the world who taught me to look more closely at money, and to consider how it's a symbol of our values.

CHAPTER EIGHT

Gilt Complex

The art on money

Coin collecting is a hobby for boys, an investment for fathers, and a windfall for grandfathers.
—*D. Wayne Johnson*[1]

And the parrot would say, with great rapidity, "Pieces of eight! Pieces of eight! Pieces of eight!" till you wondered that it was not out of breath, or till John threw his handkerchief over the cage.
—*Robert Louis Stevenson*[2]

Of all antiquities coins are the smallest; yet, as a class, the most authoritative in record, and the widest in range. No history is so unbroken as that which they tell; no geography so complete; no art so continuous in sequence, nor so broad in extent; no mythology so ample and so various. Unknown kings, and lost towns, forgotten divinities and new schools, if not new styles of art, have here their authentic record. Individual character is illustrated, and the tendencies of races defined.
—*Reginald Stuart Poole*[3]

Sufi Mostafizur Rahman and me at Wari-Bateshwar, in rural Bangladesh. He has found hoards of ancient coins from these ruins that are from an ancient, lost civilization.

I had one day to spend in Dhaka, Bangladesh, to learn about the coins from a lost civilization. And I picked the wrong day. The country was in the midst of a political dispute. The opposition party had taken to the streets to protest, creating a citywide blockade that devolved into deadly violence.[4]

I wasn't leaving my hotel, so Sufi Mostafizur Rahman, an archaeologist at Jahangirnagar University, visited me. He is leading the excavation of forty-eight archaeological sites that are roughly fifty miles from Dhaka and known as Wari-Bateshwar. The ruins date back to at least 450 BC. He believes that the ruins are of an ancient city, Sounagora, part of Gangaridae, an area near the Ganges River known for trade and referenced by Virgil, Plutarch, and Ptolemy.[5]

"Ptolemy mentioned many cities on the subcontinent that are now lost. Now archaeologists are trying to find them," he says.[6]

Rahman arrived at this hypothesis because of the many artifacts that his team has unearthed, including hoards of coins.

Noticing my intrigue, he whispered, "Would you like to visit the ruins?"

"Yes, but how?" I replied, remembering the blockade.

"We'll have to start early," he said.

The next morning, we threaded the blockade with only a few protesters banging on the van door and escaped to the hinterland, where a majestic set of ruins of an ancient walled city awaited.[7]

"One of the best ways to identify this civilization is to study its coins," Rahman tells me. He says that it's from coins that we can learn about a society's economy, trading routes, political leaders, and cultural traditions.[8]

More than one thousand silver punch-mark coins have been found at Wari-Bateshwar. The coins are of similar weight at 57.6 grams, which suggests that a central authority with uniform weights made them. The fronts of many of the coins have punch marks, which indicate how they were created. The coins don't have the names of rulers but bear their symbols. For example, a moon and triple arches are the mark of rulers during the Mauryan Empire. These coins also bear images of boats, fish, flowers, trees, and the sun—more than one hundred symbols. Sometimes these symbols represented the head official at the mint or whoever was in charge of the monetary system. The symbols on the backs of these coins were made by bankers to denote different denominations and give them status as legal tender. Scholars have classified the coins in two groups: *janapada* (which refers to a series of ancient Indian kingdoms) and imperial. The *janapada* series were issued from 600 BC to 400 BC, before the Mauryan Empire. The imperial coins were made from 400 BC to 200 BC, during the Mauryan Empire, one of the world's largest empires during that era.

The *janapada* series coins are an incredible discovery because they challenge the commonly held belief that civilization didn't take root in this area until 300 BC. These coins indicate the existence of an urban center that participated in commerce, banking, and trade—with areas throughout the subcontinent, and maybe even the Mediterranean world. "This means it was the earliest state in Bangladesh and in the Indian subcontinent as well," says Rahman.[9] Not only that—these coins were made around the same time as those in Lydia, making them some of the oldest in the world. "These coins are symbols of a lost civilization," he says.

In the first chapter, we explored Paleolithic cave art from 40,000 years ago. Those symbols are a record of early human expression. They demonstrate man's capacity for symbolic thought. Symbolic art from this era is the beginning of man's creative story. Symbolic understanding gave rise to the invention of money. In order to define and denote the various denominations and types of money, we emblazon it with art, images, and insignias that represent us. We put symbols on symbols. It follows that money can be a guide to cultural history and our collective past.

Like a fossil, money can help us remember and understand a society. Because coins are made from durable metals, they survive over the years and provide clues about the place and period in which they were made. People often stored coins in jars and buried them because they didn't have access to banks or wanted to preserve their wealth from, say, an invading army. Some of these hoards were forgotten, only to be discovered centuries later with their unspoiled coins.

Many scholars see antique money as a type of art, especially because many pieces were designed by artisans and craftsmen. For example, the famous Indian Head cent of the nineteenth century was crafted by portraitist James Longacre, who also served as chief engraver of the US Mint. One of the most widely viewed portraits in the world is of George Washington, which was painted by Gilbert Stuart and is found on the one-dollar bill. A curator at the Museum of Fine Arts in Boston, the late Cornelius Vermeule III, observed that early American coins with patriotic images inspired other artisans to include similar depictions on furniture, glassware, needlework, and even cookie cutters. For example, in 1892, the Central Glass Company made glass tables with a "Coin" pattern, which had replicas of US coins embedded in the design. However, the US government prohibited this line because of counterfeiting concerns.[10] Vermeule explains the aesthetic movement: "As the nineteenth century progressed, patriotism, publicity, and national numismatic motifs were intermixed."[11] He writes that money, especially coins, is a type of democratic art, accessible to the people and worthy of study:

> The United States coinage represents a great attempt, still in process, to provide democracy with instruments of visual beauty...Coins are the one form of art to which every American is exposed at every moment. They are the only class of sculpture that a large segment of the population ever handles...knowledge that coins...are a form of official, historical art designed to reach citizens in every epoch of United States affairs makes an aesthetic study worthwhile.[12]

In 1970, UNESCO officially recognized the historical importance of "cultural property" such as coins that are more than one hundred years old, and suggested ways to regulate the trade of them.[13]

Coin collectors, or numismatists, are especially good at interpreting the symbols found on these cultural properties. Numismatics, the study and collection of money, is an ancient activity. Archaeologists have found coin collections that date back to the Roman Empire. Even Emperor Augustus Caesar, who lived in the first century AD, collected coins from distant lands and gave them to friends. Around AD 250, the Roman mint issued commemorative coins with images of several of the emperors. During the Italian Renaissance, in the fourteenth century, the scholar and poet Petrarch was renowned for his collection of ancient coins. In fifteenth-century Europe, collecting money was called a "hobby of kings," as many members of royal families and aristocrats built their collections.[14] Sixteenth-century collector Guillaume Budé wrote one of the first numismatic texts, *Libellus de Moneta Craeca*, or "A pamphlet of Greek coins." In 1834, the first numismatics magazine, *Blätter für Münzkunde*, or "Hannover's Numismatics," was published in Hannover, Germany.[15] During the twentieth century, well-known collectors included King Farouk of Egypt and Josiah Lilly, who ran pharmaceutical giant Eli Lilly and Company; a coin that has been owned by a famous collector usually is considered to have a pedigree because of the record of ownership, and is thus more valuable. Also during the twentieth century, this hobby of kings was practiced by the masses, as coin collecting was democratized with the creation of local coin clubs, conventions for traders, and an online market.

According to the US Mint, 147 million people collected coins as part of the 50 States Quarters Program. In 1997, after years of work by numismatists and debate among congressmen, President Bill Clinton signed the program into law; the quarters program was "to promote the diffusion of knowledge among the youth of the United States about the individual States, their history and geography, and the rich diversity of the national heritage."[16] The law also stipulated that the design of each coin was to be "dignified" and something of which US citizens would be "proud."[17] A rigorous process for the selection of each coin's design was established. Many of the designs were created by professional artists who participated in the US Mint's Artistic Infusion Program, the website for which says, "The designs on United States coins and medals are more than simple illustrations on small metal discs; they are expressions of the values, aspirations, and shared heritage of our Nation. They serve as illustrations to the world of the essence and the story of America."[18]

One of those stories is that of Caesar Rodney. He is on the Delaware quarter, which was the first one issued as part of the program because Delaware was the first state to ratify the Constitution. Caesar Rodney was born in Delaware, and he eventually served as Speaker of the state house and as a state supreme court justice. However, he also suffered from asthma and cancer. In 1776, during the Second Continental Congress, the two members of the Delaware delegation were in disagreement regarding whether to vote for independence. Rodney, also a member, was many miles away, at home. According to Jim Noles, the author of *A Pocketful of History*, there is a popular legend in which Rodney was notified of the impasse, and despite his sickness, jumped on his horse and galloped in the rain toward Philadelphia, where he yelled to awaiting delegates, "I vote for independence!"[19] Rodney's fateful ride is portrayed on the Delaware quarter.

Every US quarter, and every coin, tells a part of America's story, from Duke Ellington on the Washington, DC, quarter to Sacagawea on the dollar coin. American numismatist Frank Meyer writes that every citizen should take the time to understand the story that American money tells:

> Coins of the United States serve not only as a medium of exchange, but also as an expression of the ideals and aspirations of a people. They contain a symbolism which should be understood and prized by every American citizen. While these coins are commonly used, they carry devices and legends which are little noted or seldom comprehended. It will be, therefore, a profitable experience for all students to study and gain an appreciation for the symbolic significance of the coins of their country.[20]

But it's not just US citizens who should look more closely at their country's coins. People all around the world can enrich their civic and cultural understanding by studying their nations' past and present money. This is what I tried to do, as the culmination of my quest to understand money and how its history has shaped us.

To discover more about the symbols on the symbols, the story that money tells, I met with numismatists in many countries, in the spare moments away from my day job. Herein are but a few conversations from collectors in Vietnam, Thailand, Philippines, Sri Lanka, and the United States. I asked them to choose a few coins that best symbolize their countries. I sought their opinions for how and why the symbols represented the nation in which they lived. In doing so, I hoped to discover how money can be a symbol of national values. Most of all, I listened to their stories and began to see how collecting coins has shaped them and can reveal much about their countries and cultural identities.

These numismatists helped me see that one may lose oneself in the accumulation of money, but remember oneself in the study of it. If making and understanding symbols are part of what makes us human, then the symbols we put on our money help to tell our collective story.

The Satan of Numismatics

Howard Daniel didn't attend school until the fifth grade. He had rheumatic fever as a kid, so he was homeschooled. To enliven his history lessons, his parents brought him stamps from around the world, which sparked his curiosity and sense of adventure.

"I grew up poor white cracker trash in Florida," he explained. We met at a café in Ho Chi Minh City (formerly Saigon), Vietnam, where we sipped sour *limon chanh* drinks. His mother always seemed to squander money, so he resolved that one day he would be wealthy.

In 1959, at the age of seventeen, he enlisted in the US Army. His career in army intelligence took him all over the world. In 1964, he met a senior enlisted member of the US Air Force in Okinawa, Japan—a numismatist who specialized in Japanese money. He was trying to convince other military personnel to study the money of East Asia. He insulted Howard's intelligence by saying, "Vietnamese money will be too difficult for you to understand." Howard doesn't like to be doubted.

Vietnam became an integral part of his life. Howard was stationed in Vietnam during the war, married a Vietnamese woman, and still lives for half the year in the country.

"In the military, we destroy things; a numismatist creates something," he explains. Over time, he amassed a collection of thousands of coins, worth at least $400,000, which he keeps in two refrigerators in his home in Virginia. He has 31 gigabytes of digital pictures of money saved on a hard drive. He has authored several books on the money of Southeast Asia and is considered a leading expert on the topic. He would probably be the president of the Numismatics Society of Vietnam—if there were one. But

Vietnam's communist government frowns upon the capitalist hobby of collecting money.

"I'm known as the 'Satan of Numismatics,' because I'm brutally honest," he said.

Once at a money convention in the United States, a dealer with a dubious reputation pestered Howard to do business with him. Instead, Howard yelled at the top of his lungs, "Get the fuck out of my face! You are as worthless as tits on a boar hog!" The dealer left with his reputation in tatters, and Howard left with a new nickname.

He demonstrated his characteristic bluntness during our conversation.

"I like it raw," he stated. *Raw* means money that isn't sealed in a case. *Slabbed* is money that is sealed in a (usually, plastic) case. It's a debate that has historically divided numismatists. "I like to touch the money. Collectors like me preserve things better, anyways. In the old days, Vietnam's museums weren't equipped to preserve ancient money. The financial history of Vietnam is disappearing, and that's why I collect money, to help the next generation learn about it."

With a gap of forty years between us, I am part of this next generation. So I asked him, what coin best represents Vietnam?

"It makes sense to start at the beginning," he explains.

Dinh Bo Linh coins are Vietnam's first. After Vietnam was liberated from the Southern Han Dynasty of China in the tenth century AD, its people fell into civil war. Through a series of battles and political maneuvers, one of the chieftains, Dinh Bo Linh, gained power and unified his country, becoming the emperor known as "Thai Binh" and ruling from 968 to 979.[21] To unify his kingdom, he issued his own currency: "cash"-style coins that resembled Chinese coins with a square hole in the middle. The coins weighed anywhere from 2.28 to 4.32 grams. Heavier coins indicate the robustness of the economy in which they were issued, since they have a higher content of copper, a rare metal. Coins that weigh less were issued during a less prosperous and wartime era. They had a lower content of copper and higher amounts of zinc and lead, which were less valuable. Lighter coins indicate a period of war because copper and other hard metals were used to make arms.[22]

These early coins had the ruler's name, Thai Binh Hung Bao, on the front. On the reverse was "Dinh," the name of the dynasty.[23] On coins from

this era, when the characters on the money look clear and in precise calligraphy, it's considered an indication that the ruler was well educated, surrounded himself with scholars, and was interested in the education of his
people. However, if the characters are illegible and the calligraphy is poor,
it suggests a ruler who lacked a strong education and was a warlord with
a military background. It's also considered a sign that the ruler wasn't as
interested in the well-being and education of his people.[24]

At first glance, the coins of this period are nothing more than metal
disks with holes in the middle. But on further analysis, they are symbols
of economic prosperity and hardship, war and peace, and a clue to the
priorities of the ruler. I didn't learn anything about ancient Vietnamese
history in school. But I learned a bit about this country's past by looking
more closely at its money.

From Brooklyn to Bangkok, by Way of Vietnam

A Brooklyn accent is hard to shake. Even if you haven't been back since 1974.
Born in Brooklyn, Ron Cristal completed his law degree and volunteered to
serve during the Vietnam War as a judge advocate officer in 1968. After a
month in Vietnam, he was sent by train to an eastern province of Thailand
to help American soldiers who had been accused of starting a fire that had
destroyed a town.

"I knew this was the place for me . . . I was home here," he explains in
his Brooklyn accent.

His fateful train ride in 1969 started a lifelong commitment to Thailand.
He studied the Thai language and speaks enough to get by. He has run
a law firm in Bangkok since 1988 and became a Thai citizen in 1998. Ron
also changed his name to Ronachai Krisadaolarn, which he picked because
it sounded similar to his American name, and it has a grand meaning in
Thai, "Victorious Battle, Majestic Power."

He has been interested in collecting coins since he was ten, and he
channeled this passion into learning about his adopted country. He eventually became an expert on Thai money, so much so that the president of
the Numismatic Association of Thailand, who is also a Thai police captain,
wrote the preface to the book that Ronachai coauthored on Thai money;

Thai monetary officials consult him on the design of new Thai money; and the king of Thailand has thanked him for his contributions to Thailand's cultural legacy.

We met in his office, on the seventeenth floor of a skyscraper in downtown Bangkok. It resembles an old newsroom, with many interior windows but with none of the reporters. Dressed in a half-sleeve button-down shirt, Ronachai ushered me into a room with a giant, off-white colored safe in which he keeps his coin collection. I asked him the same thing I asked Howard. What coins best represent this country?

It's not an easy question because Thailand has a diverse history, having been ruled by many different kings and influenced by several other civilizations. For example, during the Funan period, from the second to seventh centuries AD, India heavily influenced the region, and coins made by Bengalis circulated in Southeast Asia. Some of these coins had images of Lakshmi, the Hindu goddess of wealth. At the beginning of the nineteenth century, coins with marks in two or three languages were made in the Kra Isthmus, in southern Thailand. After giving it some thought, Ronachai, like Howard, started with his country's first indigenous money, *pot duang*.

During the thirteenth century, the first Thai kingdom, known as Sukhothai, was established. King Ramkhamhaeng is believed to have introduced *pot duang*, or "bullet coins," which were chunky, made by hand, and looked like bullets. Each bears the symbol of the ruler who issued the coins. For example, the chakra, a Hindu symbol found on *pot duang* issued between 1782 and 1886, represented the Chakri Dynasty.

Experts still debate where the use of *pot duang* as a currency originated. Some think that they were made to resemble cowrie shells, which were known to function as currency in China; others believe they derived from money that looked like bracelets circulating in Southeast Asia.[25] Whatever the reason for their introduction and shape, *pot duang* circulated for six hundred years, until 1904. They remain an important part of Thailand's monetary history.

As Thailand advanced, so did its money. Gold and silver coins with the inscription "Krung Thep" ("city of angels") were handmade in Bangkok during the reign of King Rama IV. These were flat, modern-looking coins that resemble early English hammered coins.[26] It is fitting that King Rama IV introduced these coins because they symbolize the modernity that he embraced. Thailand still issued *pot duang* during his reign, whereas most other countries minted flat coins. By adopting flat coinage, King Rama IV was helping to modernize Thailand's monetary system. In addition, he opened his kingdom to Western powers, signing commercial treaties with the United Kingdom and the United States; he was the inspiration for the king in the 1944 novel *Anna and the King of Siam* and the subsequent musical *The King & I*.[27] Eventually, Queen Victoria gave Rama IV a hand-powered machine for making coins in Thailand.

Ronachai let me hold his prized gold Krung Thep coin.

"By holding it, you can feel Thailand's cultural history. This coin is art," he explained.

"Is that why you collect money?" I asked.

"Some people raise orchids, I collect coins," he deadpanned.[28]

Two Coins, Four Hundred Years

Two coins can explain four hundred years of Filipino history: Dos Mundos are a symbol of Spain's ascent as a world power and its conquest of the Philippines; counterstamped coins are symbols of Spain's descent and exit from the Philippines.

I learned about Dos Mundos coins from William "Willie" Villareal, a leader of the Philippine Numismatic & Antiquarian Society (PNAS), which was founded in 1929. But first he ran me through his thoughts on the state of numismatics in the Philippines. We met at the Polo Club in Manila, where he is a life member. Willie is as sharp as a razor, cracking colorful jokes while holding a tumbler of scotch in his right hand.

"We meet whenever we want to get drunk," he says with a laugh. "In the old days, we traded wives, but now that we've run out of wives, we trade coins."

Despite his irreverence, Willie sees PNAS as a highly respected organization. The eighty-five-year history of PNAS has made it one of the oldest institutions in the country and a de facto curator of Filipino culture. Amateurs and collectors who occasionally stumble upon a hoard of coins often first consult with PNAS on the legitimacy or significance of the coins before they bring them to the national museum. The PNAS has become a filter and adviser for several museums.

"Soon everyone will be just zeros and ones on a computer chip. We do this to preserve our identities."

He paused and turned his attention on me.

"The problem with your generation is that you have no heroes—because you haven't struggled. Do you even know who General MacArthur is?" he asked.

Willie believes that it is through understanding the symbols, portraits, and legends on money that young people can remember a nation's heroes and its history. By looking at George Washington and Abraham Lincoln, for example, we are reminded of their deeds and the courage they demonstrated in making difficult decisions. We remember what it means to survive and sacrifice—and these are virtues to which citizens should aspire. He believes money not only reflects these historic figures but can connote a larger narrative of an entire era.

"Young man, every coin tells a story," he declared.

"So tell me one," I said.

He obliged.

Once upon a time, more specifically in 1732, Spain adopted precise guidelines for the design of a new coin that became known as "Dos Mundos" ("Two Worlds"). These coins were meant to replace previously issued odd-shaped silver or gold pieces, called "cobs," that bore images of the Spanish shield and the Christian cross, with marks indicating ruler, dates, and mints. Cobs were irregular chunks of metal, cut to certain predetermined weights, but were easily clipped, shaved, debased, and counterfeited due to their irregular shapes.

Dos Mundos were designed for frequent and international usage: consistent weight and purity with a floral edge, a design with flowers on the rims, to protect against debasers shaving the edges. The thoughtful design enabled the coins to withstand counterfeiting, debasement, and the wear and tear of heavy usage, as it became a dominant world currency. Over time, Dos Mundos became one of the most famous coins in history.

The symbols on the coin show Spain for what it was—a proud and supreme power with an empire that spanned the world and on which the sun never set. The front of the coin features the Spanish ruler's coat of arms and an "8" that signals its denomination. The silver coin became commonly known for its value, referred to as *ocho reales*, or "pieces of eight." It also bears the saying D.G. HISPAN ET IND REX, which is translated to mean "By the grace of God, King of Spain and the Indies." The back of the coin features the date on which the coin was minted, with the words UTRAQUE UNUM—"both worlds are one"—a claim made by Spanish kings that they effectively ruled the old and the new worlds. It also has a mint mark indicating in which colony the coin was struck. In the center are two hemispheres of the world, which overlap underneath a Spanish crown. The hemispheres, floating on an ocean, are flanked by what's supposedly two pillars of Hercules, representing the promontories that frame the Strait of Gibraltar. These crowned pillars have a ribbon around them that reads PLUS ULTRA, or "There is more beyond." In the Philippines, as in other Spanish colonies, these coins were also known as *columnarias* after the two pillars, and as a result, they have also been referred to as "pillar dollars." In sum, it is a beautiful coin with perfect symmetry.

Dos Mundos coins achieved what the drachma and the denarius did a thousand years earlier—they flowed beyond the borders of the seat of power. One reason that they flowed so freely was that they were intended for use across the vast lands that composed the Spanish Empire. There was also a huge quantity of these coins made. From 1732 to 1772, the Mexico Mint produced 478,305,907 of them.[29] They were also minted in smaller numbers in other Spanish colonies, including Chile, Colombia, Guatemala, and Peru. These coins even circulated throughout the British colonies in North America. The coins spread across the Pacific Ocean via galleons, the sailing ships measuring up to 160 feet in length. The galleon trade route between Manila and Acapulco, initiated by Spain in the late sixteenth century, took approximately four months by ship, one way, to link East and West. For hundreds of years, Manila, then known as the "Pearl of the Orient," gathered and exported spices, ivories, porcelain, and silks on these ships. In return, Acapulco sent European and American goods, as well as silver in the form of Dos Mundos coins.

The galleon trade fueled economic growth in the Philippines. As planned, religious institutions and the Spanish aristocracy gained control of the galleon trade and benefited the most financially from it. Because Dos Mundos were used to buy silk from Chinese merchants for export, they became known as "silk money." These coins circulated in places like Canton and Macau because of their intrinsic worth and high silver content. In 1772, for fiscal reasons, King Carlos III issued coins with lower silver content and placed his portrait on the Dos Mundos, a precedent that future rulers followed. The several types and grades of coins in circulation caused a degree of monetary confusion such that Chinese merchants occasionally placed a chop mark of a Chinese character on a Dos Mundos coin to denote its authenticity and acceptability.

Because the galleons were carrying so many valuables, the Spanish sent security vessels to accompany them on their long voyages. However, sometimes the galleons would arrive late, be captured by pirates, or capsize because of treacherous weather. In 1690, a galleon named *Nuestra Señora del Pilar*, en route to Manila, sank near what is now Guam after striking a reef. It's thought that the ship was transporting up to two million silver Dos Mundos coins, said to be worth an estimated $1 billion.[30] When a ship didn't reach Manila, it caused suffering in the Philippines, since the entire economy rose and fell on the fate of galleons. The lucrative trade route was eventually halted in the early nineteenth century, during the Mexican War of Independence, as the decline of the Spanish Empire accelerated. Another Filipino coin tells this tale.

To learn about this later story, I met with another numismatist, Percival "Boyet" Manuel. He became interested in collecting money when he was eight years old. His father was a marine officer who brought money from his travels back home. Now a youthful-looking forty-year-old intellectual, Boyet remains passionate about numismatics. He has become a leading expert on Filipino money and runs a comprehensive website on the topic.

Dressed in blue jeans and a checkered shirt, he joined me in Manila for a lunch of chicken adobo, french fries with mayonnaise, and carrot juice.

"Preservation is crucial. We have a fragmented past. Money has helped us forge a national identity," he said.

The Philippines is indeed geographically diverse, composed of more than seven thousand islands. The islands were a Spanish colony for more than three hundred years and then were governed by the United States until 1946, when they became an autonomous nation. The influence of other cultures is everywhere. Filipino food is a mash-up of different cuisines—ground beef picadillo from Spain, fried chicken from America, egg rolls from China. You can ride between the many Manila shopping malls in a festively decorated "Jeepney," vehicles originally adapted from US military jeeps after World War II.

Even its money has been multicultural. I asked Boyet what money best represents his country. He answered without hesitation: counterstamped coins—they illustrate the decline of the Spanish Empire and the fusion of two cultures. He even took me on a guided tour of the Money Museum at the Philippines Central Bank to see some of these coins.

During the nineteenth century, many Latin American colonies sought independence from Spain. With the cessation of the galleon trade, Spain still needed money for other parts of its empire, so it did the unthinkable. Spain used the "rebel" coins issued by its Latin American colonies that were in the midst of revolutions. These coins were inscribed with revolutionary mottos "Libre" and "Independencia," but they also entered and circulated in the Philippines. It was embarrassing that the once-proud Spanish crown that had issued beautiful Dos Mundos was forced to use money from colonies in revolt. This would be like the United Kingdom using US dollars for circulation in another British colony like India—after the United States had declared independence. To picture what these counterstamped coins look like, imagine a US quarter. Now envision the top of George Washington's profile, which is on the front of the coin, and it has been struck over with a small oval that bears another image, say, a British crown.

Spanish officials were also concerned that these coins would stir revolutionary spirits in the Philippines. In 1828, Don Mariano Ricafort, a Spanish official who had jurisdiction over the Philippines, decreed that coins made by "*provincias insurectas y gobiernos revolucionarios*" would be altered.[31] These coins would be stamped over, or "counterstamped," with slogans like "*Habilitado Por El Rey N.S.D. Fern VII*," giving credit to the monarch and sometimes obliterating the revolutionary mottos. They were also stamped with the name Manila to limit the use of these coins to the Philippines, but after five years the die used to make the counterstamp had worn out. Because counterstamps were the indication of legitimacy, sometimes even

Dos Mundos were revalidated by counterstamp. In 1834, Spain established a mint in Manila to create local coins. But there weren't enough trained workers to staff it, nor was there enough precious metal available. Therefore Queen Isabel II's officials continued the practice of counterstamping coins, which had begun under her predecessor, King Ferdinand VII.

Counterstamps were made by screw-pressing machines in the shape of ovals that bore the seal of Spanish rulers. For example, an eight-Mexican-reals coin made in 1830 was stamped with a large "F.7." seal of King Ferdinand VII. An eight-escudos from Colombia made in 1826 was stamped with "Y.II.," a small seal of Ysabella (Isabella) II, the queen of Spain. In some cases, coins were counterstamped twice with the seals of both rulers so that they would be valid during the reign of each.

Spain stopped counterstamping coins in 1836 because the process wasn't regulated properly and counterfeiters had duplicated the die that was used to counterstamp. Many counterfeit coins were introduced into circulation. The government ceased counterstamping to regain control over the coins in circulation. In addition, as Spain recognized the independence of its Latin American colonies, it lost access to vast amounts of silver. Lacking these resources, Spain permitted other foreign coins to circulate in the Philippines, including American and Latin American coins. By 1852, the peso was introduced in the form of banknotes and fractional coinage.

That Spain had to reuse and counterstamp money from its former colonies highlights what was a deteriorating economic situation made worse by many local factors. First, the Philippines lacked the natural resources to create enough coins locally. Second, there was a plague of smallpox, and an earthquake struck the Philippines during the years when counterstamping colonial and foreign coins was implemented, and so the Spanish needed money to pay for hospitals and medicine. Third, the prolific galleon trade had slowed. Spain recognized that a currency famine could have led to more political instability.

"Counterstamped coins are examples of two clashing civilizations," Boyet explains. These coins are tangible manifestations of the relationship between Spain and the Philippines—a country and its colony. They show a foreign culture pressed upon an indigenous one.

The mash-up of symbols fascinates Boyet, who collects these scarce coins. He is on the lookout for a rare counterstamped coin from Colombia made from gold.

"It's more likely that I will be struck by lightning," he quipped.

A Galaxy of Money

It took an astrophysicist for me to see how universal the symbols on our money can be.

Kavan Ratnatunga left Sri Lanka in 1978 and studied at Australia National University for his PhD in astrophysics. He worked at Princeton's Institute for Advanced Study (where Albert Einstein worked the last twenty-one years of his life) and the NASA Goddard Space Flight Center. At Johns Hopkins University, he used automated image analysis to study the first quad gravitational lens found with the NASA Hubble Space Telescope (a lensed image is created when the gravitational field of a large entity distorts the image of a more remote entity).[32] In 2005, Kavan retired and returned to his native country.

And that's where we met, in Colombo, the capital of Sri Lanka, on a sweltering, sticky day. As the president of the Sri Lankan Numismatic Society, Kavan was eager to share his research on indigenous money.

"I used to map the universe, now I map the galaxy of Lankan[33] money," he said.

In 1998, he launched his website, which has high-resolution images of more than six hundred Lankan coins, by far the most comprehensive on the Internet. Kavan has become a guru to Lankan monetary officials, who consult with him when they curate their numismatic exhibitions. He also has a degree in museology and is working toward his second PhD, this one in archaeology. This astrophysicist-turned-archaeologist didn't just come back to earth; he goes beneath it, so to speak, analyzing the metallic makeup of once-buried coins.

Kavan uses a rigorous scientific approach to study the physical properties of coins. He once procured a hoard of one hundred copper coins made during the tenth-century AD reign of Rajaraja Chola I of Lanka. He measured the weight, thickness, and diameter of each coin and graphed the results. He found a correlation between the weight and the thickness.

But there was no correlation between the weight and the diameter. This allowed him to infer that the coins were likely struck from cooling drops of molten metal rather than a cold planchet, a metal disk with which coins are made.[34] Determining how a coin was made can reveal clues about the society in which it was created—for example, whether coin makers were using primitive technology or advanced techniques learned from trading partners. This astrophysicist is able to turn a hoard of coins into a forensic treasure chest of historical knowledge.

"Archaeology isn't so different from astronomy. In both cases, you are observing the past and can't experiment," he declared. "There are also many astronomical symbols on ancient Lankan money."

The oldest so-called Puranas coins found in Lanka date back to the third century BC and are made from silver. On the front is the sun, which was the mark of the Magadha Kingdom, which ruled what's now eastern India. The sun may represent King Bimbisara, a patron of Buddha, or Ashoka, who dispatched his son to Lanka to spread Buddhism.[35] There is another coin that blends Kavan's interests of money and space—a copper one that was issued during the reign of King Mahasena in the third century AD. On the back are four dots inside a circle. Kavan hints that this symbol looks like a quad gravitational lens but it is definitely something else, though it's too worn-out to determine.[36] A more modern coin, one of irregular shape, was made from copper during the ninth century AD and exhibits the influence of the First Pandyan Empire, which lasted from the sixth to tenth centuries AD and stretched from southern India to northern Lanka. On the front is a crescent moon with a bull seated beneath it.[37] In the sixteenth century, an even more modern coin, the Venetian gold ducat, which was probably used by the Portuguese who had settled Ceylon (as Sri Lanka was formerly called), was adorned with astronomical symbols, thirteen stars that surround Jesus Christ.

Kavan kept returning to the astronomical symbols that we put on our money, such as the sun, the moon, and stars. These celestial objects are universal, found on money no matter what era, as evidenced by thousands of years of Lankan money, and no matter what geographical area, as in the thirteen stars on the 1838 Liberty Seated Half Dime in the United States, and the sun on the 1813 one-real coin of the Provincias del Rio de la Plata in Argentina. The reasons for using these symbols vary, from honoring a sun god to equating a king with the divine or symbolizing various colonies.

Art historian Rudolf Wittkower explains that the recurrence of symbols isn't a coincidence but an example of cultural diffusion. For example, he considers the symbol of an eagle fighting a snake, which recurs in many cultures over thousands of years. He traces the symbol to an ancient Babylonian legend known as the Etana Epic, in which the gods choose a man named Etana to be king. However, his wife cannot produce an heir, so Etana must obtain a special birth plant found in heaven. Etana discovers a languishing eagle, which he rescues, and it takes him to heaven.[38] The conflict between the eagle and the serpent is a subplot of Etana's story, as the eagle lives atop a tree and the serpent at the bottom. Though they've promised Shamash the Sun God that they will live together harmoniously, the eagle eats the serpent's young. The serpent hides inside a dead bull's stomach, and when the eagle feeds upon the bull, the serpent captures the bird and banishes him to die. Etana rescues the eagle, and the eagle helps to restore man's line of succession.[39]

Wittkower finds that this symbol first appears in the ancient Near East and, over time, migrated to more distant areas. He reasons that the symbol wasn't invented anew but was spread from one culture to the next. For instance, the symbol appears on an Indian pendant from 3000 BC but not on jewelry from the regions of Punjab or Sindh, which suggests that it isn't an indigenous symbol. The eagle and snake images found in India resemble those found in Mesopotamia, and archaeologists have also discovered other links between ancient Mesopotamia and the Indus River civilization.

Similar eagle and snake symbols have appeared across different geographies over thousands of years: a Babylonian seal from 3000 BC, ancient Greek coins, ancient Roman coins, an Indian seal from the fifth century AD, the emblem of Pope Clement IV during the thirteenth century, the current-day seal of Mexico (which appears on the peso), and the state seal of New Mexico.[40] The ribbon in the beak of the eagle on the Great Seal on US money resembles a snake. Indeed, the eagle-and-snake myth took on new meanings and interpretations in different cultures. The eagle found on the Great Seal represents power and freedom. In India and Sri Lanka, the symbols came to represent a bird known as Garuda, who carries in its beak a snake known as Naga.

Kavan helped me recognize that some monetary symbols aren't just astronomical but universal. When you spend a dollar, you aren't just handing over something with an American emblem; you are exchanging something bearing a symbol that has been used by humans in various cultures over thousands of years. Despite the many ways in which countries try to make their money unique, some symbols continue to shine on.

The Dean

Dorothy had it right in *The Wizard of Oz*—there's no place like home. And in the field of numismatics, there's no place like my adopted hometown of New York City, with its many collectors, exhibitions, and shops. Arguably the best-known coin shop in the world is Stack's, on West Fifty-Seventh Street close to Carnegie Hall. It was founded in the 1930s by two brothers, Joseph and Morton Stack, who traded almost anything to make ends meet during the Great Depression—statues, stamps, rare coins, and even tooth fillings. They couldn't afford dealing in all of these items, so they specialized in coins that have intrinsic value and can be melted into base metals. Over the decades, Stack's has hosted more than eight hundred public auctions, becoming perhaps the leading auction house of rare coins.

One dreary winter morning I visited Stack's. Inside was only one customer, a man in his mid-thirties who had recently lost his job. He was selling a gold coin that he had owned for fifteen years so that he could pay his bills—he made $350. I wanted to discuss his collection, but I had to move on. Unlike Dorothy, I wasn't searching for Oz; I was looking for the dean.

At eighty-five years old, Harvey Stack is a human encyclopedia of numismatics, the dean of coin dealers. In the early 1940s, Morton brought his son Harvey into the shop to sort paperwork, wash showcases, sweep the floors, and make runs to the post office. Harvey began working full-time at Stack's in 1947 and learned from many great numismatists who all worked at Stack's, such as Henry Grunthal, curator of the American Numismatics Association; and Elvira and Vladimir Stefanelli, curators of the American Numismatics

Collection at the Smithsonian. For decades, Stack's was known as a club-house, open on Saturdays so collectors from the tri-state area could meet there. There was much to discuss as World War II soldiers returned home and brought coins to Stack's that they gathered from bombed-out banks and museums abroad and wanted to sell. Harvey absorbed much knowledge from these conversations, and with it he developed an impressive career.

Harvey's résumé in numismatics is peerless. He has sixty-five years' experience as a professional numismatist, has conducted the most auctions in the industry, has been a member of the American Numismatics Association for more than fifty years, receiving the group's "Numismatist of the Year" honor in 1997, and served as head of the Professional Numismatists Guild.[41] In 1995 he was one of the people who testified before Congress to propose the creation of the 50 State Quarters Program.[42] I was excited to meet the man behind the money.

"What kind of gun is that?" I asked, surprised to see an armed security guard waiting for me when the elevator door opened.

"A real one," Harvey said, laughing. "But we tell them not to shoot anyone," he whispered. He was dressed in a navy coat, gray slacks, silver sweater, and his trademark yellow-tinted eyeglasses. Forty years ago he contracted the measles and developed encephalitis on his optic nerve, so he wears glasses to shield his eyes from bright light. He steered me into his office and offered me a Diet Coke.

I asked Harvey what I asked the others—what coins best represent his country? He had difficulty choosing, and not because of the many options but because of a lack of them. Antebellum coinage such as half cents and large cents were influenced by Grecian and Roman designs because the Greek and Roman eras were seen as periods of high culture. From 1892 to 1916, when Charles Barber was chief engraver of the US Mint, coins had Grecian heads. The symbols weren't the best representatives of the United States. Moreover, there was a law that prohibited changing the design of coins for a twenty-five-year period so that they could be traded without hesitation across the country. Many nineteenth-century US coins had images of Native Americans, and twentieth-century US coins have depictions of US presidents like George Washington and Abraham Lincoln. But Harvey doesn't believe these coins are aesthetically riveting, truly representative of America the Beautiful.

Finally, Harvey said with a broad smile, "You can't go wrong with the double eagle."

The "double eagle" $20 gold piece, made between 1907 and 1933, is one of the most famous coins in American history, renowned for its beauty. It took the friendship of an artist and a president to make it happen, he explained.

President Theodore Roosevelt was obsessed with extolling the United States. He came of age after the Civil War, during Reconstruction, and he knew many Americans still defined themselves as being from the North or South. As president, he looked to unify the country by trumpeting Americana: He signed the Antiquities Act, which gave the president power to designate public lands for conservation. He used this to create eighteen monuments and fifty-one bird sanctuaries and protect more than 100 million acres of forest.[43] He came to the same conclusion as Ralph Waldo Emerson and Walt Whitman, who thought that America should have an indigenous and representative art so that it could unmoor itself from Europe.[44]

When it came to money, Roosevelt wanted to unify the country with common, triumphant symbols that expressed a national self-identity. He described the US coins designed by Charles Barber as "atrocious hideousness."[45] He turned to his friend the sculptor Augustus Saint-Gaudens for help. Saint-Gaudens had already designed the inaugural medal for then vice president Roosevelt, who said it was "a real addition to the national sum of permanent achievement."[46] In 1904, Roosevelt wrote to the Treasury secretary, "Would it be possible, without asking permission from Congress, to employ a man like Saint-Gaudens to give us a coinage that would have some beauty?"[47] It was the first time that a US coin was designed by someone not working for the US Mint and so was a slight to Barber and the rest of the mint staff.

The $20 gold double eagle was initially designed in 1849 by portraitist James Longacre. On the front was Lady Liberty with a tiara surrounded by thirteen stars. On the back was a wreath and an eagle with the denomination and "United States of America" written around the edge. The coin received a lukewarm reception for its shabby appearance, an "imperfectly formed" eagle that looked "ashamed of itself."[48]

Saint-Gaudens, who was also a numismatist, was paid five thousand dollars to improve these coins, as well as ones of other denominations. His version would be known as the "MCMVII double eagle." Not only did Roosevelt authorize Saint-Gaudens, but he provided him artistic input:

> How is the gold coinage design coming along? I want to make a suggestion... I was looking up some gold coins of Alexander the Great today, and I was struck by their high relief. Would it be well to have our coins in high relief, and also to have the rims raised? The point of having the rim raised would be, of course, to protect the figure of the coins; and if we have the figures in high relief, like figures on the old Greek coins, they will surely last longer. What do you think of this?[49]

Saint-Gaudens welcomed Roosevelt's suggestions and agreed with his analysis. However, Saint-Gaudens was skeptical that the US Mint would approve a high-relief coin because of the technical requirements and Barber's lingering resentment at being excluded from the design. Roosevelt explained to the Treasury secretary that this was his "pet baby."[50] Roosevelt thought the secretary saw him as a "crack-brained lunatic on the subject."[51] But in the end, the secretary had "no earthly objection to having those coins as artistic as the Greeks could desire."[52]

Despite dying in 1907 from cancer, Saint-Gaudens had his work live on through his coins. On the front is Liberty striding with a torch in her right hand, olive branch in her left. On the back is an eagle soaring, facing left, over the rising sun, with the denomination and "United States of America" above. The coins required seven blows from the press to create the dramatic relief that Saint-Gaudens envisioned. His design lacked the words "In God We Trust," as US law didn't require its inclusion, which generated controversy, so Congress restored it. As a coin, the double eagle was seen as unequaled in American coinage. Roosevelt was thrilled. The market price of these coins moved sharply higher from a face value of $20 to around $30. The coin remained in circulation until 1933, when Roosevelt's fifth cousin

President Franklin Roosevelt's Gold Reserve Act required that Americans hand over their gold to the US government.

David Bowers, legendary numismatist and business partner of Harvey Stack, writes, "In the annals of American numismatics, [it] has been a 'trophy coin' *par excellence*...This coin...represents the epitome of American coinage art."[53] Some five thousand MCMVII double eagles exist today, and almost everyone gasps when one comes up for auction. In fact, the 1933 double eagle once held by King Farouk of Egypt, who had bought it for $1,575, was auctioned for $7.6 million (including commission) in 2002, the highest ever for a rare coin.[54] The company that helped run the auction? Well, I was sitting in their office, and its dean had just offered me a Diet Coke.

Listen Closely

It's been said that "money talks," and indeed it does—through the images and depictions found on it. Every numismatist I met urged me to look closely and study the symbols on the coins. There wasn't one dramatic takeaway from my conversations, as each collector can interpret a coin differently. But it seemed fitting to end my quest with where I began, examining the creative and symbolic capabilities that we possess that led to the invention of money and drives the reinvention of it. I haven't started a coin collection as a result, but I examine the unusual coins that I come across and try to work out the meaning of their symbols. These monetary symbols have something to say about our civic and cultural history. They have become symbols of our national values. They are reminders that *we* can shape money, even as it continues to shape us.

Epilogue

I realized that my quest to better understand money had turned into an obsession when I disregarded the US Department of State's travel warnings while in Dhaka, Bangladesh. I was determined to see the hoards of coins unearthed at Wari-Bateshwar, even if that meant racing past an angry mob of political protesters. I had become consumed with seeing money in new ways, trying to answer my governing question, "What is it about money that makes the world go 'round?" I circumnavigated the globe in search of answers but also found myself, at times, going in circles trying to understand this all-encompassing topic. I took solace when I learned that John Maynard Keynes spent at least five years in search of the beginnings of money, scouring ancient texts. He wrote that he "became absorbed to the point of frenzy."[1] Keynes even referred to his study as "Babylonian madness."[2]

Perhaps the reason for my obsession is that studying money is a never-ending pursuit. It's always changing, redefined by our needs and reinvented by our imagination. My initial task of writing a black-and-white book on such a colorful topic was to capture the essence of money. Despite looking at this subject through different kaleidoscopic lenses, money can be seen throughout as a symbol of value.

My biological investigation into the origin of exchange suggests that cooperation and symbolic thought led to the creation of this symbol of value. Humans could see items for their potential, symbolic value. The psychological lens shows that a reward region of the brain, the nucleus accumbens, fires at the thought of gaining monetary benefits, obviously registering that money is a symbol of value, something to be desired. From the Maoris of New Zealand to apartment movers in Montreal, anthropologists have discovered that the journey of this symbol through a community can define the shape of human relationships and contours of a society. Regardless of whether it's hard, soft, or intangible, money remains something that is desired, and for some, an item to be controlled. Across different faiths, even God recognizes money as a symbol of value, providing detailed instructions on how to handle material wealth. Look more closely at money and it reveals a symbol of our values with telling images struck on ancient and modern coins alike.

Regardless of how we look at money, it stares back at us. But it isn't waiting. It's always moving, shifting, and encroaching on various parts of our lives, and we often don't realize it. Only with deliberate reflection can we see how its history has shaped us, from helping to control or democratize a society, to obtaining the resources necessary to live. This symbol of value activates our minds, steers our bodies, and helps determine the fate of our souls.

Because everyone interprets this symbol differently, it takes real, conscious thought to work out what it means to you. But that doesn't mean I won't help.

Recently I had dinner with an Iranian American friend. I shared some of my research from this book with him. He mentioned that in 2009, during the political protests in Iran, protesters wrote antigovernment messages on paper money.[3] It proved to be a good way to spread a message through the community.

The next day, on my walk to work, I passed by a tall lady wearing a gabardine skirt and an indigo scarf on the street and handed her a dollar bill. She was surprised, at first declining it, perhaps not wanting to take on a debt that she couldn't repay, but she eventually accepted. I had scribbled a message on it, in hopes that it will find you. In the meantime, until it reaches you, you will just have to look more closely at the money that comes your way.

Acknowledgments

Culo quadrato: the Italian expression for someone who sits in a chair working so long that he or she gets a "square butt." It's the nickname that some of my friends call me because of this book, which took many years to complete. While working at J. P. Morgan and fulfilling my duties as a US Navy reservist, I wrote in the morning, late at night, on weekends, and during the holidays (sorry, Mom!)—on planes, trains, automobiles, and even a submarine base. Without a doubt, it's the most intellectually demanding project of which I've ever been a part, and also the most rewarding.

Because of the book's breadth, I had to get up to speed on many different disciplines. I relied on many experts for each chapter. I'm grateful to those who read the manuscript, spotted mistakes, and helped me get (most of) it right:

Chapter 1: Rachel Gittman and Lindsey Carr, both PhD candidates at the University of North Carolina at Chapel Hill (UNC); Leandro Vaca, Galapagos Science Center lab and field coordinator; Stephen Walsh, professor of geography at UNC and codirector of the Galapagos Science Center; Carlos Valle, professor of evolutionary biology at the Galapagos Science Center; Haim Ofek, professor of economics at the State University of New York at Binghamton.

Chapter 2: Kenway Louie, research assistant professor, Center for Neural Science at New York University (NYU); Gijs Brouwer, postdoctoral fellow and research scientist in neuroscience at NYU; Brian Knutson, associate professor of psychology and neuroscience at Stanford University; Camelia Kuhnen, associate professor of finance at the University of North Carolina's Kenan-Flagler Business School; Dilip Soman, professor of marketing at Rotman School of Management, University of Toronto; Kevin Bynum, BlackRock; Tim Kubarych, Harding Loevner.

Chapter 3: Randall Wray, professor of economics at the University of

Missouri–Kansas City; John Sherry, professor of anthropology at the University of Notre Dame; Steven Garfinkle, professor of history at Western Washington University; Sergei Kan, professor of anthropology and Native American studies at Dartmouth College; Dan Chamby, BlackRock; and Shayne Ebudo, formerly an executive director at J. P. Morgan.

Chapter 4: Ute Wartenberg Kagan, executive director of American Numismatic Society; Steven Garfinkle; David Sear, formerly at B. A. Seaby and author of *Roman Coins and Their Values*; Wayne G. Sayles, author of *Ancient Coin Collecting*; Randall Wray; Lawrence Stack and Harvey Stack, Stack's Bowers Gallery.

Chapter 5: Benn Steil, director of international economics at the Council on Foreign Relations; Farley Grubb, professor of economics at the University of Delaware; Justin Leverenz, Oppenheimer; Steve Mariotti, NFTE; Nicolas Rodriguez-Brizuela, Artisan Partners; Nirat Lertchitvikul, Stack's Bowers Gallery in Hong Kong; Harvey Stack; Lawrence Stack; Chirag Garg; Shayne Ebudo; Kevin Bynum.

Chapter 6: Balaji Srinivasan, Andreessen Horowitz; Tom Trentman, Sands Capital; Suchit Das, former senior product manager at PayPal; Tientsin Huan, J. P. Morgan; Charles Allen, BitcoinShop; Michal Handerhan, BitcoinShop; Moshe Cohen, Columbia University.

Chapter 7: Reverend Steven Paulikas; Monzer Kahf, scholar of Islamic finance; Paul Courtright, professor of religion at Emory University; Susannah Heschel, professor of Jewish studies at Dartmouth College; Larry Kahaner; Umar Moghuls; Nicolas Rodriguez-Brizuela; Charles Boxenbaum.

Chapter 8: Howard Daniel, Quoc Hoang Nguyen, Ronachai Krisadaolarn, Willie Villareal, Percival "Boyet" Manuel, Kavan Ratnatunga, Harvey Stack, Lawrence Stack. As well as Ravi Shankar Sharma, secretary of Numismatics Society of Calcutta; and H. S. Saggu, treasurer of the Numismatics Society of Calcutta; Morena Ramos, PNAS; Ed Nocom, PNAS; Mr. Thieu in Hanoi; D. Wayne Johnson; Wayne Homren, editor of the *E-Sylum*.

I'm thankful for the contributions of these smart folks: Jon Anderson, Arjun Dev Arora, Sundeep Ahuja, John Baxter, Danielle Bernstein, Frank Bisignano, Vicki Black, Michael Bossidy, Josh Bower, Katie Clark, Bishawjit Das, Mike Derham, Mitul Desai, Jasmin Eichler, Corine Farhat, Hussein Fazal, David Gardner, Jono Gasparro, Sophie Geng, Henedina Somoza Gonzales,

Adam Jackson, Moushumi Khan, Sarah Labowitz, Dennis Lockhart, Frederick Mbari, Lisa Miller, Seema Mody, Maroof Mohsin, Lamiya Morshed, Lakshay Nirula, Jared O'Connell, Anne Phyfe Palmer, Chirayu Patel, Sufi Mostafizur Rahman, Benjamin Richter, Jafar Rizvi, Sorin Roibu, Patrick Scholtes, Geoff Schwarten, Manuel Sevillano, Katherine Snedeker, Vivek Sodera, Adam Starr, Lev Sviridov, Paul Volcker, Michael Welch, David Wertime, Brian Westover, John Williams, Andreas Xenachis, Andrew Young, Muhammad Yunus, and everyone who provided testimonials for the book and helped with obtaining pictures. I am especially thankful for Archduke Julian Boxenbaum, who was always available to discuss the book and how to improve it. Thank you to Ariana Pieper, dear friend and editor, who has helped me write for years; you read early drafts, researched diligently, and provided invaluable edits. I appreciate your brilliance and support.

I'm thankful to J. P. Morgan for being a wonderful place at which to learn about money and capital markets, and to my managers and colleagues, who are some of the smartest and most diligent people I've ever known. I'm also grateful to the New York Public Library, an incredible resource, as well as their research librarians. Thank you, Professor Gretchen Young, a magnificent friend and my masterful editor at Hachette. You helped conceive of this book and shepherded it to success. Along the way you provided wise counsel, encouraged me, and made this text infinitely better. Everyone needs a Gretchen in their life. Thank you to the entire team at Hachette and Grand Central Publishing, including Jamie Raab, Rick Wolff, Allyson Rudolph, Jamie Snider, Marlene Plasencia, Caitlin Mulrooney-Lyski, and Thomas Pitoniak. My agent, Gillian MacKenzie, was remarkable in shaping the direction of the manuscript and providing counsel.

My loving family sustained me during this project: Raghbir, Surishtha, and Kashi. When I would tire of writing, I would walk circles around Madison Square Park, chatting with my mother, who offered sage advice.

My mentor, Douglas Brinkley, is splendid, available at late hours to talk shop and help me hone this craft. He and his wife, Anne, have been incredibly generous to me over the years. I'm proud to be a lifelong student and disciple of his. And to you, the reader, for joining me on this journey.

List of Illustrations

Selected Bibliography

Akerlof, George A., and Robert J. Shiller. *Animal Spirits*. Princeton, NJ: Princeton University Press, 2009.

Andreessen, Marc. "Why Bitcoin Matters." *New York Times*, January 21, 2014. http://dealbook.nytimes.com/2014/01/21/why-bitcoin-matters/?_php=true&_type=blogs&_r=0.

Aristotle. *The Politics and Economics of Aristotle*. Trans. E. Walford. London: George Bell & Sons, 1876.

Balter, Michael. "On the Origin of Art and Symbolism." *Science* 323 (February 6, 2009): 709–11. http://www.sciencemag.org/content/323/5915/709.full?ijkey=PVlAWrnJDMlhE&keytype=ref&siteid=sci.

Beinhocker, Eric D. *The Origin of Wealth*. Boston: Harvard Business School Press, 2006.

Belsky, Gary, and Thomas Gilovich. *Why Smart People Make Big Money Mistakes*. New York: Simon & Schuster, 2009.

Benedict, Ruth. *The Chrysanthemum and the Sword*. New York: First Mariner Books, 2005.

Bhatt, S. R. "The Concept of Moksa—An Analysis." *Philosophy and Phenomenological Research* 36, no. 4 (1976): 564–70.

Board of Governors of the Federal Reserve System. *The Federal Reserve System: Purposes and Functions*. 9th ed. Washington, DC: Publications Committee of the Board of Governors of the Federal Reserve System, 2005.

Bordo, Michael David. "The Classical Gold Standard: Some Lessons for Today." Federal Reserve Bank of St. Louis, May 1981. http://research.stlouisfed.org/publications/review/81/05/Classical_May1981.pdf.

Brooks, David. "The Inverse Logic of Life." Aspen Institute, July 16, 2013. https://www.youtube.com/watch?v=WlJnNRdVHHw.

Buchanan, Mark. *The Social Atom*. Kindle ed. New York: Bloomsbury USA, 2007.

Cobert, Beth, Brigit Helms, and Doug Parker. "Mobile Money: Getting to Scale in Emerging Markets." McKinsey & Company, Insights and Publications, May 2012. http://www.mckinsey.com/insights/social_sector/mobile_money_getting_to_scale_in_emerging_markets.

Colander, David, et al. "The Financial Crisis and the Systemic Failure of Academic Economics." Social Science Research Network, March 9, 2009. http://papers.ssrn.com/sol3/papers.cfm?abstract_id=1355882.

Coyle, Daniel. *The Talent Code*. Kindle ed. New York: Random House, 2009.

Darwin, Charles. *The Descent of Man*. New York: D. Appleton, 1871.

———. *The Expression of the Emotions in Man and Animals*. Oxford University Press, 1998.

———. *The Origin of Species*. Amherst, NY: Prometheus Books, 1991.

Davidson, Paul. "Monetary Policy in the Twenty-First Century in the Light of the Debate Between Chartalism and Monetarism." In Jeff Biddle et al., eds., *Economics Broadly Considered*. New York: Routledge, 2001, pp. 335–47.

Dawkins, Richard. *The Greatest Show on Earth*. New York: Free Press, 2009.

———. *The Selfish Gene*. Oxford: Oxford University Press, 1989.

d'Errico, Francesco, and Lucinda Blackwell, eds. *From Tools to Symbols*. Johannesburg: Wits University Press, 2005.

Duhigg, Charles. *The Power of Habit*. Kindle ed. New York: Random House, 2012.

Eagleton, Catherine, et al. *Money: A History*. New York: Firefly Books, 2007.

Eichengreen, Barry. *Exorbitant Privilege*. Kindle ed. New York: Oxford University Press, 2011.

Eichengreen, Barry, and Peter Temin. "The Gold Standard and the Great Depression." *NBER Working Paper Series*. June 1997. http://www.nber.org/papers/w6060.pdf?new_window=1.

Erwann, Michel-Kerjan, and Paul Slovic, eds. *The Irrational Economist*. New York: PublicAffairs, 2010.

Federal Reserve Bank of Boston. "History of Colonial Money." http://www.bos.frb.org/education/pubs/historyo.pdf.

Feller, Ray. "Collecting Away Their Suffering: Meaningful Hobbies and the Processing of Traumatic Experience." Diss., Antioch University New England, 2001. https://etd.ohiolink.edu/ap/0?0:APPLICATION_PROCESS%3DDOWNLOAD_ETD_SUB_DOC_ACCNUM:::F1501_ID:antioch1317735299%2Cattachment.

Ferguson, Niall. *The Ascent of Money*. New York: Penguin Group, 2008.

Fet, Victor. "Kozo-Polyansky's Life." In B. M. Kozo-Polyansky, ed., *Symbiogenesis: A New Principle of Evolution*. Cambridge, MA: Harvard University Press, 2010.

Ford, Brian J. *The Secret Language of Life: How Animals and Plants Feel and Communicate*. New York: Fromm International, 1999.

Fox, Justin. *The Myth of the Rational Market*. New York: HarperCollins, 2009.

Francis, Pope. "Apostolic Exhortation Evangelii Gaudium. Vatican." 2013. http://www.vatican.va/holy_father/francesco/apost_exhortations/documents/papa-francesco_esortazione-ap_20131124_evangelii-gaudium_en.html#No_to_the_new_idolatry_of_money.

Frank, Tenney. *An Economic History of Rome.* New York: Cooper Square, 1962.

Franklin, Benjamin. "A Modest Enquiry Into the Nature and Necessity of a Paper-Currency." *Colonial Currency Reprints.* Boston: John Wilson & Son, 1911, pp. 335–57.

Friedman, Milton, and Rose D. Friedman. *Free to Choose.* New York: Harcourt Brace Jovanovich, 1980.

Friedman, Walter A. *Fortune Tellers.* Princeton, NJ: Princeton University Press, 2014.

Glimcher, Paul W. *Foundations of Neuroeconomic Analysis.* New York: Oxford University Press, 2011.

Gordon, Barry J. "Aristotle, Schumpeter, and the Metalist Tradition." *Quarterly Journal of Economics* 75, no. 4 (November 1961): 608–14.

Gordon, Deborah. *Ants at Work: How an Insect Society Is Organized.* New York: Free Press, 1999.

Gowa, Joanne S. *Closing the Gold Window: Domestic Politics and the End of Bretton Woods.* Ithaca, NY: Cornell University Press, 1983.

Graeber, David. *Debt: The First 5,000 Years.* Kindle ed. Brooklyn: Melville House, 2011.

Graham, Benjamin. *The Intelligent Investor.* New York: Harper, 2006.

Greco, Thomas H. *The End of Money and the Future of Civilization.* Kindle ed. White River Junction, VT: Chelsea Green, 2009.

Greenspan, Alan. *Age of Turbulence.* New York: Penguin, 2008.

———. *The Map and the Territory.* New York: Penguin, 2013.

Greenspan, Stanley I., and Stuart Shanker. *The First Idea.* Cambridge, MA: Da Capo Press, 2004.

Grubb, Farley. "Benjamin Franklin and the Birth of Paper Money." Federal Reserve Bank of Philadelphia, March 3, 2006. https://www.philadelphiafed.org/publications/economic-education/ben-franklin-and-paper-money-economy.pdf.

Guthrie, R. Dale. *The Nature of Paleolithic Art.* Chicago: University of Chicago Press, 2005.

Hamilton, Alexander. *The Works of Alexander Hamilton.* Vol. 2. Ed. J. C. Hamilton. New York, 1850.

Harris, William V. *The Monetary Systems of the Greeks and Romans.* Oxford Scholarship Online ed. New York: Oxford University Press, 2008.

Hyde, Lewis. *The Gift.* New York: Random House, 2007.

Ingham, Geoffrey. " 'Babylonian Madness': On the Historical and Sociological Origins of Money." In John N. Smithin, ed., *What Is Money?* New York: Routledge, 2000.

Jacob, Margaret C. *The Enlightenment: A Brief History with Documents.* Boston: Bedford / St. Martin's, 2001.

Kahaner, Larry. *Values, Prosperity, and the Talmud.* Hoboken, NJ: John Wiley & Sons, 2003.

Kahneman, Daniel. *Thinking, Fast and Slow.* Kindle ed. New York: Farrar, Straus & Giroux, 2011.

Kahneman, Daniel, and Angus Deaton. "High Income Improves Evaluation of Life but Not Emotional Well-being. *PNAS* 107, no. 38 (September 21, 2010): 1–5. http://www.pnas.org/content/107/38/16489.long.

Kahneman, Daniel, and Amos Tversky. "Prospect Theory: An Analysis of Decision Under Risk." *Econometrica* 47, no. 2 (1979): 263–92.

Karimzadi, Shahvazar. *Money and Its Origins.* New York: Routledge, 2013.

Keller, Timothy. "Treasure vs. Money." Redeemer Presbyterian Church, May 2, 1999. http://sermons2.redeemer.com/sermons/treasure-vs-money.

Keynes, John Maynard. *The Collected Writings of John Maynard Keynes.* Vol. 11. Cambridge: Cambridge University Press, 1983.

———. *Treatise on Money: The Pure Theory of Money.* New York: Palgrave Macmillan, 1971.

Khan, Muhammad Arkan. *Islamic Economics and Finance: A Glossary.* New York: Routledge, 1990.

Kindleberger, Charles P., and Robert Z. Aliber. *Manias, Panics, and Crashes.* 6th ed. New York: Palgrave Macmillan, 2011.

Knapp, Georg Friedrich. *The State Theory of Money.* London: Macmillan, 1924.

Knutson, Brian. "Emotion Is Peripheral." January 15, 2014. http://edge.org/print/response-detail/25466.

Knutson, Brian, et al. "Anticipation of Monetary Reward Selectively Recruits Nucleus Accumbens." *Journal of Neuroscience* 21 (2001): RC159.

Komter, Aafke E. *Social Solidarity and the Gift.* Cambridge: Cambridge University Press, 2005.

Krugman, Paul. "The Theory of Interstellar Trade." Princeton University, July 1978. http://www.princeton.edu/~pkrugman/interstellar.pdf.

Kurlansky, Mark. *Salt.* New York: Penguin, 2002.

Landy, Joshua. "In Defense of Humanities." Stanford University, December 7, 2010. http://news.stanford.edu/news/2010/december/humanities-defense-landy-120710.html.

Lebra, Takie Sugiyama. *Japanese Patterns of Behavior.* Honolulu: University Press of Hawaii, 1976.

Lewis, C. S. *Mere Christianity.* New York: HarperCollins, 1980.

Lewis, Hunter. *How Much Money Does an Economy Need?* Mount Jackson, VA: Axios Press, 2007.

Lewis-Williams, David P. *Inside the Neolithic Mind.* London: Thames & Hudson, 2005.

Lowenstein, Roger. *When Genius Failed.* New York: Random House, 2000.

Luscombe, Belinda. "Do We Need $75,000 a Year to Be Happy?" *Time,* September 6, 2010. http://content.time.com/time/magazine/article/0,9171,2019628,00.html.

Mahalakshmi, R. *The Book of Lakshmi.* New Delhi: Penguin, 2009.

Martin, Felix. *Money: The Unauthorized Biography.* London: Bodley Head, 2013.

Marx, Karl. *Capital*. Vol. 1. 1867. Online ed. Progress Publishers. https://www.marxists
.org/archive/marx/works/1867-c1/ch04.htm.

Mauss, Marcel. *The Gift*. London: Norton, 1990.

McTaggart, Lynne. *The Bond*. New York: Free Press, 2011.

Mellor, Mary. *The Future of Money: From Financial Crisis to Public Resource*.
New York: Pluto Press, 2010.

Mills, Cynthia L. *The Theory of Evolution*. Hoboken, NJ: John Wiley & Sons, 2004.

Mises, Ludwig von. *Human Action: A Treatise on Economics*. San Francisco: Fox &
Wilkes, 1996. http://mises.org/Books/humanaction.pdf.

——. *The Theory of Money and Credit*. New Haven, CT: Yale University Press, 1953.

Mlodinow, Leonard. *Subliminal*. Kindle ed. New York: Random House, 2012.

Murphy, Antoin E. *John Law: Economic Theorist*. Oxford: Oxford University Press, 1997.

Noles, James L. *A Pocketful of History*. Cambridge, MA: Da Capo Press, 2008.

Ofek, Haim. *Second Nature: Economic Origins of Human Evolution*. Kindle ed. Cambridge: Cambridge University Press, 2001.

Piketty, Thomas. *Capital in the Twenty-First Century*. Cambridge, MA: Harvard University Press, 2014.

Plato. *The Laws*. Trans. T. J. Saunders. London: Penguin Books, 1970.

Principe, Lawrence. *The Secrets of Alchemy*. Chicago: University of Chicago Press, 2013.

Rand, Ayn. *Atlas Shrugged*. New York: Penguin, 2005.

Rickards, James. *Currency Wars*. New York: Penguin, 2011.

Roach, John. "Ant Study Shows Link Between Single Gene, Colony Formation." National
Geographic News, January 24, 2002. http://news.nationalgeographic.com/news/
pf/17495718.html.

Roberts, Renea, dir. *Gifting It: A Burning Embrace of Gift Economy*. 2002.

Rothbard, Murray N. "The Monetary Breakdown of the West." Ludwig von Mises Institute, n.d. http://mises.org/money/4s3.asp.

——. "What Has Government Done to Our Money?" Ludwig von Mises Institute, n.d.
https://mises.org/money/4s1.asp.

Rupp, Katherine. *Gift-Giving in Japan: Cash, Connections, Cosmologies*. Stanford, CA:
Stanford University Press, 2003.

Samuelson, Robert J. *The Great Inflation and Its Aftermath*. New York: Random
House, 2008.

Sandel, Michael J. *What Money Can't Buy*. New York: Farrar, Straus & Giroux, 2012.

Sapp, Jan. *Evolution by Association: A History of Symbiosis*. New York: Oxford
University Press, 1994.

Schumpeter, Joseph A. *History of Economic Analysis*. New York: Oxford University
Press, 1994.

Seaford, Richard. *Money and the Early Greek Mind*. Cambridge: Cambridge University
Press, 2004.

Smith, Adam. *The Wealth of Nations.* New York: Knopf, 1991.

Smith, Vernon L. *Rationality in Economics.* New York: Cambridge University Press, 2008.

Smithsonian National Museum of Natural History. "Bigger Brains: Complex Brains for a Complex World." http://humanorigins.si.edu/human-characteristics/brains.

Sowell, Thomas. *On Classical Economics.* New Haven, CT: Yale University Press, 2006.

Steil, Benn. *The Battle of Bretton Woods.* Princeton, NJ: Princeton University Press, 2013.

Swensen, David F. *Unconventional Success.* Kindle ed. New York: Simon & Schuster, 2005.

Taylor, Mark C. *Confidence Games.* Chicago: University of Chicago Press, 2004.

Thaler, Richard H. "Mental Accounting Matters." *Journal of Behavioral Decision Making* 12 (1999): 183–206.

Tien-tsin Huang. *Payment Processing: Payments Market Share Handbook.* J. P. Morgan, 2013.

Vermeij, Geerat J. *Nature: An Economic History.* Princeton, NJ: Princeton University Press, 2004.

Weatherford, Jack. *The History of Money.* New York: Three Rivers Press, 1997.

Wenger, Albert. "Bitcoin as Protocol." Union Square Ventures, October 31, 2013. http://www.usv.com/posts/bitcoin-as-protocol.

Witherington, Ben, III. *Jesus and Money.* Grand Rapids, MI: Brazos Press, 2010.

Woo, David. "Bitcoin: A First Assessment." Bank of America Merrill Lynch, 2013.

Wray, L. Randall. *Credit and State Theories of Money: The Contributions of A. Mitchell Innes.* Cheltenham, England, and Northampton, MA: Edward Elgar, 2004.

Xinyue Zhou, Kathleen D. Vohs, and Roy F. Baumeister. "The Symbolic Power of Money." *Psychological Science* 20, no. 6 (2009): 700–706.

Zaman, Asad. "Islamic Economics: A Survey of the Literature: II." *Islamic Studies* 48, no. 4 (2009): 525–66.

Zweig, Jason. *Your Money and Your Brain.* Kindle ed. New York: Simon & Schuster, 2007.

Notes

Epigraph

1. Voltaire, *A Philosophical Dictionary*, n.d., University of Adelaide, retrieved March 11, 2014, from http://ebooks.adelaide.edu.au/v/voltaire/dictionary/chapter332.html.
2. Italo Calvino, *Invisible Cities*, Kindle ed. (Orlando, FL: Harcourt, 2012).

Chapter 1. *It's a Jungle Out There*

1. William Whewell, *History of the Inductive Sciences*, vol. 2 (London: J. W. Parker, 1837), p. 185.
2. Adam Smith, *The Wealth of Nations* (New York: Knopf, 1991), p. 13.
3. Charles Darwin, *The Origin of Species* (Amherst, NY: Prometheus Books, 1991), pp. 47–48.
4. Richard L. Lesher and George J. Howick, *Assessing Technology Transfer* (Washington, DC: National Aeronautics and Space Administration, 1966), p. 9.
5. BBC, *History of Life on Earth*, retrieved March 3, 2013, from http://www.bbc.co.uk/nature/history_of_the_earth.
6. Darwin, *The Origin of Species*, pp. 1–20.
7. Paul D. Stewart, *Galápagos: The Islands That Changed the World* (New Haven, CT: Yale University Press, 2007), pp. 147–50.
8. National Oceanic and Atmospheric Administration, *National Ocean Service Education*, March 25, 2008, http://oceanservice.noaa.gov/education/kits/corals/media/supp_coral02bc.html.
9. E. M. Bik, "Composition and Function of the Human-Associated Microbiota," *Nutritional Reviews* 67 (2009): S164–71.
10. Haim Ofek, *Second Nature: Economic Origins of Human Evolution*, Kindle ed. (Cambridge: Cambridge University Press, 2001), loc. 67.
11. Ian Sample, "With a Little Help from Your Friends You Can Live Longer," *Guardian*, July 27, 2010, http://www.theguardian.com/lifeandstyle/2010/jul/27/friendship-relationships-good-health-study.
12. Robert W. Bauman, *Microbiology* (San Francisco: Pearson, 2006), pp. 85–86.
13. Victor Fet, "Kozo-Polyansky's Life," in Boris Mikhaylovich Kozo-Polyansky, *Symbiogenesis: A New Principle of Evolution* (Cambridge, MA: Harvard University Press, 2010).

14. Jeanna Bryner, "Dinosaur-Era Insects Frozen in Time During Oldest Pollination," *Live Science*, May 14, 2012, retrieved March 3, 2013, from http://www.livescience.com/20304-amber-insects-oldest-pollination.html.

15. In evolutionary biology, the reproductive success (RS) has become known as the currency of natural selection. RS is determined by the number of offspring that an individual produces, and which survives to reproduce. Professor Carlos Valle points out that energy is a good proxy for RS. For example, the optimal foraging theory suggests that individuals use energy as currency and seek to maximize it.

16. William C. Burger, *Flowers: How They Changed the World* (Amherst, NY: Prometheus Books, 2006), pp. 81–90.

17. Adam Cole, "Honey, It's Electric: Bees Sense Charge on Flowers," NPR, February 22, 2013, retrieved March 3, 2013, from http://www.npr.org/2013/02/22/172611866/honey-its-electric-bees-sense-charge-on-flowers.

18. Bauman, *Microbiology*, pp. 141–63.

19. Jack Weatherford, *The History of Money* (New York: Three Rivers Press, 1997), p. 48.

20. Anahit Galstyan et al., "The Shade Avoidance Syndrome in Arabidopsis: A Fundamental Role for Atypical Basic Helix-loop-helix Proteins as Transcriptional Cofactors," *Plant Journal* 66, no. 2 (2011): 258–67.

21. Mark Kurlansky, *Salt* (New York: Penguin, 2002), pp. 10–11.

22. Karl Marx, *Capital*, vol. 1 (1887), online ed. (Progress Publishers, n.d.), https://www.marxists.org/archive/marx/works/1867-c1/ch04.htm.

23. Lynne McTaggart, *The Bond* (New York: Free Press, 2011), pp. xx–xxi.

24. John A. Moore, *Heredity and Development*, 2nd ed. (Washington, DC: National Academies Press, 1972), pp. 7–18.

25. Charles Darwin, *The Descent of Man* (New York: Appleton, 1871), p. 79.

26. Robert Axelrod, *The Evolution of Cooperation*, Kindle ed. (New York: Perseus Book Group, 2009), pp. 7–9.

27. Ibid., pp. 50–51.

28. Ibid., pp. 40–41.

29. Ibid., p. 123.

30. Richard Dawkins, *The Selfish Gene* (Oxford: Oxford University Press, 1989), p. 229.

31. Ibid., p. 203.

32. Ludwig von Mises, *Human Action: A Treatise on Economics* (San Francisco: Fox & Wilkes, 1996), http://mises.org/Books/humanaction.pdf, p. 144.

33. McTaggart, *The Bond*, p. 80.

34. Ibid.

35. Bernadette Boden-Albala et al., "Social Isolation and Outcomes Post Stroke," *Neurology* 64, no. 11 (2005): 1888–92.

36. McTaggart, *The Bond*, p. 80; Julianne Holt-Lunstad, Timothy B. Smith, and J. Bradley Layton, "Social Relationships and Mortality Risk: A Meta-analytic Review," *PLOS*

Medicine 7, no. 7 (July 10, 2010), http://www.plosmedicine.org/article/info:doi/10.1371/journal.pmed.1000316.

37. Dawkins, *The Selfish Gene*, p. 258.

38. Susanne Shultz, Christopher Opie, and Quentin D. Atkinson, "Stepwise Evolution of Stable Sociality in Primates," *Nature* 479 (November 10, 2011): 219–22.

39. Celia W. Dugger and John Noble Wilford, "New Hominid Species Discovered in South Africa," *New York Times*, April 8, 2010, retrieved March 4, 2013, from http://www.nytimes.com/2010/04/09/science/09fossil.html?pagewanted=all&_r=0.

40. Martin Reuter et al., "Investigating the Genetic Basis of Altruism: The Role of the COMT Val158Met Polymorphism," *Social Cognitive and Affective Neuroscience* (2010), http://scan.oxfordjournals.org/content/early/2010/10/28/scan.nsq083.full.

41. "Researchers in Bonn Find an 'Altruism Gene,'" press release, University of Bonn, Bonn, Germany, http://www3.uni-bonn.de/Press-releases/researchers-in-bonn-find-an-201caltruism-gene201c.

42. Adam L. Penenberg, "Social Networking Affects Brains like Falling in Love," *Fast Company*, July 1, 2010, http://www.fastcompany.com/1659062/social-networking-affects-brains-falling-love.

43. Mark Honigsbaum, "Oxytocin: Could the 'Trust Hormone' Rebond Our Troubled World?," *Guardian*, August 20, 2011, http://www.guardian.co.uk/science/2011/aug/21/oxytocin-zak-neuroscience-trust-hormone.

44. Zack Lynch, *The Neuro Revolution* (New York: St. Martin's Press, 2009), pp. 97–108.

45. C. H. Declerck, Christopher Boone, and Toko Kiyonari, "The Effect of Oxytocin on Cooperation in a Prisoner's Dilemma Depends on the Social Context and a Person's Social Value Orientation," *Social Cognitive and Affective Neuroscience* (2013), http://www.ncbi.nlm.nih.gov/pubmed/23588271.

46. Axelrod, *The Evolution of Cooperation*, p. 94.

47. Peter T. Boag and Peter R. Grant, "Intense Natural Selection in a Population of Darwin's Finches (Geospizinae) in the Galapagos," in Kathleen Donohue, ed., *Darwin's Finches* (Chicago: University of Chicago Press, 2011), p. 286.

48. Martin H. Wikelski, "Darwin's Finches," *eLS* (2001): 3–4.

49. Smith, *The Wealth of Nations*, pp. 4–7.

50. Ann Gibbons, *The First Human* (New York: Anchor Books, 2007), pp. 36–39.

51. British Museum, "A History of the World in 100 Objects: Olduvai Handaxe," n.d., retrieved March 18, 2013, from http://www.bbc.co.uk/ahistoryoftheworld/about/transcripts/episode3.

52. Francisco J. Ayala, *Am I a Monkey?* (Baltimore: Johns Hopkins University Press, 2010), pp. 3–10.

53. Mises, *Human Action*, p. 176.

54. John F. Hoffecker, *Landscape of the Mind* (New York: Columbia University Press, 2011), pp. 15–66.

55. Ofek, *Second Nature*, locs. 1499–1503.

56. Michael Balter, "On the Origin of Art and Symbolism," *Science* 323 (February 6, 2009): 709–11, http://www.sciencemag.org/content/323/5915/709.full?ijkey=PVlAWrnJDMlhE &keytype=ref&siteid=sci.

57. Marek Kohn and Steven Mithen, "Handaxes: Products of Sexual Selection?," *Antiquity* 73 (1999): 518–26.

58. Catherine de Lange, "Our Ancestors Had to Grow Bigger Brains to Make Axes," *New Scientist*, November 4, 2010, retrieved March 18, 2013, from http://www.newscientist .com/article/dn19677-our-ancestors-had-to-grow-bigger-brains-to-make-axes.html.

59. Peter N. Peregrine and Melvin Ember, eds., *Encyclopedia of Prehistory*, vol. 1 (New York: Springer, 2001), pp. 3–7.

60. Jonathan Kingdon, *Self-Made Man* (New York: John Wiley, 1993), pp. 47–49.

61. Maev Kennedy, "Invention of Cooking Made Having a Bigger Brain an Asset for Humans," *Guardian*, October 22, 2012, http://www.theguardian.com/science/2012/ oct/22/cooking-supports-increased-human-brain-power.

62. Ferris Jabr, "Does Thinking Really Hard Burn More Calories?," *Scientific American*, July 18, 2012, http://www.scientificamerican.com/article.cfm?id=thinking-hard-calories.

63. "Bigger Brains: Complex Brains for a Complex World," Smithsonian National Museum of Natural History, n.d., retrieved March 20, 2013, from http://humanorigins.si.edu/ human-characteristics/brains.

64. "Glacial and Interglacial Cycles of the Pleistocene," *Encyclopaedia Britannica*, retrieved March 20, 2013, from http://www.britannica.com/EBchecked/ topic/121632/climate-change/275791/Glacial-and-interglacial-cycles-of-the-Pleistocene.

65. Stanley I. Greenspan, *The First Idea* (Cambridge, MA: Da Capo Press, 2004), pp. 169–71.

66. Hoffecker, *Landscape of the Mind*, pp. 3–8.

67. R. Dale Guthrie, *The Nature of Paleolithic Art* (Chicago: University of Chicago Press, 2005), pp. 7–26, 335–39.

68. Hoffecker, *Landscape of the Mind*, p. x.

69. Ibid., pp. 5–6.

70. Ibid., p. 77.

Chapter 2. *A Piece of My Mind*

1. Alan Greenspan, *Age of Turbulence* (New York: Penguin, 2008), p. 47.

2. Daniel Kahneman, *Thinking, Fast and Slow*, Kindle ed. (New York: Farrar, Straus & Giroux, 2011), p. 288.

3. Adam Levy, "Brain Scans Show Link Between Lust for Sex and Money," Bloomberg, February 1, 2006.

4. Michael S. Sweeney, *Brain: The Complete Mind* (Washington, DC: National Geographic Society, 2009), pp. 1–2.

5. Conor Dougherty and Kelly Evans, "Economy in Worst Fall Since '82," *Wall Street Journal*, February 28, 2009.

6. Alan Greenspan, *The Map and the Territory* (New York: Penguin, 2013), p. 7.

7. Ibid., p. 8.

8. Ibid., p. 3.

9. Gregory S. Berns et al., "Predictability Modulates Human Brain Response to Reward," *Journal of Neuroscience* 21, no. 8 (2001): 2793–98.

10. Jason Zweig, *Your Money and Your Brain*, Kindle ed. (New York: Simon & Schuster, 2007), loc. 2995.

11. Walter A. Friedman, *Fortune Tellers* (Princeton, NJ: Princeton University Press, 2014), p. iv.

12. Ibid., p. 6.

13. Ibid., p. 8.

14. Efficient markets theory was an application of rational expectations. See Thomas J. Sargent, "Rational Expectations," *The Concise Encyclopedia of Economics*, n.d., retrieved May 3, 2014, from http://www.econlib.org/library/Enc/RationalExpectations.html.

15. Justin Fox, *The Myth of the Rational Market* (New York: HarperCollins, 2009), pp. xiv–xv.

16. Ibid., pp. xiii–xiv.

17. Ibid., pp. 47–57.

18. Zweig, *Your Money and Your Brain*, locs. 98–100.

19. Professor Dilip Soman raises an interesting point: When we make our own financial decisions, we may allow emotions to play a factor without realizing it. But when others, for example a wealth manager, make financial decisions for us, they may be more dispassionate about it. In this case, Markowitz may have benefited from a wealth adviser who could have put aside emotions when allocating the money.

20. Toshio Yamagishi et al., "In Search of *Homo economicus*," *Psychological Science* (2014), http://www.ncbi.nlm.nih.gov/pubmed/25037961?dopt=Abstract.

21. Peter Coy, "What Good Are Economists Anyway?," *Bloomberg Businessweek*, April 15, 2009.

22. "Why Economists Failed to Predict the Financial Crisis," Knowledge@Wharton, May 13, 2009, retrieved May 5, 2014, from http://knowledge.wharton.upenn.edu/article/why-economists-failed-to-predict-the-financial-crisis.

23. David Colander et al., "The Financial Crisis and the Systemic Failure of Academic Economics," March 9, 2009, Social Science Research Network, http://papers.ssrn.com/sol3/papers.cfm?abstract_id=1355882.

24. Cited in Fox, *The Myth of the Rational Market*, p. xi.

25. Cited in Greenspan, *The Map and the Territory*, p. 8.

26. Ibid., p. 14.

27. Kahneman, *Thinking, Fast and Slow*, p. 211.

28. Ibid., pp. 7–8.

29. Michael R. Cunningham, "Weather, Mood, and Helping Behavior: Quasi Experiments with the Sunshine Samaritan," *Journal of Personality and Social Psychology* 37, no. 11 (1979): 1947–56.

30. David Hirshleifer and Tyler Shumway, "Good Day Sunshine: Stock Returns and the Weather," *Journal of Finance* 58, no. 3 (2003): 1009–32.

31. Leonard Mlodinow, *Subliminal*, Kindle ed. (New York: Random House, 2012), pp. 23–24.

32. Adrian C. North, "The Effect of Background Music on the Taste of Wine," *British Journal of Psychology* 103, no. 3 (2012): 293–301.

33. Kahneman, *Thinking, Fast and Slow*, pp. 130–31.

34. Ibid., p. 216.

35. Ibid., pp. 212–15.

36. David F. Swensen, *Unconventional Success*, Kindle ed. (New York: Simon & Schuster, 2005), locs. 3532–37.

37. Kahneman, *Thinking, Fast and Slow*, p. 216.

38. George A. Akerlof and Robert J. Shiller, *Animal Spirits* (Princeton, NJ: Princeton University Press, 2009).

39. Markus K. Brunnermeier and Christian Julliard, "Money Illusion and Housing Frenzies," *Review of Financial Studies* 21, no. 1 (2008): 135–80.

40. Carl R. Chena, Peter P. Lung, and F. Albert Wang, "Stock Market Mispricing: Money Illusion or Resale Option?," *Journal of Financial and Quantitative Analysis* 44, no. 5 (2009): 1125–47.

41. Louis N. Christofides and Amy Chen Peng, "The Determinants of Major Provisions in Union Contracts: Duration, Indexation, and Non-Contingent Wage Adjustment," unpublished paper, University of Cyprus, 2004.

42. Bernd Weber et al., "The Medial Prefrontal Cortex Exhibits Money Illusion," *Proceedings of the National Academy of Sciences* 106, no. 13 (2009): 5025–28.

43. Daniel Kahneman and Amos Tversky, "Prospect Theory: An Analysis of Decision Under Risk," *Econometrica* 47 no. 2 (1979): 263–92.

44. Daniel Kahneman, "Daniel Kahneman—Biographical," 2002, retrieved April 27, 2013, from http://www.nobelprize.org/nobel_prizes/economics/laureates/2002/kahneman-autobio.html.

45. Mebane Faber, "Dow 300 Point Days and Volatility Clustering," MEB Faber Research, August 7, 2008, retrieved May 30, 2014, from http://mebfaber.com/2008/08/07/dow-300-point-days-and-volatility-clustering.

46. Gary Belsky and Thomas Gilovich, *Why Smart People Make Big Money Mistakes* (New York: Simon & Schuster, 2009), pp. 48–49.

47. Stephen J. Brown and Onno W. Steenbeek, "Doubling: Nick Leeson's Trading Strategy," *Pacific-Basin Finance Journal* 9, no. 2 (2001): 83–99.

48. Paul Pierson, "The New Politics of the Welfare State," *World Politics* 48, no. 2 (1996): 143–79.

49. Devin G. Pope and Maurice E. Schweitzer, "Is Tiger Woods Loss Averse? Persistent Bias in the Face of Experience, Competition, and High Stakes," *American Economic Review* 101 (2011): 129–57.

50. Christopher Trepel, Craig R. Fox, and Russell A. Poldrack, "Prospect Theory on the Brain? Toward a Cognitive Neuroscience of Decision Under Risk," *Cognitive Brain Research* (2005): 34–50.

51. Benedetto De Martino, Colin F. Camerer, and Ralph Adolphs, "Amygdala Damage Eliminates Monetary Loss Aversion," *Proceedings of the National Academy of Sciences* 107, no. 8 (2010): 3788–92.

52. Katie Moisse, "What Happens in the Amygdala…Damage to Brain's Decision-Making Area May Encourage Dicey Gambles," *Scientific American*, February 9, 2010.

53. Richard H. Thaler, "Mental Accounting Matters," *Journal of Behavioral Decision Making* 12 (1999): 183–206.

54. Mathias Pessiglione et al., "How the Brain Translates Money into Force: A Neuroimaging Study of Subliminal Motivation," *Science* 316 (2007): 904–6.

55. Xinyue Zhou, Kathleen D. Vohs, and Roy F. Baumeister, "The Symbolic Power of Money," *Psychological Science* 20, no. 6 (2009): 700–706.

56. Mathias Pessiglione, "How the Brain Translates Money into Force: A Neuro-imaging Study of Subliminal Motivation," *SCitizen*, May 24, 2007.

57. J. F. Stein and Catherine Stoodley, *Neuroscience* (New York: Wiley, 2006), pp. 36–37.

58. Sandra Blakeslee, "Brain Experts Now Follow the Money," *New York Times*, June 17, 2003.

59. Cristina Becchio et al., "How the Brain Responds to the Destruction of Money," *Journal of Neuroscience, Psychology, and Economics* 4, no. 1 (2011): 1–10.

60. Ibid.

61. Dean Buonomano, *Brain Bugs* (New York: Norton, 2011), pp. 19–46.

62. David Linden, *The Accidental Mind* (Cambridge, MA: Belknap Press of Harvard University Press, 2007), pp. 28–32.

63. Don Ross, "Introduction to Neuroeconomics: Neural Information Processing," Society for Neuroeconomics, n.d., retrieved April 27, 2013, from http://www.neuroeconomics .org/teaching/course-introduction-to-neuroeconomics-ec-490-syllabus-lectures/EC%20 490%20lecture%203%20neural%20information%20processing.pdf/at_download/file.

64. Buonomano, *Brain Bugs*, pp. 19–46.

65. Stanley I. Greenspan, *The First Idea* (Cambridge, MA: Da Capo Press, 2004), pp. 24–27.

66. Ibid.

67. Brian Knutson et al., "Anticipation of Monetary Reward Selectively Recruits Nucleus Accumbens," *Journal of Neuroscience* 21 (2001): RC159.

68. Zweig, *Your Money and Your Brain*, loc. 729.

69. Hans C. Breiter et al., "Acute Effects of Cocaine on Human Brain Activity and Emotion," *Neuron* 19, no. 3 (1997): 591–611; Patricia Wen, "An Addictive Thrill: MGH Study Finds Gambling, Cocaine Affect Same Region of Brain," *Boston Globe*, May 24, 2001, p. A.1.

70. Zweig, *Your Money and Your Brain*, loc. 143.

71. Adam Levy, "Mapping the Trader's Brain," *Bloomberg Markets*, February 1, 2006.

72. Alan G. Sanfey et al., "The Neural Basis of Economic Decision-Making in the Ultimatum Game," *Science* 300 (2003): 1755–58.

73. Zweig, *Your Money and Your Brain*, loc. 3890.

74. Sanfey et al., "The Neural Basis of Economic Decision-Making in the Ultimatum Game."

75. Brian Knutson, "*Emotion Is Peripheral*," Edge, January 15, 2004, retrieved May 15, 2014, from http://edge.org/print/response-detail/25466.

76. Brian Knutson et al., "Distributed Neural Representation of Expected Value," *Journal of Neuroscience* 25, no. 19 (2005): 4806–12.

77. Brian Knutson et al., "Nucleus Accumbens Activation Mediates the Influence of Reward Cues on Financial Risk Taking," *NeuroReport* 19 (2008): 509–13.

78. "Brain Scam?," editorial, *Nature Neuroscience* 7, no. 683 (2004).

79. Brian Knutson et al., "Neural Predictors of Purchases," *Neuron* 53, no. 1 (2007): 147–56.

80. Camelia M. Kuhnen and Brian Knutson, "The Neural Basis of Financial Risk Taking," *Neuron* 47 (2005): 763–70.

81. Ibid.

82. Camelia M. Kuhnen, Brian Knutson, and Gregory R. Samanez-Larkin, "Serotonergic Genotypes, Neuroticism, and Financial Choices," *PLoS ONE* 8, no. 1 (2013): e54632.

83. Ibid.

84. Paul Gabrielsen, "Stanford Scholar Looks to Genes to Make Sense of the Dollars You Invest," Stanford News Service, March 4, 2013, retrieved April 4, 2013, from http://news.stanford.edu/pr/2013/pr-genes-invest-attitude-030413.html.

85. Blakeslee, "Brain Experts Now Follow the Money."

86. Josh Fischman, "The Marketplace in Your Brain," *Chronicle of Higher Education*, September 4, 2012.

87. Paul W. Glimcher, *Foundations of Neuroeconomic Analysis* (New York: Oxford University Press, 2011), p. 427.

88. Blakeslee, "Brain Experts Now Follow the Money."

89. Fischman, "The Marketplace in Your Brain."

90. Ibid.

91. Many use the terms *nucleus accumbens* and *ventral striatum* interchangeably, even though nucleus accumbens is a part of the ventral striatum (along with ventral putamen and ventral caudate).

92. Gregory Berns and Sara E. Moore, "A Neural Predictor of Cultural Popularity," *Journal of Consumer Psychology* (2011).

93. Anna Teo, "Spotlight on Neuroeconomics," *Business Times*, March 1, 2013.

Chapter 3. *So in Debt*

1. Michael Lewis, *Liar's Poker* (New York: Norton, 1989), p. 99.

2. Lewis Hyde, *The Gift* (New York: Random House, 2007), p. 13.

3. Charles Dickens, *David Copperfield* (New York: Random House, 2000), p. 166.

4. Katherine Rupp, *Gift-Giving in Japan: Cash, Connections, Cosmologies* (Stanford, CA: Stanford University Press, 2003).

5. Benjamin Okaba, *Why Nigerians Bury Their Money: An Ethnography of Ijo Contemporary Burial Ceremonies* (Port Harcourt: Emhai, 1997).

6. "Factors Affecting Reserve Balances," Federal Reserve, March 27, 2014, http://www.federalreserve.gov/releases/h41/20140327.

7. Professor Steven Garfinkle prefers the word *commercial* instead of *market* sphere. He suggests that *market* has a connotation found in economics that may suggest "capitalist."

8. Adam Smith, *The Wealth of Nations* (New York: Knopf, 1991), pp. 19–22.

9. Adam Smith, *An Inquiry Into the Nature and Causes of the Wealth of Nations*, vol. 1, ed. W. Playfair (Hartford: O. D. Cooke, 1811), p. 17.

10. L. Randall Wray, ed., *Credit and State Theories of Money: The Contributions of A. Mitchell Innes* (Cheltenham, England, and Northampton, MA: Edward Elgar, 2004), pp. 16–18.

11. Ibid.

12. Caroline Humphrey, "Barter and Economic Disintegration," *Man* 20, no. 1 (March 1985): 48–72.

13. David Graeber, *Debt: The First 5,000 Years*, Kindle ed. (Brooklyn: Melville House, 2011), loc. 540.

14. Ibid., loc. 627–29.

15. Ibid., loc. 648–60.

16. Ibid., loc. 773–89.

17. Paul Sillitoe, "Why Spheres of Exchange?," *Ethnology* 45, no. 1 (2006): 1–23.

18. Ibid.

19. Marcel Mauss, *The Gift* (London: Norton, 1990).

20. Hyde, *The Gift*, pp. xx–xxii.

21. Ibid., pp. 20–25.

22. Aafke E. Komter, *Social Solidarity and the Gift* (Cambridge: Cambridge University Press, 2005), pp. 58–60.

23. Ibid.

24. Mauss, *The Gift*, pp. 23–24.

25. Hyde, *The Gift*, pp. 13–20.

26. Komter, *Social Solidarity and the Gift*, pp. 58–59.

27. Hyde, *The Gift*, p. 18.

28. Lakshmi Gandhi, "The History Behind the Phrase 'Don't Be an Indian Giver,'" NPR, September 2, 2013, http://www.npr.org/blogs/codeswitch/2013/09/02/217295339/the -history-behind-the-phrase-dont-be-an-indian-giver.

29. Hyde, *The Gift*, pp. 3–5.

30. Ibid., pp. 35–40. Kwakiutl is part of the larger Kwakwaka'wakw society.

31. Gail Ringel, "The Kwakiutl Potlatch: History, Economics, and Symbols," *Ethnohistory* 26, no. 4 (1979): 347–62. Sergei Kan points out that the new chief could also be the firstborn or most capable son of the sister of the old chief in matrilineal societies such as the Tlingit.

32. Ibid.

33. Homer G. Barnett, "The Nature of the Potlatch," *American Anthropologist* 40, no. 3 (1938): 349–58.

34. Ringel, "The Kwakiutl Potlatch."

35. Barnett, "The Nature of the Potlatch."

36. Joseph Masco, "Competitive Displays: Negotiating Genealogical Rights to the Potlatch at the American Museum of Natural History," *American Anthropologist* 98, no. 4 (December 1996): 837–52.

37. Ringel, "The Kwakiutl Potlatch."

38. Markus Giesler, "Consumer Gift Systems," *Journal of Consumer Research* (2006): 283–90.

39. Ibid.

40. Ibid.

41. "Kickstarter Stats," retrieved March 27, 2014, from http://www.kickstarter.com/help/ stats.

42. Rob Trump, "Why Would You Ever Give Money Through Kickstarter?," *New York Times Magazine*, February 8, 2013, http://www.nytimes.com/2013/02/10/magazine/why-would -you-ever-give-money-through-kickstarter.html?pagewanted=all&_r=0.

43. Komter, *Social Solidarity and the Gift*, p. 67.

44. Ibid., pp. 56–57.

45. Ibid., pp. 42–43.

46. George Lakoff, *Moral Politics: How Liberals and Conservatives Think* (Chicago: University of Chicago Press, 2002), pp. 4–8.

47. George Lakoff and Mark Johnson, "Conceptual Metaphor in Everyday Language," *Journal of Philosophy* 77, no. 8 (1980): 453–86.

48. Shawn Tully, "The Toughest Guy on Wall Street," *Fortune*, March 2006, http://features .blogs.fortune.cnn.com/2012/05/13/jamie-dimon-jpmorgan.

49. Marc Sandalow, "Bush Claims Mandate, Sets 2nd-term Goals," *San Francisco Chronicle*, November 5, 2004, http://www.sfgate.com/politics/article/Bush-claims-mandate -sets-2nd-term-goals-I-2637116.php.

50. Wilfred Dolfsma, Rene van der Eijk, and Albert Jolink, "On a Source of Social Capital: Gift Exchange," *Journal of Business Ethics* 89, no. 3 (October 2009): 315–29.

51. David B. Wooten, "Qualitative Steps Toward an Expanded Model of Anxiety in Gift-Giving," *Journal of Consumer Research* 27, no. 1 (2000): 84–95.

52. Jean-Sébastien Marcoux, "Escaping the Gift Economy," *Journal of Consumer Research* 36, no. 4 (2009): 671–85.

53. Ibid.

54. Ibid.

55. Rupp, *Gift-Giving in Japan*, pp. 1–3.

56. Ruth Benedict, *The Chrysanthemum and the Sword* (New York: First Mariner Books, 2005), pp. 100–108. Her account is somewhat dated, but her main points are important and relevant to gift giving in Japan today.

57. Ibid.

58. Ibid., pp. 100–104.

59. Ibid., pp. 112–18.

60. Ibid., pp. 132–36.

61. Ibid., pp. 146–48.

62. Takie Sugiyama Lebra, *Japanese Patterns of Behavior* (Honolulu: University Press of Hawaii, 1976), pp. 96–100.

63. Rupp, *Gift-Giving in Japan*, pp. 105–8.

64. Professor John Sherry raises a thought-provoking point about the wedding registries in Western society. Newlyweds can use the registry to give themselves gifts by invoking the social debt that their guests may feel. The newlyweds are able to obtain items that may have been difficult otherwise, and without taking on financial debt. By accepting these gifts, the newlyweds continue their role in the circle of gift giving, and will be expected to reciprocate, perhaps, at a later date. Some $19 billion is spent on gifts via registries per year. For more, read Tonya Williams Bradford and John F. Sherry Jr., "Orchestrating Rituals Through Retailers: An Examination of Gift Registry," *Journal of Retailing* 89, no. 2 (2013): 158–75.

65. Rupp, *Gift-Giving in Japan*, pp. 57–59.

66. Ibid., pp. 68–70.

67. Fritz M. Heichelheim, *An Ancient Economic History* (Leiden: A. W. Sijthoff, 1958), pp. 54–56.

68. Ibid.

69. Jamie Stokes, ed., *Encyclopedia of the Peoples of Africa and the Middle East* (New York: Facts on File, 2009), pp. 664–65.

70. Steven J. Garfinkle, "Turam-ili and the Community of Merchants in the Ur III Period," *Journal of Cuneiform Studies* 54 (2002): 29–48.

71. Steven J. Garfinkle, "Shepherds, Merchants, and Credit: Some Observations on Lending Practices in Ur III," *Journal of the Economic and Social History of the Orient* 47, no. 1 (2004): 1–30.

72. Ibid.

73. Ibid.

74. Steven Garfinkle, email correspondence, June 22, 2014 (K. Sehgal, interviewer).

75. Douglas Garbutt, "The Significance of Ancient Mesopotamia in Accounting History," *Accounting Historians Journal* 11, no. 1 (1984): 83–101.

76. Garfinkle, "Shepherds, Merchants, and Credit."

77. Michael Hudson, "How Interest Rates Were Set, 2500 BC–1000 AD: Máš, Tokos and Fœnus as Metaphors for Interest Accruals," *Journal of the Economic and Social History of the Orient* 43, no. 2 (2000): 132–61. According to Steven Garfinkle, *máš* means "goat."

78. Garbutt, "The Significance of Ancient Mesopotamia in Accounting History."

79. Hudson, "How Interest Rates Were Set, 2500 BC–1000 AD."

80. Suzanne Daley, "Paris Journal; A Green Light for Sinful Drivers: It's Election Time," *New York Times*, March 26, 2002, http://www.nytimes.com/2002/03/26/world/paris -journal-a-green-light-for-sinful-drivers-it-s-election-time.html.

81. Marvin A. Powell, "Money in Mesopotamia," *Journal of the Economic and Social History of the Orient* 39, no. 3 (1996): 224–42.

82. Steven Garfinkle, email correspondence, June 22, 2014 (K. Sehgal, interviewer).

83. Hudson, "How Interest Rates Were Set, 2500 BC–1000 AD."

84. Ibid.

85. François Thureau-Dangin, "Sketch of a History of the Sexagesimal System," *Osiris* (1939): 95–141.

86. Hudson, "How Interest Rates Were Set, 2500 BC–1000 AD."

87. U.S. Department of State, "Trafficking in Persons Report," 2012, http://www.state.gov/ documents/organization/192587.pdf.

88. Alain Testart, "The Extent and Significance of Debt Slavery," *Revue française de sociologie* 43 (2002): 173–204.

89. Instead of being just an instrument of governance, as Garfinkle notes, the Code of Hammurabi may have been "royal propaganda" that wasn't always enforced.

90. Graeber, *Debt*, locs. 3591–92.

91. Testart, "The Extent and Significance of Debt Slavery."

92. Edward M. Harris, "Did Solon Abolish Debt-Bondage?," *Classical Quarterly* 52, no. 2 (2002): 415–30.

93. Richard Ford, "Imprisonment for Debt," *Michigan Law Review* 25, no. 1 (November 1926): 24–49.

94. Walter Thornbury, "The Fleet Prison," *Old and New London* 2 (1878): 404–16, http:// www.british-history.ac.uk/report.aspx?compid=45111.

95. Jason Zweig, "Are Debtors' Prisons Coming Back?," *Wall Street Journal*, August 28, 2012, http://blogs.wsj.com/totalreturn/2012/08/28/are-debtors-prisons-coming-back.

96. Ford, "Imprisonment for Debt."

97. Charles J. Tabb, "The History of the Bankruptcy Laws in the United States," *American Bankruptcy Institute Law Review* (1995): 5–51.

98. U.S. Department of State, "Trafficking in Persons Report."

99. Jessica Silver-Greenberg, "Welcome to Debtors' Prison, 2011 Edition," *Wall Street Journal*, March 16, 2011, http://online.wsj.com/article/SB10001424052748704396504576204553811636610.html.

100. Susie An, "Unpaid Bills Land Some Debtors Behind Bars," NPR, December 12, 2011, http://www.npr.org/2011/12/12/143274773/unpaid-bills-land-some-debtors-behind-bars.

Chapter 4. *Hard and Heavy*

1. This quote is inscribed on the wall next to the door to the vault in the basement of the Federal Reserve Bank of New York building.

2. Aristotle, *Politics*. trans. Benjamin Jowett (New York: Dover, 2000), p. 42.

3. David Boyle, ed., *The Money Changers* (London: Earthscan, 2002), p. 41.

4. Federal Reserve Bank of New York, "Gold Vault," retrieved June 16, 2013, from http://www.newyorkfed.org/aboutthefed/goldvault.html.

5. Ibid.

6. HowStuffWorks, "How Much Gold Is There in the World?," retrieved June 20, 2013, from http://money.howstuffworks.com/question213.htm.

7. Georg Friedrich Knapp, *The State Theory of Money* (London: Macmillan, 1924).

8. U.S. Department of Treasury, "Legal Tender Status," retrieved June 1, 2014, from http://www.treasury.gov/resource-center/faqs/currency/pages/legal-tender.aspx.

9. Paul Davidson, "Monetary Policy in the Twenty-First Century in the Light of the Debate Between Chartalism and Monetarism," in Jeff Biddle, John B. Davis, Steven G. Medema, eds., *Economics Broadly Considered* (New York: Routledge, 2001), pp. 335–47.

10. Jacob Goldstein and David Kestenbaum, "The Island of Stone Money," NPR, December 10, 2010, retrieved May 25, 2013, from http://www.npr.org/blogs/money/2011/02/15/131934618/the-island-of-stone-money.

11. Mark Kurlansky, *Salt* (New York: Penguin, 2002), p. 63.

12. Wayne G. Sayles, email correspondence, June 28, 2014 (K. Sehgal, interviewer).

13. François Velde, "A Brief History of Minting Technology," June 18, 1997, retrieved April 5, 2014, from http://frenchcoins.net/links/technolo.pdf.

14. Ute Kagan, email correspondence, June 16, 2014 (K. Sehgal, interviewer).

15. J. N. Postgate, *Early Mesopotamia: Society and Economy at the Dawn of History* (London: Routledge, 1994), p. 18.

16. Ibid., p. 204.

17. Ibid., p. 53.

18. Ibid., p. 51.

19. Stephen Bertman, *Handbook to Life in Ancient Mesopotamia* (Oxford: Oxford University Press, 2005), p. 249.

20. Postgate, *Early Mesopotamia*, pp. 202–203.

21. Karen Rhea Nemet-Nejat, *Daily Life in Ancient Mesopotamia* (Peabody, MA: Hendrickson, 2002), pp. 267–68.

22. Bertman, *Handbook to Life in Ancient Mesopotamia*, p. 257.

23. Luca Peyronel, "Ancient Near Eastern Economics: The Silver Question Between Methodology and Archaeological Data," *Proceedings of the 6th International Congress on the Archaeology of the Ancient Near East* (2010): 926–27.

24. Catherine Eagleton et al., *Money: A History* (New York: Firefly Books, 2007), p. 17.

25. Ibid., p. 19.

26. Ibid., p. 18.

27. Nemet-Nejat, *Daily Life in Ancient Mesopotamia*, p. 264.

28. Eagleton, *Money*, p. 18.

29. Ibid., p. 19.

30. Wendy Christensen, *Empire of Ancient Egypt* (New York: Chelsea House, 2009), pp. 9–10.

31. Barry J. Kemp, *Ancient Egypt: Anatomy of a Civilization* (London: Routledge, 1989), pp. 124–25.

32. Ibid., pp. 124–26.

33. A. Rosalie David, *Handbook to Life in Ancient Egypt* (New York: Facts on File, 2003), pp. 318–20.

34. Ibid.

35. Ibid., pp. 318–21.

36. Eagleton, *Money*, p. 21.

37. British Museum, "The Wealth of Africa," retrieved July 1, 2013, from http://www.british museum.org/explore/online_tours/africa/the_wealth_of_africa/ancient_egypt.aspx.

38. David P. Silverman, ed., *Ancient Egypt* (New York: Oxford University Press, 1997), pp. 64–65.

39. Peter Tyson, "Where Is Punt?," December 1, 2009, retrieved April 22, 2014, from NOVA: http://www.pbs.org/wgbh/nova/ancient/egypt-punt.html.

40. David, *Handbook to Life in Ancient Egypt*, pp. 334–56.

41. Silverman, *Ancient Egypt*, p. 40.

42. Rosemarie Klemm and Dietrich Klemm, *Gold and Gold Mining in Ancient Egypt and Nubia* (New York: Springer, 2013), pp. 20–28.

43. David, *Handbook to Life in Ancient Egypt*.

44. Christensen, *Empire of Ancient Egypt*, pp. 73–89.

45. G. K. Jenkins, "An Egyptian Gold Coin," *British Museum Quarterly* 20, no. 1 (1955): 10–11.

46. "Lydia," *The Metropolitan Museum of Art Bulletin* 26, no. 5 (1968): 199–200.

47. Koray Konuk, "Asia Minor to the Ionian Revolt," in W. E. Metcalf, ed., *The Oxford Handbook of Greek and Roman Coinage* (New York: Oxford University Press, 2012), pp. 43–60.

48. Forthcoming research suggests that electrum was man-made and not naturally occurring in the mountains or nearby river.

49. Donald Kagan, "The Dates of the Earliest Coins," *American Journal of Archaeology* 86, no. 3 (1982): 343–60.

50. Glyn Davies, *A History of Money: From Ancient Times to the Present Day* (Cardiff: University of Wales Press, 1994), p. 63.

51. Robert W. Wallace, "The Origin of Electrum Coinage," *American Journal of Archaeology* 91, no. 3 (1987): 385–97.

52. Richard Seaford, *Money and the Early Greek Mind* (Cambridge: Cambridge University Press, 2004), pp. 136–46.

53. Eagleton, *Money*, p. 24.

54. Konuk, "Asia Minor to the Ionian Revolt."

55. Jack M. Balcer, "Herodotus, the 'Early State,' and Lydia," *Historia: Zeitschrift für Alte Geschichte* 43, no. 2 (1994): 246–49.

56. David M. Schaps, "The Invention of Coinage in Lydia, in India, and in China," 2006, retrieved July 6, 2013, from XIV International Economic History Congress, Session 30.

57. Ibid.

58. Madhukar K. Dhavalikar, "The Beginning of Coinage in India," *World Archaeology* 6, no. 3 (1975): 330–38.

59. Seaford, *Money and the Early Greek Mind*, pp. 102–14.

60. Ute Wartenberg Kagan notes that there were more weight standards than just the Attic one.

61. Davies, *A History of Money*, p. 80.

62. Peter G. Van Alfen, "The Coinage of Athens, Sixth to First Century B.C.," in *The Oxford Handbook of Greek and Roman Coinage*, ed. William E. Metcalf (New York: Oxford University Press, 2012), pp. 88–104.

63. There were still barter and debt transactions in Athens. In the rest of Greece, it took more time for coinage to flourish.

64. Edward E. Cohen, "The Elasticity of the Money-Supply at Athens," in W. V. Harris, ed., *The Monetary Systems of the Greeks and Romans* (Oxford: Oxford University Press, 2008), pp. 66–83.

65. C. J. Howgego, *Ancient History from Coins* (New York: Routledge, 1995), pp. 1–23.

66. Jack Weatherford, *The History of Money* (New York: Three Rivers Press, 1997), pp. 34–35.

67. Ibid.

68. Ron Owens, *Solon of Athens* (Portland, OR: Sussex Academic Press, 2010), pp. 130–34.

69. Léopold Migeotte, *The Economy of the Greek Cities* (Berkeley: University of California Press, 2009), pp. 173–79.

70. Weatherford, *The History of Money*, pp. 41–42.

71. Plato, *The Laws*, trans. T. J. Saunders (London: Penguin Books, 1970), p. 159.

72. Davidson, "Monetary Policy in the Twenty-First Century in the Light of the Debate Between Chartalism and Monetarism."

73. Shahzavar Karimzadi, *Money and Its Origins* (New York: Routledge, 2013), pp. 139–50.

74. Aristotle, *The Politics and Economics of Aristotle*, trans. E. Walford (London: George Bell, 1876), pp 21–22.

75. Joseph A. Schumpeter, *History of Economic Analysis* (New York: Oxford University Press, 1994), pp. 62–64.

76. Barry J. Gordon, "Aristotle, Schumpeter, and the Metalist Tradition," *Quarterly Journal of Economics* 75, no. 4 (1961): 608–14.

77. Scott Meikle, "Aristotle on Money," *Phronesis* 39, no. 1 (1994): 26–44.

78. Ibid.

79. Aristotle, *The Politics and Economics of Aristotle*, p. 25.

80. Tenney Frank, *An Economic History of Rome* (New York: Cooper Square, 1962), pp. 69–89.

81. "Gresham's Law," *Encyclopaedia Britannica*, retrieved August 6, 2013, from http://www.britannica.com/EBchecked/topic/245850/Greshams-law.

82. Bernhard E. Woytek, "The Denarius Coinage of the Roman Republic," in W. E. Metcalf, ed., *The Oxford Handbook of Greek and Roman Coinage* (New York: Oxford University Press, 2012), pp. 315–34.

83. Andrew Meadows, "J. W. Moneta and the Monuments: Coinage and Politics in Republican Rome," *Journal of Roman Studies* 91 (2001): 27–49.

84. Eagleton, *Money*, pp. 39–61.

85. Alfred Wassink, "Inflation and Financial Policy Under the Roman Empire to the Price Edict of 301 A.D.," *Historia: Zeitschrift für Alte Geschichte* 40, no. 4 (1991): 465–93.

86. Mary E. Thornton, "Nero's New Deal," *Transactions and Proceedings of the American Philological Association* 102 (1971): 621–29.

87. Gary Richardson, Alejandro Komai, and Michael Gou, "Roosevelt's Gold Program," Federal Reserve History, retrieved April 22, 2014, from http://www.federalreservehistory.org/Events/DetailView/24.

88. Wassink, "Inflation and Financial Policy Under the Roman Empire to the Price Edict of 301 A.D."

89. Thornton, "Nero's New Deal."

90. Ulrich W. Hiesinger, "The Portraits of Nero," *American Journal of Archaeology* 79, no. 2 (1975): 113–24.

91. Weatherford, *The History of Money*, pp. 46–63.

92. C. H. V. Sutherland, "Denarius and Sestertius in Diocletian's Coinage Reform," *Journal of Roman Studies* 51 (1961): 94–97.

93. World Gold Council, "Demand and Supply," retrieved July 29, 2013, from http://www.gold.org/about_gold/story_of_gold/demand_and_supply.

94. World Steel Association, "World Crude Steel Output Increases by 1.2% in 2012," January 22, 2013, retrieved July 29, 2013, from http://www.worldsteel.org/media-centre/press-releases/2012/12-2012-crude-steel.html.

95. Andrew Ross Sorkin, "Render Unto Caesar, but Who Backs Bitcoin?," *New York Times*, November 25, 2013.

96. James Grant, "All About Gold" (Charlie Rose, interviewer), December 5, 2010.

97. Virginia Morell, "Feature Article: Bowerbirds," *National Geographic*, July 2010.

98. Paul T. Keyser, "Alchemy in the Ancient World: From Science to Magic," *Illinois Classical Studies* 15, no. 2 (1990): 361.

99. Ibid., 353–78.

100. Lynn Thorndike, *A History of Magic and Experimental Science* (New York: Columbia University Press, 1923), p. 194.

101. Keyser, "Alchemy in the Ancient World."

102. Lawrence Principe, *The Secrets of Alchemy* (Chicago: University of Chicago Press, 2013), pp. 13–18.

103. Ibid., pp. 30–38.

104. Ibid., pp. 65–70.

105. Lawrence Principe, "Alchemy Restored," *Isis* 102, no. 2 (2011): 305–12.

106. Ibid., p. 307.

107. Davies, *A History of Money*, pp. 29–30.

Chapter 5. *Some Like It Soft*

1. Marco Polo, *The Travels*. trans. Ronald Latham (London: Penguin Books, 1958), pp. 147–48.

2. Lawrence Lande and Tim Congdon, "John Law and the Invention of Paper Money," *RSA Journal*, 139, no. 5414 (January 1991): 916–28.

3. Bill Gross, "Investment Outlook: The Scouting Party," January 2002, http://www.pimco.com/EN/Insights/Pages/IO_01_2002.aspx.

4. The story is inspired by a Wall Street currency trader whose name has been changed.

5. Neil Irwin, "This One Number Explains How China Is Taking Over the World," *Washington Post*, December 3, 2013, http://www.washingtonpost.com/blogs/wonkblog/wp/2013/12/03/this-one-number-explains-how-china-is-taking-over-the-world.

6. Barry J. Eichengreen, *Exorbitant Privilege*, Kindle ed. (New York: Oxford University Press, 2011).

7. Ibid.

8. "All Signs Pointing to Gold," U.S. Global Investors, September 17, 2012, http://www.usfunds.com/investor-resources/frank-talk/all-signs-pointing-to-gold/#.Uiky_Dash8E.

9. Milton Friedman and Rose D. Friedman, *Free to Choose* (New York: Harcourt, 1980), p. 249.

10. "Monetarists Anonymous," *Economist*, 2012, http://www.economist.com/node/21563752.

11. Gordon Tullock, "Paper Money—A Cycle in Cathay," *Economic History Review* 9, no. 3 (1957): 393–407.

12. Federal Reserve, "How Much U.S. Currency Is in Circulation?," August 2, 2013, retrieved August 8, 2013, from http://www.federalreserve.gov/faqs/currency_12773.htm.

13. The Federal Reserve tracks several measures of the money supply. Two of the standards are M1 and M2. Both include currency in circulation, but they do not include the bank reserves kept at the Fed. M1 is a measure of the most easily accessible types of money, and includes circulating currency, travelers' checks, and demand deposits or accounts similar to "checking accounts." M2 includes these categories plus some that are not quite as liquid since they are meant for household saving or investment, like savings and money market accounts, certificates of deposit worth less than $100,000 (CDs or "small time deposits"), and the funds parked in retail money market mutual funds. In June 2013, M1 totaled $2.5 trillion. M2 was over $10.5 trillion.

14. Economist Irving Fisher's work led to the first clear differentiation between nominal and real interest rates. In his description of the relationship, the nominal interest rate approximates the real interest rate plus the inflation rate, thus anticipated changes in the inflation rate will be reflected in the nominal interest rate. See "Irving Fisher," *Concise Encyclopedia of Economics*, retrieved June 1, 2014, from http://www.econlib .org/library/Enc/bios/Fisher.html.

15. The example works out to $97.09.

16. The example works out to $27.683 million.

17. Hunter Lewis, *How Much Money Does an Economy Need?* (Mount Jackson, VA: Axios Press, 2007), pp. 6–7.

18. Marc Shell, "Money and the Mind: The Economics of Translation in Goethe's Faust," *MLN* 95, no. 3 (April 1980): 516–62.

19. Jack Weatherford, *The History of Money* (New York: Three Rivers Press, 1997), pp. 137–40.

20. Mark Levine, "Can a Papermaker Help to Save Civilization?," *New York Times Magazine*, February 17, 2012, http://www.nytimes.com/2012/02/19/magazine/timothy-barrett -papermaker.html?pagewanted=all.

21. Tsuen-Hsuin Tsien, "Raw Materials for Old Papermaking in China," *Journal of the American Oriental Society* 93, no. 4 (1973): 510–19.

22. Thomas F. Carter, *The Invention of Printing in China and Its Spread Westward* (New York: Ronald Press, 1955).

23. Metropolitan Museum of Art, "Tang Dynasty (618–906)," retrieved April 10, 2014, from http://www.metmuseum.org/toah/hd/tang/hd_tang.htm.

24. Tullock, "Paper Money—A Cycle in Cathay."

25. Liansheng Yang, *Money and Credit in China: A Short History* (Cambridge, MA: Harvard University Press, 1952), pp. 51–52.

26. Nirat Lertchitvikul calls the notes from this era "warlord paper money," since they depended heavily on the appointed governor and local warlords.

27. Yang, *Money and Credit in China*, pp. 51–52.

28. Kojiro Tomita, Andrew McFarland Davis, and Ch'üan Pu Tung Chih, "Ancient Chinese Paper Money as Described in a Chinese Work on Numismatics," *Proceedings of the American Academy of Arts and Sciences* 53, no. 7 (June 1918): 467–647.

29. Yang, *Money and Credit in China*, pp. 5–6.

30. Ibid., p. 52.

31. Richard Von Glahn, "Monies of Account and Monetary Transition in China, Twelfth to Fourteenth Centuries," *Journal of the Economic and Social History of the Orient* (2010): 463–505.

32. Richard Von Glahn, "Cycles of Silver in Chinese Monetary History, in Billy K. L. So, ed., *The Economy of Lower Yangzi Delta in Late Imperial China: Connecting Money, Markets, and Institutions* (New York: Routledge, 2013), pp. 17–71.

33. Von Glahn, "Monies of Account and Monetary Transition in China, Twelfth to Fourteenth Centuries."

34. Tsien, "Raw Materials for Old Papermaking in China."

35. Yang, *Money and Credit in China*, p. 53.

36. Tullock, "Paper Money—A Cycle in Cathay."

37. Von Glahn, "Cycles of Silver in Chinese Monetary History."

38. Richard Von Glahn, "Silver and the Transition to a Paper Money Standard," Von Gremp Workshop in Economic and Entrepreneurial History, 2010, University of California, Los Angeles, pp. 1–31, http://www.econ.ucla.edu/workshops/papers/History/Von%20Glahn.pdf.

39. Von Glahn, "Cycles of Silver in Chinese Monetary History."

40. Yang, *Money and Credit in China*, p. 55.

41. Von Glahn, "Monies of Account and Monetary Transition in China, Twelfth to Fourteenth Centuries."

42. Ibid.

43. Ibid.

44. Richard Von Glahn, "The Origins of Paper Money in China," in William N. Goetzmann and K. Geert Rouwenhorst, eds., *The Origins of Value: The Financial Innovations That Created Modern Capital Markets* (New York: Oxford University Press, 2005), pp. 65–91.

45. John W. Dardess, "From Mongol Empire to Yüan Dynasty: Changing Forms of Imperial Rule in Mongolia and Central Asia," *Monumenta Serica* (1972–73): 117–65.

46. Von Glahn, "Monies of Account and Monetary Transition in China, Twelfth to Fourteenth Centuries."

47. "Kublai Khan," *Encyclopaedia Britannica*, http://www.britannica.com/EBchecked/topic/324254/Kublai-Khan/3994/Social-and-administrative-policy.

48. Weatherford, *The History of Money*, pp. 125–28.

49. Yang, *Money and Credit in China*, pp. 64–66.

50. Von Glahn, "Monies of Account and Monetary Transition in China, Twelfth to Four-teenth Centuries."

51. Yang, *Money and Credit in China*, pp. 64–66.

52. Tullock, "Paper Money—A Cycle in Cathay."

53. Von Glahn, "Monies of Account and Monetary Transition in China, Twelfth to Four-teenth Centuries."

54. Lande, "John Law and the Invention of Paper Money."

55. Antoin E. Murphy, *John Law: Economic Theorist* (Oxford: Oxford University Press, 1997), pp. 31–40.

56. Niall Ferguson, *The Ascent of Money* (New York: Penguin Group, 2008), p. 132.

57. Stephen Quinn and William Roberds, "How Amsterdam Got Fiat Money," Federal Reserve Bank of Atlanta, December 2010, https://www.frbatlanta.org/documents/pubs/wp/wp1017.pdf.

58. Earl J. Hamilton, "John Law of Lauriston: Banker, Gamester, Merchant, Chief?," *American Economic Review* 57, no. 2 (1967): 273–82.

59. H. Montgomery Hyde, *John Law: The History of an Honest Adventurer* (London: Home & Van Thal, 1969), p. 83.

60. Antoin E. Murphy, "John Law," in William N. Goetzmann and K. Geert Rouwenhorst, eds., *The Origins of Value: The Financial Innovations That Created Modern Capital Markets* (New York: Oxford University Press, 2005), pp. 225–38.

61. Ibid.

62. Earl J. Hamilton, "Prices and Wages at Paris under John Law's System," *Quarterly Journal of Economics*, 51, no. 1 (November 1936): 42–70.

63. Ibid.

64. Ferguson, *The Ascent of Money*, pp. 138–49.

65. Lande, "John Law and the Invention of Paper Money."

66. Ferguson, *The Ascent of Money*, pp. 140–45.

67. Murphy, "John Law."

68. Ferguson, *The Ascent of Money*, pp. 138–49.

69. Lande, "John Law and the Invention of Paper Money."

70. Ferguson, *The Ascent of Money*, pp. 138–49.

71. Lande, "John Law and the Invention of Paper Money."

72. Murphy, "John Law."

73. Lande, "John Law and the Invention of Paper Money."

74. Ferguson, *The Ascent of Money*, pp. 138–57.

75. Eichengreen, *Exorbitant Privilege*, pp. 10–11.

76. Farley Grubb, "Benjamin Franklin and the Birth of Paper Money," Federal Reserve Bank of Philadelphia, March 3, 2006, https://www.philadelphiafed.org/publications/economic-education/ben-franklin-and-paper-money-economy.pdf.

77. Ibid.

78. Charles W. Calomiris, "Institutional Failure, Monetary Scarcity, and the Depreciation of the Continental," *Journal of Economic History* 48, no. 1 (1988): 47–69.

79. Benjamin Franklin, "A Modest Enquiry into the Nature and Necessity of a Paper-Currency," in *Colonial Currency Reprints* (Boston: John Wilson, 1911), pp. 335–57.

80. Grubb, "Benjamin Franklin and the Birth of Paper Money."

81. Robert Garson, "The US Dollar and American Nationhood, 1781–1820," *Journal of American Studies* 35, no. 1 (2001): 21–46.

82. Farley Grubb, email correspondence, May 27, 2014 (K. Sehgal, interviewer). Grubb points out that this was because of time discounting; colonial paper money was structured in a way similar to US savings bonds.

83. Ibid.

84. Calomiris, "Institutional Failure, Monetary Scarcity, and the Depreciation of the Continental."

85. Declaration of Independence, July 4, 1776, http://www.archives.gov/exhibits/charters/declaration_transcript.html.

86. Grubb, email correspondence, May 27, 2014.

87. Robert Shaw, "History of the Dollar," *Analysts Journal* 14, no. 2 (1958): 77–79.

88. Farley Grubb, "The Continental Dollar: How Much Was Really Issued?," *Journal of Economic History* 68, no. 1 (March 2008): 283–91.

89. Massachusetts Historical Society, "United States Continental Paper Currency," http://www.masshist.org/findingaids/doc.cfm?fa=fao0005.

90. Grubb, email correspondence, May 27, 2014.

91. Alexander Hamilton, *The Works of Alexander Hamilton*, vol. 2, ed. John C. Hamilton (New York: J. F. Trow, 1850), p. 271.

92. Garson, "The US Dollar and American Nationhood, 1781–1820."

93. Eichengreen, *Exorbitant Privilege*, pp. 10–14.

94. Grubb, email correspondence, May 27, 2014.

95. Constitution of the United States of America, http://www.archives.gov/exhibits/charters/constitution_transcript.html.

96. Weatherford, *The History of Money*, pp. 136–40.

97. Ronald W. Michener and Robert E. Wright, "State 'Currencies' and the Transition to the U.S. Dollar: Clarifying Some Confusions," *American Economic Review* 95, no. 3 (June 2005): 682–703.

98. Abraham Lincoln, *Abraham Lincoln: Speeches and Writings, 1859–1865* (New York: Library of America, 1989), p. 397.

99. Heather Cox Richardson, *The Greatest Nation on Earth* (Cambridge, MA: Harvard University Press, 1997), pp. 1–7.

100. Marc Egnal, "The Greenback Is Born," *New York Times*, February 27, 2012, http://opinionator.blogs.nytimes.com/2012/02/27/the-greenback-is-born/?_php=true&_type=blogs&_r=0.

101. Ibid.

102. Grubb, email correspondence, May 27, 2014.

103. University of Groningen, "American History: From Revolution to Reconstruction and Beyond," retrieved May 31, 2014, from http://www.let.rug.nl/usa/essays/general/a-brief-history-of-central-banking/national-banking-acts-of-1863-and-1864.php.

104. "Resumption Act of 1875," *Encylopaedia Britannica*, retrieved September 8, 2013, from http://www.britannica.com/EBchecked/topic/499805/Resumption-Act-of-1875.

105. Murray N. Rothbard, "What Has Government Done to Our Money?," Ludwig von Mises Institute, https://mises.org/money/4s1.asp.

106. Nathan Lewis, "The 1870–1914 Gold Standard: The Most Perfect One Ever Created," *Forbes*, January 3, 2013, http://www.forbes.com/sites/nathanlewis/2013/01/03/the-1870-1914-gold-standard-the-most-perfect-one-ever-created.

107. Michael David Bordo, "The Classical Gold Standard: Some Lessons For Today," Federal Reserve Bank of St. Louis, May 1981, http://research.stlouisfed.org/publications/review/81/05/Classical_May1981.pdf.

108. Barry Eichengreen and Peter Temin, "The Gold Standard and the Great Depression," June 1997, NBER Working Paper Series, http://www.nber.org/papers/w6060.pdf?new_window=1.

109. Murray N. Rothbard, "The Monetary Breakdown of the West," Ludwig von Mises Institute, http://mises.org/money/4s3.asp.

110. Ibid.

111. James Rickards, *Currency Wars* (New York: Penguin, 2011), p. 66.

112. Eichengreen, "The Gold Standard and the Great Depression."

113. Benn Steil, *The Battle of Bretton Woods* (Princeton, NJ: Princeton University Press, 2013), p. 24.

114. Eichengreen, "The Gold Standard and the Great Depression."

115. Steil, *The Battle of Bretton Woods*, p. 25.

116. Jacob Goldstein and David Kestenbaum, "Why We Left the Gold Standard," NPR, April 21, 2011, http://www.npr.org/blogs/money/2011/04/27/135604828/why-we-left-the-gold-standard.

117. Steil, *The Battle of Bretton Woods*, p. 27.

118. Joanne S. Gowa, *Closing the Gold Window: Domestic Politics and the End of Bretton Woods* (Ithaca, NY: Cornell University Press, 1983), pp. 34–40.

119. Rickards, *Currency Wars*, p. 78.

120. Miller Center, "American President: A Reference Resource," http://millercenter.org/president/lbjohnson/essays/biography/4.

121. Stephen Daggett and Nina M. Serafino, "Costs of Major U.S. Wars," Congressional Research Service, 2010, http://www.fas.org/sgp/crs/natsec/RS22926.pdf.

122. Leonard Dudley and Peter Passell, "The War in Vietnam and the United States Balance of Payments," *Review of Economics and Statistics* 50, no. 4 (1968): 437–42.

123. Julian E. Zelizer, "The Nation: Guns and Butter; Government Can Run More Than a War," *New York Times*, December 30, 2001, http://www.nytimes.com/2001/12/30/weekinreview/the-nation-guns-and-butter-government-can-run-more-than-a-war.html.

124. Robert J. Samuelson, *The Great Inflation and Its Aftermath* (New York: Random House, 2008), p. 4.

125. Ibid., pp. 63–65.

126. Benjamin Klein, "Our New Monetary Standard: The Measurement and Effects of Price Uncertainty, 1880–1973," *Economic Inquiry* 13, no. 4 (December 1975): 461–84.

127. Allan H. Meltzer, "Origins of the Great Inflation," *Review* (2005): 145–76, http://research.stlouisfed.org/publications/review/05/03/part2/Meltzer.pdf.

128. Joseph E. Gagnon and Marc Hinterschweiger, *Flexible Exchange Rates for a Stable World Economy* (Washington, DC: Peterson Institute for International Economics, 2011), pp. 12–13.

129. Gowa, *Closing the Gold Window*, pp. 140–50.

130. President Richard M. Nixon, "Address to the Nation Outlining a New Economic Policy: 'The Challenge of Peace,'" August 15, 1971, http://www.presidency.ucsb.edu/ws/?pid=3115#axzz2fZeubBDa.

131. Rickards, *Currency Wars*, pp. 85–93.

132. Roger Lowenstein, "The Nixon Shock," *Bloomberg Businessweek*, August 4, 2011, http://www.businessweek.com/printer/articles/870-the-nixon-shock.

133. Steil, *The Battle of Bretton Woods*, p. 353.

134. Henry Ford, *My Life and Work* (Garden City, NY: Doubleday, Page, 1922), p. 179.

135. Board of Governors of the Federal Reserve System, *The Federal Reserve System: Purposes and Functions* (Washington, DC: Publications Committee of the Board of Governors of the Federal Reserve System, 2005), p. 1.

Chapter 6. *Back to the Future*

1. Alex Crippen, "CNBC Buffett Transcript Part 2: The 'Zebra' That Got Away," CNBC, March 2, 2011, http://www.cnbc.com/id/41867379.

2. Erick Schonfeld, "Jack Dorsey on Charlie Rose: 'It's Really Complex to Make Something Simple,'" Tech Crunch, January 11, 2011, http://techcrunch.com/2011/01/11/jack-dorsey-charlie-rose.

3. Peter H. Diamandis and Steven Kotler, *Abundance: The Future Is Better Than You Think* (New York: Free Press, 2012).

4. Andrew Ross Sorkin, "A Revolution in Money," *New York Times*, April 1, 2014, http://dealbook.nytimes.com/2014/04/01/a-revolution-in-money/?_php=true&_type=blogs&_r=0.

5. Nick Barisheff, *$10,000 Gold: Why Gold's Inevitable Rise Is the Investor's Safe Haven* (Mississuaga, Ontario: John Wiley & Sons Canada, 2013).

6. Ibid., pp. 164–68.

7. Natasha Lennard, "Ben Bernanke Tells Ron Paul What Gold Is," *Salon*, July 14, 2011, http://www.salon.com/2011/07/14/bernanke_ron_paul_is_gold_money.

8. John C. Williams, "Cash Is Dead! Long Live Cash!," Federal Reserve Bank of San Francisco 2012 Annual Report, http://www.frbsf.org/files/2012_Annual_Report_Essay.pdf.

9. Robert Lee Hotz, "Why You Shouldn't Put Your Money Where Your Mouth Is," *Wall Street Journal*, April 18, 2014, http://online.wsj.com/news/articles/SB100014240527023 03456104579489510784385696.

10. Mark Koba, "$2 Trillion Underground Economy May Be Recovery's Savior," CNBC, April 24, 2013, http://www.cnbc.com/id/100668336.

11. John Cook, "After Bootstrapping to $10M in Sales, BizX Scores Real Cash for Virtual Currency," Geek Wire, April 16, 2013, http://www.geekwire.com/2013/after-bootstrapping -to-10m-in-sales-bizx-scores-cash-for-virtual-currency.

12. Meritxell Mir, "In Hard-Hit Spain, Bartering Becomes Means of Getting By," *USA Today*, February 20, 2013, http://www.usatoday.com/story/news/world/2013/02/20/ spanish-bartering/1894365.

13. John Stonestreet, "Spain Barter Economy Wins Followers in Grip of Crisis," Reuters, February 20, 2010, http://www.reuters.com/article/2012/02/20/us-spain-barter-idUST RE81J0NJ20120220.

14. Rachel Donadio, "Battered by Economic Crisis, Greeks Turn to Barter Networks," *New York Times*, October 1, 2011, http://www.nytimes.com/2011/10/02/world/europe/ in-greece-barter-networks-surge.html?_r=0&adxnnl=1&pagewanted=all&adxnnl x=1381862981-8waQus1MLcdWO4mVYjdxsA.

15. Ibid.

16. Mir, "In Hard-Hit Spain, Bartering Becomes Means of Getting By."

17. International Reciprocal Trade Association, "Modern Trade and Barter," http://www .irta.com/index.php/about/modern-trade-barter.

18. Michael Burawoy and Pavel Krotov, "The Soviet Transition from Socialism to Capitalism: Worker Control and Economic Bargaining in the Wood Industry," *American Sociological Review* (1992): 16–38.

19. David M. Woodruff, "The Russian Barter Debate: Implications for Western Policy," *PONARS*, 1998, http://personal.lse.ac.uk/woodruff/_private/materials/pm_0038.pdf.

20. Barbara A. Cellarius, " 'You Can Buy Almost Anything with Potatoes': An Examination of Barter During Economic Crisis in Bulgaria," *Ethnology* (2000): 73–92.

21. Mary Mellor, *The Future of Money: From Financial Crisis to Public Resource* (New York: Pluto Press, 2010), pp. 152–76.

22. "Confidence in Institutions," Gallup, June 1, 2013, http://www.gallup.com/poll/1597/ confidence-institutions.aspx#1.

23. World Bank, "Participatory Budgeting in Brazil," http://www-wds.worldbank.org/ external/default/WDSContentServer/WDSP/IB/2009/11/03/000333037_20091103015 746/Rendered/PDF/514180WP0BR0Bu10Box342027B01PUBLIC1.pdf.

24. Dana Khromov, "Ithaca Hours Revival Would Require Community Support," April 13, 2011, http://www.ithaca.com/news/article_175100c4-65d6-11e0-bd73-001cc4c002e0.html.

25. Gretchen M. Herrmann, "Special Money: Ithaca Hours and Garage Sales," *Ethnology* 45, no. 2 (2006): 125–41.

26. "The Birth of the Dollar Bill," NPR, December 7, 2012, http://www.npr.org/blogs/money/2012/12/07/166747693/episode-421-the-birth-of-the-dollar-bill.

27. "Funny Money," *Economist*, December 20, 2005, http://www.economist.com/node/5323615.

28. Cary Stemle, "Starbucks Reports Continued Growth in Mobile App Usage," MobilePaymentsToday.com, January 24, 2014, http://www.mobilepaymentstoday.com/articles/starbucks-reports-continued-growth-in-mobile-app-usage.

29. Paul Kemp-Robertson, "Bitcoin. Sweat. Tide. Meet the Future of Branded Currency," TED, July 2013, http://www.ted.com/talks/paul_kemp_robertson_bitcoin_sweat_tide_meet_the_future_of_branded_currency.html.

30. Thomas H. Greco, *The End of Money and the Future of Civilization*, Kindle ed. (White River Junction, VT: Chelsea Green, 2009), loc. 3442.

31. Kathleen Gallagher, "Peer to Peer Lending Sites Attracting Investors," *Milwaukee Wisconsin Journal Sentinel*, November 9, 2013, http://www.jsonline.com/business/peer-to-peer-lending-sites-attracting-investors-b99137303z1-231300731.html.

32. Greco, *The End of Money and the Future of Civilization*, loc. 3486.

33. bitcoinmining.com, "What is Bitcoin Mining?," April 9, 2013, https://www.youtube.com/watch?v=GmOzih6I1zs.

34. "Getting Started," Bitcoin Mining, http://www.bitcoinmining.com/getting-started.

35. "Frequently Asked Questions," http://bitcoin.org/en/faq.

36. David Woo, Ian Gordon, and Vadim Iaralov, "Bitcoin: A First Assessment," Bank of America Merrill Lynch, 2013.

37. Steven Perlberg, "Bernanke: Bitcoin 'May Hold Long-Term Promise,'" *Business Insider*, November 18, 2013, http://www.businessinsider.com/ben-bernanke-on-bitcoin-2013-11#ixzz2nDsX0xSR.

38. Paul Krugman, "Bitcoin Is Evil," *New York Times*, December 28, 2013, http://krugman.blogs.nytimes.com/2013/12/28/bitcoin-is-evil/?_php=true&_type=blogs&_r=0.

39. Robin Sidel, Eleanor Warnock, and Takashi Mochizuki, "Almost Half a Billion Worth of Bitcoins Vanish," *Wall Street Journal*, February 28, 2014, http://online.wsj.com/news/articles/SB10001424052702303801304579410010379087576.

40. Patricia Hurtado, "Ex-Bitcoin Foundation's Shrem Indicted After Plea Talks," Bloomberg, April 14, 2014, http://www.bloomberg.com/news/2014-04-14/ex-bitcoin-foundation-s-shrem-indicted-by-u-s-after-plea-talks.html.

41. Scott Lee, "FBI Seized $28.5 Million In Bitcoins from Silk Road Owner Ross Ulbricht," TechBeat, October 29, 2013, http://techbeat.com/2013/10/fbi-seized-28-5-million-bitcoins-silk-road-owner-ross-ulbricht.

42. Richard Rubin and Carter Dougherty, "Bitcoin Is Property, Not Currency, in Tax System: IRS," Bloomberg, May 25, 2014, http://www.bloomberg.com/news/2014-03-25/bitcoin-is-property-not-currency-in-tax-system-irs-says.html.

43. Michael Carney, "Bitcoin, You Have a China Problem," *PandoDaily*, November 6, 2013, http://pando.com/2013/11/26/bitcoin-you-have-a-china-problem.

44. Alex Hern, "Chinese Bitcoin Exchange Closes Deposits After Central Bank Clampdown," *Guardian*, April 3, 2014, http://www.theguardian.com/technology/2014/apr/03/chinese-bitcoin-exchange-closes-after-central-bank-clampdown.

45. Matthew Philips, "Bitcoin Isn't Really Banned in China—and It's Quickly Gaining Ground," *Bloomberg Businessweek*, March 20, 2014, http://www.businessweek.com/articles/2014-03-20/btc-chinas-bobby-lee-bitcoin-isnt-really-banned-in-china-and-its-quickly-gaining-ground.

46. François R. Velde, "Bitcoin: A Primer," Chicago Fed Letter, December 2013, http://www.chicagofed.org/digital_assets/publications/chicago_fed_letter/2013/cfldecember2013_317.pdf.

47. Marc Andreessen, "Why Bitcoin Matters," *New York Times*, January 21, 2014, http://dealbook.nytimes.com/2014/01/21/why-bitcoin-matters/?_php=true&_type=blogs&_r=0.

48. Brian Fung, "Marc Andreessen: In 20 Years, We'll Talk About Bitcoin Like We Talk About the Internet Today," *Washington Post*, May 21, 2014, http://www.washingtonpost.com/blogs/the-switch/wp/2014/05/21/marc-andreessen-in-20-years-well-talk-about-bitcoin-like-we-talk-about-the-internet-today/?tid=pm_business_pop.

49. A good explanation is in Andreessen, "Why Bitcoin Matters."

50. Timothy Carmody, "Money 3.0: How Bitcoins May Change the Global Economy," *National Geographic*, October 14, 2013, http://news.nationalgeographic.com/news/2013/10/131014-bitcoins-silk-road-virtual-currencies-internet-money.

51. Kevin Fitchard, "Square Retools Consumer Mobile Payments, Replacing Wallet with a New App Called Order," GigaOm, May 12, 2014, http://gigaom.com/2014/05/12/square-retools-consumer-mobile-payments-replacing-wallet-with-a-new-app-called-order.

52. Jane Martinson, "Apple's In-App Game Charges: How My Kids Ran Up Huge Bills," *Guardian*, March 26, 2013, http://www.theguardian.com/technology/shortcuts/2013/mar/26/apples-in-app-game-charges-kids-bills.

53. I was engaging in a CNP (card not present) transaction, which is riskier (and less profitable for Square and Visa) because the vendor can't verify that I actually have the credit card. Several cases of fraud have been reported.

54. Edward Bellamy, *Looking Backward* (New York: Dover Thrift Editions, 1996).

55. "Credit Card," *Encyclopaedia Britannica*, http://www.britannica.com/EBchecked/topic/142321/credit-card.

56. Jack Weatherford, *The History of Money* (New York: Three Rivers Press, 1997), pp. 225–32.

57. US Census Bureau, "2012 Credit Cards—Holders, Number, Spending, and Debt, 2000 and 2009, and Projections, 2012," http://www.census.gov/compendia/statab/2012/

tables/12s1188.pdf; Tien-tsin Huang, "Payment Processing: Payments Market Share Handbook," J. P. Morgan, 2013.

58. Emily Steel, "Using Credit Cards to Target Web Ads," *Wall Street Journal*, October 11, 2011, http://online.wsj.com/news/articles/SB1000142405297020400230457662703065133 9352.

59. "War of the Virtual Wallets," *Economist*, November 17, 2012, http://www.economist .com/news/finance-and-economics/21566644-visa-mastercard-and-other-big-payment-networks-need-not-be-victims-shift/print.

60. "Secret History of the Credit Card," *Frontline*, PBS, November 23, 2004, http://www .pbs.org/wgbh/pages/frontline/shows/credit/etc/script.html.

61. Bradley Johnson, "100 Leading National Advertisers," *Advertising Age*, June 20, 2011, http://adage.com/article/news/ad-spending-100-leading-national-advertisers/228267/.

62. "MasterCard Advisors' Cashless Journey," MasterCard, September 2013, http://news room.mastercard.com/wp-content/uploads/2013/09/Cashless-Journey_WhitePaper _FINAL.pdf.

63. Steve Barnett and Nigel Chalk, "Building a Social Safety Net," International Monetary Fund, September 2010, http://www.imf.org/external/pubs/ft/fandd/2010/09/pdf/ barnett.pdf.

64. Shan-Jing Wei, "Why Do the Chinese Save So Much?," *Forbes*, February 2, 2010, http:// www.forbes.com/2010/02/02/china-saving-marriage-markets-economy-trade.html.

65. Simon Kuper, "Debt: Another Word for Guilt," *FT*, January 14, 2011, http://www.ft.com/ intl/cms/s/2/a2c51e14-1ded-11e0-badd-00144feab49a.html#axzz2zOkYgJ7C.

66. Huang, "Payment Processing."

67. Mark Zandi, Virendra Singh, and Justin Irving, "The Impact of Electronic Payments on Economic Growth," Moody's, February 2013, http://corporate.visa.com/_media/ moodys-economy-white-paper.pdf.

68. Scott Schmith, "Credit Card Market: Economic Benefits and Industry Trends," Visa, March 2008, http://corporate.visa.com/_media/ita-credit-card-report.pdf.

69. Chris G. Christopher Jr. and Erik Johnson, "Emerging Consumer Markets: The New Drivers of Global Economic Growth," *Supply Chain Quarterly*, 2011, http://www .supplychainquarterly.com/columns/201104monetarymatters.

70. David Humphrey et al., "What Does It Cost to Make a Payment?," *Review of Network Economics* 2, no. 2 (June 2003), http://www.riksbank.se/Upload/Dokument_riksbank/ Kat_foa/Cost%20of%20Making.pdf.

71. Community Merchants USA, "The Benefits of Small Business Card Acceptance," http:// communitymerchantsusa.com/resources/the-benefits-of-small-business-card-acceptance.

72. But until credit card companies make the economics more favorable, there may not be mass adoption among small merchants.

73. International Telecommunication Union, 2013 Facts and Figures, http://www.itu.int/ en/ITU-D/Statistics/Documents/facts/ICTFactsFigures2013.pdf.

74. "Gartner Says Worldwide Mobile Payment Users to Reach 141 Million in 2011," Gartner, July 21, 2011, http://www.gartner.com/newsroom/id/1749114.

75. Huang, "Payment Processing."

76. Ibid.

77. Jennifer Van Grove, "Square Sets New Record: $2M Processed in One Day," Mashable, April 29, 2011, http://mashable.com/2011/04/29/square-payments.

78. Leena Rao, "Visa Makes a Strategic Investment in Disruptive Mobile Payments Startup Square," Tech Crunch, April 27, 2011, http://techcrunch.com/2011/04/27/visa -makes-a-strategic-investment-in-disruptive-mobile-payments-startup-square.

79. A Square merchant can be a high risk. Square is a "merchant acquirer" that aggregates all of its customers. In order for it to be profitable, it needs to have favorable rates from the credit card companies. The problem is that Square's customers turn over quickly, so credit card companies charge Square high fees.

80. Donna Tam, "PayPal Wants to Get Rid of Your Wallet," *CNET*, May 21, 2013, http://www .cnet.com/news/paypal-wants-to-get-rid-of-your-wallet. Square has launched its "Order" application, which enables users to order ahead from restaurants.

81. Jason Del Rey, "Starbucks Has Bigger Plans in Mobile Payments Than Most People Realize," *Re/code*, July 17, 2014, http://recode.net/2014/07/17/starbucks-has-bigger-plans -in-mobile-payments-than-most-people-realize.

82. Sarah Clark, "NTT Docomo to Take Japanese Mobile Wallet Global," NFC World, October 11, 2012, http://www.nfcworld.com/2012/10/11/318353/ntt-docomo-to-take -japanese-mobile-wallet-global.

83. Bill Siwicki, "It's Official: Mobile Devices Surpass PCs in Online Retail," Internet Retailer, October 1, 2013, http://www.internetretailer.com/2013/10/01/its-official-mobile -devices-surpass-pcs-online-retail.

84. "Why Does Kenya Lead the World in Mobile Money?," *Economist*, May 27, 2013, http:// www.economist.com/blogs/economist-explains/2013/05/economist-explains-18.

85. Fiona Graham, "M-Pesa: Kenya's Mobile Wallet Revolution," BBC, November 22, 2010, http://www.bbc.co.uk/news/business-11793290.

86. "Mobile Threats Around the World," Lookout, retrieved April 20, 2014, from https://www .lookout.com/resources/know-your-mobile/mobile-threats-around-the-world.

87. "Mobile-Payments Fraud Concerns Consumers," *ISO & Agent*, July 14, 2011.

88. Jon M. Chang, "PayPal Galactic Looks to Solve Payments in Space," ABC News, June 27, 2013, http://abcnews.go.com/Technology/paypal-galactic-launches-answer-questions -space-transactions/story?id=19498683.

89. "Galactic Credit Standard," Wookieepedia, retrieved November 12, 2013, from http:// starwars.wikia.com/wiki/Galactic_Credit_Standard.

90. "PayPal, SETI Launch Program to Explore Space Currency," *International Business Times*, June 27, 2013.

91. Matt Peckham, "Space Payments: PayPal Galactic Aims for Infinity and Beyond," *Time*, June 27, 2013, http://techland.time.com/2013/06/27/space-payments-paypal-galactic-aims-for-infinity-and-beyond.

92. "New Currency for Space Travellers," BBC, October 5, 2007, http://news.bbc.co.uk/2/hi/business/7029564.stm.

93. Brian Dodson, "PayPal Galactic—Don't Leave Earth Without It," *GizMag*, July 2, 2013, http://www.gizmag.com/paypal-galactic-financial-infrastructure-for-space-travel/28116.

94. Paul Krugman, "The Theory of Interstellar Trade," July 1978, http://www.princeton.edu/~pkrugman/interstellar.pdf.

95. "Starship Enterprises," *Economist*, October 23, 2013, http://www.economist.com/news/science-and-technology/21588350-dismal-scientists-also-speculating-about-space-flight-starship-enterprises.

96. Cotton Delo, "Your Klout Score Could Get You into American Airlines' First Class Lounge," *Advertising Age*, May 7, 2013, http://adage.com/article/digital/american-airlines-opens-lounge-high-klout-scorers/241336.

97. "Man or Machine," *Wall Street Journal*, June 29, 2012, http://online.wsj.com/news/articles/SB10001424052702304782404577490533504354976.

98. Andrew Ross Sorkin, "A Revolution in Money," *New York Times*, April 1, 2014, http://dealbook.nytimes.com/2014/04/01/a-revolution-in-money/?_php=true&_type=blogs&_r=0.

99. Hal E. Hershfield et al., "Increasing Saving Behavior Through Age-Progressed Renderings of the Future Self," *Journal of Marketing Research* 48 (November 2011): S23–S37.

Chapter 7. *Angel Investors*

1. *New American Standard Bible* (Carol Stream, IL: Creation House, n.d.), p. 324.

2. *Pirke Avot* (New York: UAHC Press, 1993), p. 56.

3. R. Mahalakshmi, *The Book of Lakshmi* (New Delhi: Penguin, 2009), p. 96.

4. "The Casualties: Faith in Hard Work and Capitalism," Pew Research Global Attitudes Project, July 2, 2012, http://www.pewglobal.org/2012/07/12/chapter-4-the-casualties-faith-in-hard-work-and-capitalism.

5. One of the best-known studies on this topic was conducted by Professors Angus Deaton and Daniel Kahneman at Princeton, who analyzed 450,000 responses of Americans from a Gallup poll about their personal happiness and income. They make a distinction between two types of happiness: 1) emotional well-being, one's daily happiness; and 2) life evaluation, a longer-lasting satisfaction. They found that income and life evaluation are positively correlated: The more money you make, the more satisfied you are with your life. They also found that emotional well-being and income are positively correlated but that the improvement in emotional well-being stalls around

the $75,000-a-year mark. For example, 41 percent of people with asthma who made less than $75,000 were reportedly unhappy, but only 21 percent of those making over $75,000 said they were unhappy. Low income worsens an already bad situation, as people have to worry about meeting their basic needs—in addition to their personal afflictions like sickness. The authors conclude that high income buys more life satisfaction but not emotional well-being after a certain point: "High incomes don't bring you happiness, but they do bring you a life you think is better." Happiness research is an emerging field in economics and psychology. It's helping to inform policy makers in distant corners of the world on how to maximize their country's happiness instead of just wealth. Canadian cities are tracking the happiness levels of their citizenry. Bhutan's Gross National Happiness (GNH) measure considers nine attributes, from cultural diversity to living standards. GNH seems to flower from Buddhism, the dominant religion in Bhutan.

6. "State of the Global Workplace," Gallup, 2013, http://www.gallup.com/strategic consulting/164735/state-global-workplace.aspx.

7. "Market of Ideas," *Economist*, April 7, 2011, http://www.economist.com/node/18527446.

8. Duncan Campbell, "Greed Is Good: A Guide to Radical Individualism," *Guardian*, March 9, 2009, http://www.theguardian.com/world/2009/mar/10/ayn-rand-capitalism.

9. Justin Fox, *The Myth of the Rational Market* (New York: HarperCollins, 2009), p. xiii.

10. Mark C. Taylor, *Confidence Games* (Chicago: University of Chicago Press, 2004), p. 4.

11. Ibid.

12. Laura Davis, "After Woman Sells Virginity for $780,000, Here Are the Results of Our Prostitution Survey," *Independent*, October 25, 2012, http://www.independent.co.uk/voices/comment/after-woman-sells-virginity-for-780000-here-are-the-results-of-our-prostitution-survey-8226025.html.

13. Michael J. Sandel, *What Money Can't Buy* (New York: Farrar, Straus & Giroux, 2012). In addition, when anything can be bought, Sandel reasons that inequality may result, since the wealthy can afford what the poor cannot; Steve Hargreaves, "How Income Inequality Hurts America," *CNNMoney*, September 25, 2013, http://money.cnn.com/2013/09/25/news/economy/income-inequality.

14. Lao Tsu, *Tao te Ching* (New York: Random House, 1997), p. 87.

15. David Graeber, *Debt: The First 5,000 Years*, Kindle ed. (Brooklyn: Melville House, 2011), p. 223.

16. Matthew 6:19–21 (New International Version), http://www.biblica.com/niv.

17. Matthew 6:21 (NIV), http://www.biblica.com/niv.

18. Matthew 6:24 (NIV), http://www.biblica.com/niv.

19. Matthew 19:16–22 (NIV), http://www.biblica.com/niv.

20. Matthew 19:23–24 (NIV), http://www.biblica.com/niv.

21. The question of who will be saved is also revealed in other passages: "With man this is impossible, but not with God; all things are possible with God" (Matthew 19:26). In

Ephesians 2:8–9, "Men are saved through God's gifts of grace, mercy, and faith." Matthew (5:3) goes further, stating, "Nothing we do earns salvation for us. It is the poor in spirit who inherit the kingdom of God."

22. Matthew 19:28–30 (NIV), http://www.biblica.com/niv.

23. Matthew 5:3 (NIV), http://www.biblica.com/niv.

24. 1 Chronicles 4:10 (NIV), http://www.biblica.com/niv.

25. Nanci Hellmich, "Is 'Jabez' for the Needy or Greedy?," *USA Today*, July 17, 2001, http://usatoday30.usatoday.com/life/books/2001-05-24-the-prayer-of-jabez.htm.

26. Laurie Goodstein, "A Book Spreads the Word: Prayer for Prosperity Works," *New York Times*, May 8, 2001, http://www.nytimes.com/2001/05/08/us/a-book-spreads-the-word-prayer-for-prosperity-works.html?pagewanted=print&src=pm.

27. Galatians 5:19–21 (NIV), http://www.biblica.com/niv.

28. Erin McClam, "Greed or Godliness? Prayer Book Creates Controversy in Georgia," *Kingman Daily Miner*, June 8, 2001, http://news.google.com/newspapers?nid=932&dat=20010608&id=DtNPAAAAIBAJ&sjid=71IDAAAAIBAJ&pg=7211,5960921.

29. Matthew 6:22–23 (NIV), http://www.biblica.com/niv.

30. Timothy Keller, "Treasure vs. Money," May 2, 1999, Redeemer Presbyterian Church, http://sermons2.redeemer.com/sermons/treasure-vs-money.

31. Juliet Schor, *The Overspent American* (New York: Harper Perennial, 1999), http://www.nytimes.com/books/first/s/schor-overspent.html.

32. Hanna Krasnova et al., "Envy on Facebook: A Hidden Threat to Users' Life," *Wirtschaftsinformatik Proceedings*, 2013, http://warhol.wiwi.hu-berlin.de/~hkrasnova/Ongoing_Research_files/WI%202013%20Final%20Submission%20Krasnova.pdf.

33. "Know What the Scriptures Say About Money and Giving," Brigham Young University, retrieved December 16, 2013, from http://personalfinance.byu.edu/?q=node/1061.

34. Luke 8:11 (NIV), http://www.biblica.com/niv.

35. Matthew 13:37 (NIV), http://www.biblica.com/niv.

36. Matthew 13:1–23 (NIV), http://www.biblica.com/niv.

37. Pope Francis, "Apostolic Exhortation Evangelii Gaudium," http://www.vatican.va/holy_father/francesco/apost_exhortations/documents/papa-francesco_esortazione-ap_20131124_evangelii-gaudium_en.html#No_to_the_new_idolatry_of_money.

38. Mark 8:35–36 (King James Version), http://www.biblegateway.com/versions/King-James-Version-KJV-Bible/#books; Matthew 16:26 (NIV), http://www.biblica.com/niv.

39. Ben Witherington III, *Jesus and Money* (Grand Rapids, MI: Brazos Press, 2010), p. 64.

40. Matthew 6:31–34 (NIV), http://www.biblica.com/niv.

41. Witherington, *Jesus and Money*, pp. 52–54.

42. Ibid., p. 51.

43. Ibid., p. 53.

44. Henry A. Sanders, "The Number of the Beast in Revelation," *Journal of Biblical Literature* 37 (1918): 95–99.

45. Luke 20:22 (NIV), http://www.biblica.com/niv.

46. Luke 20:25 (KJV), http://www.biblegateway.com/versions/King-James-Version-KJV-Bible/#books.

47. Matthew 21:13 (NIV), http://www.biblica.com/niv.

48. Luke 6:35 (NIV), http://www.biblica.com/niv.

49. Acts 2:42–47 (NIV), http://www.biblica.com/niv.

50. Mark 12:43–44 (NIV), http://www.biblica.com/niv.

51. Keller, "Treasure vs. Money."

52. C. S. Lewis, *Mere Christianity* (New York: HarperCollins, 1980), pp. 86–89.

53. Genesis 1:31 (Revised Standard Version), http://quod.lib.umich.edu/r/rsv/browse.html.

54. Deuteronomy 11:14 (RSV), http://quod.lib.umich.edu/r/rsv/browse.html.

55. Ecclesiastes 5:15 (RSV), http://quod.lib.umich.edu/r/rsv/browse.html.

56. Exodus 20:4 (RSV), http://quod.lib.umich.edu/r/rsv/browse.html.

57. Exodus 32:1–35 (RSV), http://quod.lib.umich.edu/r/rsv/browse.html.

58. Exodus 20:17 (RSV), http://quod.lib.umich.edu/r/rsv/browse.html.

59. Proverbs 18:23 (RSV), http://quod.lib.umich.edu/r/rsv/browse.html.

60. Ecclesiastes 5:10 (RSV), http://quod.lib.umich.edu/t/rsv/browse.html.

61. Deuteronomy 8:13–18 (RSV), http://quod.lib.umich.edu/r/rsv/browse.html.

62. Larry Kahaner, *Values, Prosperity, and the Talmud* (Hoboken, NJ: John Wiley & Sons, 2003), p. 15. Primary source: Babylonian Talmud, *Tamid* 32b.

63. Job 22:24 (RSV), http://quod.lib.umich.edu/r/rsv/browse.html.

64. *Encyclopedia of Torah Thoughts*, trans. Charles B. Chavel (New York: Shilo, 1980), pp. 484–89.

65. Job 22:25 (RSV), http://quod.lib.umich.edu/r/rsv/browse.html.

66. Proverbs 23:4–5 (RSV), http://quod.lib.umich.edu/r/rsv/browse.html.

67. *Encyclopedia of Torah Thoughts*, pp. 484–89.

68. Larry Kahaner, email correspondence, May 27, 2014 (K. Sehgal, interviewer).

69. Proverbs 15:15 (RSV), http://quod.lib.umich.edu/r/rsv/browse.html.

70. Proverbs 28:27 (RSV), http://quod.lib.umich.edu/r/rsv/browse.html.

71. Proverbs 11:24 (RSV), http://quod.lib.umich.edu/r/rsv/browse.html.

72. Deuteronomy 15:11 (RSV), http://quod.lib.umich.edu/r/rsv/browse.html.

73. Joseph Telushkin, *Biblical Literacy* (New York: William Morrow, 1997), p. 483.

74. Leviticus 25:36 (RSV), http://quod.lib.umich.edu/r/rsv/browse.html.

75. Ezekiel 18:12–13 (RSV), http://quod.lib.umich.edu/r/rsv/browse.html. For an in-depth look at usury in Judaism, and how moneylending was perceived in broader society, read Joseph Shatzmiller's *Shylock Reconsidered: Jews, Moneylending, and Medieval Society* (Berkeley: University of California Press, 1990).

76. Telushkin, *Biblical Literacy*, pp. 473–74. Primary source: Babylonian Talmud, *Bava Bathra* 9a.

77. Geoffrey Wigoder, ed., *The New Encyclopedia of Judaism* (Jerusalem: Jerusalem Publishing House, 2002), pp. 161–62.

78. Gerald J. Blidstein, "Tikkun Olam," in *Tikkun Olam* (Lanham, MD: Rowman & Littlefield, 1997), pp. 17–60.

79. Colin Turner, "Wealth as an Immortality Symbol in the Qur'an: A Reconsideration of the ml/amwl Verses," *Journal of Qur'anic Studies* 8, no. 2 (2006): 58–83.

80. Asad Zaman, "Islamic Economics: A Survey of the Literature: II," *Islamic Studies* 48, no. 4 (2009): 525–66.

81. *Qur'ān* (Sahih International), www.quran.com, Surat Al-Kahf 18:32–43.

82. Ibid., Surat Al-'Anfāl 8:28.

83. Ibid., Surat Al-Munāfiqūn 63:9.

84. Ibid., Surat Al-Baqarah 2:261.

85. Ibid., Surat At-Tawbah 9:24.

86. Ibid., Surat Al-Fajr 89:20–23.

87. Ibid., Surat Al-Humazah 104:101–103.

88. Turner, "Wealth as an Immortality Symbol in the Qur'an."

89. Monzer Kahf, correspondence about Islam and wealth, May 25, 2014 (K. Sehgal, interviewer).

90. Turner, "Wealth as an Immortality Symbol in the Qur'an."

91. *Qur'ān* (Sahih International), www.quran.com, Surat Ṭāhā 20:131.

92. Ibid., Surat Al-'A`rāf 7.152.

93. Ibid., Surat Ṭāhā 20:6.

94. *Qur'ān* 28:77, cited in Zaman, "Islamic Economics: A Survey of the Literature: II."

95. Michael Bonner, "Poverty and Economics in the Qur'an," *Journal of Interdisciplinary History* 35, no. 3 (2005): 391–406.

96. Muhammad Arkam Khan, *Islamic Economics and Finance: A Glossary* (New York: Routledge, 1990), p. 157.

97. *Qur'ān* (Sahih International), www.quran.com, Surat An-Nisā' 4:161.

98. M. Siddieq Noorzoy, "Islamic Laws on Riba (Interest) and Their Economic Implications," *International Journal of Middle East Studies* 14, no. 1 (1982): 3–17.

99. Muhammad Anwar, "Islamicity of Banking and Modes of Islamic Banking," *Arab Law Quarterly* 18, no. 1 (2003): 62–80.

100. "Lakshmi," BBC, August 24, 2009, http://www.bbc.co.uk/religion/religions/hinduism/deities/lakshmi.shtml.

101. Mahalakshmi, *The Book of Lakshmi*, pp. 1–20.

102. Ibid., p. 72.

103. Sharada Sugirtharajah, "Picturing God," in P. Bowen, ed., *Themes and Issues in Hinduism* (London: Cassell, 1998), pp. 161–203.

104. Mahalakshmi, *The Book of Lakshmi*, pp. 6–8.

105. Ibid., pp. 71–94.

106. "Dhanteras Symbolizes Arrival of Goddess Lakshmi," *Times of India*, November 1, 2013, http://articles.timesofindia.indiatimes.com/2013-11-01/kanpur/43591930_1_dhanteras -dhanavantri-goddess-lakshmi.

107. Wendy Doniger, *The Hindus: An Alternative History* (New York: Penguin, 2009), p. 378.

108. Albert Hall Museum, Jaipur, "Gallery Collection: Coins," http://alberthalljaipur.gov.in/ displaycontents/view/49.

109. Donald R. Davis Jr., "Being Hindu or Being Human: A Reappraisal of the Puruṣārthas," *International Journal of Hindu Studies* 8, no. 1/3 (2004): 1–27; S. R. Bhatt, "The Concept of Moksa—An Analysis," *Philosophy and Phenomenological Research* 364 (1976): 564–70.

110. Arvind Sharma, "The Puruṣārthas: An Axiological Exploration of Hinduism," *Journal of Religious Ethics* (1999): 223–56.

111. French economist Thomas Piketty asserts in his book *Capital in the Twenty-First Century* that there is a tendency for capitalism to lead to greater inequality. If this is the case, then the market divides people based on the resources allocated. Paul Courtright, a professor at Emory University, points out that if he's right then the market is *adharmic*, inherently immoral. To right this wrong, we must channel the market against itself—redistributing capital in a fairer manner. We need to make money in order to give it away.

112. "Ashrama," *Encyclopaedia Britannica*, http://www.britannica.com/EBchecked/topic/ 38363/ashrama.

113. Sharma, "The Puruṣārthas."

114. Bhagavad Gita, 5:18–22, trans. Stephen Mitchell (New York: Harmony Books, 1998), p. 85.

115. Ibid., 5:18–29, pp. 85–87.

116. "Meditation Mapped in Monks," BBC, March 1, 2002, http://news.bbc.co.uk/2/hi/ science/nature/1847442.stm.

117. Joshua Landy, "In Defense of Humanities," December 7, 2010, http://news.stanford .edu/news/2010/december/humanities-defense-landy-120710.html.

Chapter 8. *Gilt Complex*

1. D. Wayne Johnson, email correspondence, March 4, 2014 (K. Sehgal, interviewer).

2. Robert Louis Stevenson, *Treasure Island* (New Jersey: J. P. Piper Books, 2013), p. 58.

3. I discovered the quote here: R. S. Poole, "LakdivaCoins Collection," retrieved March 2, 2014, from http://coins.lakdiva.org. Original source is here: R. S. Poole, "On the Study of Coins," *Antiquary* 9 (1884): 7–10.

4. While I was in Dhaka, some of the news headlines read: "Opposition supporters hurl petrol-bomb at police vehicle in Rajshahi"; "10 injured in clash. Policeman injured after handmade bomb explodes"; "72 hour blockade effective 6:00 am. Embassy travel restrictions in effect. Exercise caution. Remain vigilant."

5. Wari-Bateshwar, retrieved February 5, 2014, from http://www.parjatan.gov.bd/wari_arc.php.

6. Reema Islam, "A Family's Passion," *Archaeology*, October 13, 2013, http://archaeology .org/issues/112–1311/letter-from/1406-wari-bateshwar-ptolemy-sounagoura-indo -pacific-beads.

7. This was a dramatic experience. In order to get us through the blockade, my friend suggested that we hire an ambulance. He explained that for 4,000 Bangladeshi taka, or 50 US dollars, we could hire an emergency vehicle with tinted windows to drive us through the blockade, and the angry mob might let us pass. I was hesitant because it didn't sound safe or ethical. Another friend, a television producer who was with us, said, "I can use my media van to get us through unharmed, but we'll need to start early, five a.m." I awoke at 4 a.m. I removed all the unnecessary items from my wallet, and I stuffed a fork from the hotel restaurant in my jean pocket—just in case. I waited in the lobby. 5:00 . . . 5:15 . . . 5:30. Finally, a vanilla white van with no decals arrives. "Where are your media credentials?" I asked. "There," he said, pointing to a sheet of white paper on the dashboard, with the word *media* scrawled in black ink. The only thing keeping me from an angry mob was a piece of paper pulled from an office HP Inkjet printer. I slid the door closed and kept my eyes shut.

8. Sufi Mostafizur Rahman, "Coins and Currency System," in Rahman, ed., *Archaeological Heritage* (Dhaka: Asiatic Society of Bangladesh, 2007), pp. 108–44.

9. Emran Hossain, "Wari-Bateshwar One of Earliest Kingdoms," *Daily Star*, March 19, 2008, http://archive.thedailystar.net/newDesign/news-details.php?nid=28431.

10. "1890s Glass Pattern Has Value Far Beyond a Few Coins," *Milwaukee Wisconsin Journal Sentinel*, March 25, 2007, http://www.jsonline.com/realestate/29340799.html.

11. Cornelius C. Vermeule, *Numismatic Art in America* (Cambridge, MA: Belknap Press of Harvard University Press, 1971), pp 20–24.

12. Ibid., Preface.

13. UNESCO, "Convention on the Means of Prohibiting and Preventing the Illicit Import, Export and Transfer of Ownership of Cultural Property," November 14, 1970, http:// portal.unesco.org/en/ev.php-URL_ID=13039&URL_DO=DO_TOPIC&URL_SECTION =201.html.

14. "Coin Collecting," *Encyclopaedia Britannica*, retrieved February 9, 2014, from http:// www.britannica.com/EBchecked/topic/124774/coin-collecting.

15. James A. Mackay, *The World Encyclopedia of Coins* (Leicestershire: Lorenz Books, 2012), pp. 58–59.

16. James L. Noles, *A Pocketful of History* (Cambridge, MA: Da Capo Press, 2008), pp. xxii–xxiii.

17. Ibid., p. xxiv.

18. "United States Mint Call for Artists: Seeking Artists to Design United States Coins and Medals," National Endowment for the Arts, retrieved May 28, 2014, from http://arts .gov/grants-individuals/united-states-mint-call-for-artists.

19. Noles, *A Pocketful of History*, pp. 1–6.

20. Frank Meyer, "The Coins of the U.S.: Symbols of a People," *Clearing House* 29, no. 2 (1954): 100–104.

21. "Dinh Bo Linh," *Encyclopaedia Britannica*, retrieved February 11, 2014, from http://www.britannica.com/EBchecked/topic/163870/Dinh-Bo-Linh.

22. Howard Daniel also said that the 1948 Viet coin is noteworthy. They were made from gold and came in three denominations. But they didn't circulate among the public. They were made for President Ho Chi Minh to present to high-ranking officials in Moscow and Beijing, a token of his gratitude for their help during the Indochina War. Ho gave the leftover coins to Vietnamese who acted valiantly during the war. Howard says these coins are special because they are a gift from the nation's hero and father. In his decades of collecting, Howard has seen only one, and that was in a museum. He would pay at least $10,000 for one.

23. R. Allan Barker, "The Historical Cash Coins of Viet Nam," 2004, http://vietnam.sudoku one.com/d1_dinh.htm.

24. Howard Daniel, email correspondence, May 28, 2014 (K. Sehgal, interviewer).

25. Ronachai Krisadaolarn and Vasilijs Milhailovs, *Siamese Coins: From Funan to the Fifth Reign* (Bangkok: River Books Press, 2010), pp. 12–13.

26. Manote Tripathi, "Coins of the Realm," *Nation*, October 22, 2012, http://www.nation multimedia.com/life/Coins-of-the-realm-30192703.html.

27. "Mongkut," *Encyclopaedia Britannica*, retrieved February 14, 2014, from http://www .britannica.com/EBchecked/topic/389268/Mongkut.

28. I think there is more to it than that. This was my second meeting with a Vietnam veteran who had stayed well past his tour of duty and become a numismatist. It's more than a coincidence. Clinical psychologist Rachel Feller thinks that collecting is a type of therapy to help people cope with difficult experiences. She interviewed many collectors and wrote her dissertation on the topic. One theme that emerged from her research may sound familiar—symbols. Collectors considered their collections to be symbols of their trauma, or symbols of the societies they once tried to destroy. These coin collections were shaping the lives of the veterans by turning them into numismatists. Building a coin collection was a way of remembering the trauma and realizing that it wouldn't destroy them. One of the veterans-turned-collectors told Feller: "There are pieces in my collection that can be tied to the traumatic experiences of my comrades. When I look at them, I often remember those men." Collectors also saw their collections as symbols of themselves, a part of their identity. Building a collection is a type of self-discovery. Some collectors preferred to discuss their collections instead of themselves—as if it were an extension of them. Ronachai's collection helped him learn about Thailand's colorful history. It helped him discover Thailand's welcoming and hospitable culture, which differs from what he calls the "rat race" found in the United States. Ronachai eventually became what he was studying all along—Thai. His

collection was no longer just a symbol of Thailand. The money had also become a symbol of him.

29. Gilbert Perez, The "Dos Mundos" Pillar Coins, Philippine Numismatic Monographs (Manila: Philippines Numismatics and Antiquarian Society, 1948).

30. Michael Richardson, "Can the Pilar Be Found? And What's in It? Deep in the Pacific a Plunge for Riches," New York Times, June 14, 2001, http://www.nytimes.com/2001/06/14/style/14iht-spang_ed3_.html.

31. Filipino Numismatist, http://www.filipinonumismatist.com/2011/10/revalidados-rare-holed-coins-of.html.

32. "Hubble Discovers New Class of Gravitational Lens for Probing the Structure of the Cosmos," HubbelSite, October 18, 1995, http://hubblesite.org/newscenter/archive/releases/1995/1995/43.

33. "Sri Lanka" is the country's modern name used since 1948. It was previously known as "Lanka."

34. Kavan Ratnatunga, "Size & Weight Analysis of 100 Copper Massa Coins," retrieved March 4, 2014, from http://coins.lakdiva.org/medievalindian/rajaraja/massa_100coins.html.

35. Kavan Ratnatunga, "Ruhuna—'Punch Mark' Silver," retrieved March 2, 2014, from http://coins.lakdiva.org/punch/punch_marked_GH442.html.

36. Kavan Ratnatunga, "Maneless Lion Type Ancient Lanka—Mahasena: 277–304," retrieved March 3, 2014, from http://lakdiva.com/coins/ancient/maneless_lion.html.

37. Kavan Ratnatunga, "Ancient Lanka—Bull and Fish Type: Pandya Influence 824–943," retrieved March 2, 2014, from http://coins.lakdiva.org/medievalindian/pandya_bull_2lrfish.html.

38. "Etana Epic," Encyclopaedia Britannica, retrieved March 6, 2014, from http://www.britannica.com/EBchecked/topic/193803/Etana-Epic.

39. British Museum, "Cuneiform Tablet Telling the Legend of Etana," retrieved May 6, 2014, from https://www.britishmuseum.org/explore/highlights/highlight_objects/me/c/cuneiform_the_legend_of_etana.aspx.

40. Rudolf Wittkower, "Eagle and Serpent. A Study in the Migration of Symbols," Journal of the Warburg Institute 2, no. 4 (April 1939): 293–325.

41. "Harvey and Larry Stack to Rejoin Stack's Bowers Galleries," CoinWeek, May 26, 2011, https://www.coinweek.com/featured-news/harvey-and-larry-stack-to-rejoin-stacks-bowers-galleries.

42. Harvey Stack, "The Phenomena of the 50-State Commemorative Quarters," Stack's Bowers, July 10, 2012, http://www.stacksbowers.com/NewsMedia/Blogs/TabId/780/ArtMID/2678/ArticleID/478/The-Phenomena-of-the-50-State-Commemorative-Quarters.aspx.

43. "Theodore Roosevelt (1858–1919)," PBS, http://www.pbs.org/nationalparks/people/historical/roosevelt.

44. *American Experience*, PBS, March 5, 2014, http://www.pbs.org/wgbh/amex/whitman/more/e_literary.html.

45. Q. David Bowers, *A Guide Book of Double Eagle Coins*, Kindle ed. (Atlanta: Whitman, 2004), loc. 5552.

46. Ibid., loc. 838.

47. William E. Hagans, "Recreating a Masterpiece," *Coins*, November 16, 2009, http://numismaster.com/ta/numis/Article.jsp?ad=article&ArticleId=8456.

48. Bowers, *A Guide Book of Double Eagle Coins*, loc. 789.

49. Ibid., loc. 5569.

50. Ibid., loc. 5604.

51. Ibid., loc. 5605.

52. Ibid., loc. 5606.

53. Ibid., loc. 5687.

54. Susan Berfield, "The Mystery of the Double Eagle Gold Coins," *Bloomberg Businessweek*. August 29, 2011, http://www.today.com/id/44288821/ns/today-today_news/t/mystery-double-eagle-gold-coins.

Epilogue

1. Cited in Geoffrey Ingham, "'Babylonian Madness': On the Historical and Sociological Origins of Money," in John N. Smithin, ed., *What Is Money?* (New York: Routledge, 2000). The original source is John Maynard Keynes, *The Collected Writings of John Maynard Keynes*, vol. 11 (Cambridge: Cambridge University Press, 1983), pp. 1–2.

2. Cited in Ingham, "'Babylonian Madness.'"

3. For further reading: "Money Talks," *Economist*, September 29, 2012.

Index

Note: Page numbers in *italics* refer to illustrations

About the Author

KABIR SEHGAL is a vice president in emerging market equities at J. P. Morgan in New York. He serves as an officer in the United States Navy Reserve, served as a speechwriter on a presidential campaign, and is a term member of the Council on Foreign Relations. He is the *New York Times* bestselling author of books including *Walk in My Shoes* (with Andrew Young), *A Bucket of Blessings*, and *Jazzocracy*. A Latin Grammy–nominated producer who has performed with Grammy Award–winning musicians as a jazz bassist, Sehgal is a graduate of Dartmouth College and the London School of Economics. To learn more about the author, you can visit CoinedBook.com.